A MANAGER'S GUIDE TO GLOBALIZATION

Second Edition

A MANAGER'S GUIDE TO GLOBALIZATION

Six Skills for Success in a Changing World

STEPHEN H. RHINESMITH

ASTD

AMERICAN SOCIETY
FOR TRAINING AND
DEVELOPMENT

1640 KING STREET
BOX 1443
ALEXANDRIA, VIRGINIA
22313-2043

McGraw-Hill

New York   San Francisco   Washington, D.C.   Auckland   Bogotá
Caracas   Lisbon   London   Madrid   Mexico City   Milan
Montreal   New Delhi   San Juan   Singapore
Sydney   Tokyo   Toronto

Mcgraw-Hill

A Division of The McGraw-Hill Companies

This publication is designed to provide accurate and authoritative information in regard to the subject matter covered. It is sold with the understanding that neither the author nor the publisher is engaged in rendering legal, accounting, or other professional service. If legal advice or other expert assistance is required, the services of a competent professional person should be sought.

From a Declaration of Principles jointly adopted by a Committee of the American Bar Association and a Committee of Publishers.

Library of Congress Cataloging-in-Publication Data

Rhinesmith, Stephen H.
    A manager's guide to globalization.: six skills for success in a changing world / Stephen H. Rhinesmith.—2nd ed.
      p. cm.
    Includes bibliographical references.
    ISBN: 978-0-07-173598-8
    1. International business enterprises—Management. 2. Executive ability. 3. Success in business. I. Title.
HD62.4.R48   1996
658'.049—dc20   95–45171

Printed in the United States of America

11 12 13 14 15 DOC/DOC 0 9 8 7 6

To Kathe

PREFACE

It is now clear that global change will be a way of life in the 1990s and beyond.

The forces of technology, political freedom, territorial dispute, ethnic rivalries, economic competition, and entrepreneurial ingenuity are stronger than all the centuries of social, political, and economic fabric that have been woven to create the world into its current form.

At the center of these changes, as always, will be people: employees, managers, and leaders of organizations struggling to adapt to the new world rushing toward them—and away from them.

NEW MANAGEMENT CHALLENGES FOR US ALL

Management is not what it used to be because the world is not what it used to be. We are currently witnessing a revolution in the nature of management that has been driven by rapid changes worldwide in social, economic, and political conditions. As companies face global competition, they are forced to radically reduce their cost structures through reengineering and downsizing initiatives that drive cost out of structures, processes, and products.

With the growth of global customers, companies are challenged to deliver products in a consistent manner to areas of the world that for many managers have been nothing more than names on a map. With new and more demanding customers asking for speedy and responsive service, companies are finding new ways to decentralize authority and responsibility. Increasing demands for quality products and services mean new forms of cooperation and new cross-functional coordination to allow global organizations to meet the needs of internal and external customers. Newly emerging markets are demanding new partnerships and joint ventures with people who have unfamiliar ways of doing business and different views of the world and their relationships with foreigners. Escalating costs of research and development in fast-changing industries like electronics, entertainment, and computers require strategic alliances and global partnerships that mean competitors have become partners, while remaining competitors. And with more highly educated workers throughout the world, managers are being asked to redefine their roles from "command and control" to "coach" in order that others can be empowered to meet the needs of a demanding marketplace, many times out of the reach of managers in a single country.

As global managers, we are supposed to have new ideas and new methods for helping others cope with massive change. But it seems that we too are struggling to understand the changes occurring, let alone creating new strategies that can help others adjust.

If you look at the transformation in science and technology since World War II, it is clear that scientific theories, methods, and applications have dramatically affected the speed, size, and ease of everything we do. In information technology, semiconductors, transportation, manufacturing, quality, and a host of other areas, we have achieved breakthroughs that were unthinkable even a decade ago. But if we look at the methods of social science and education we are using to train people to deal with accelerating technological changes, we see that there are few new ways to prepare people, other than some outdoor team-adventure training, action learning, and rudimentary interactive video-computer techniques. In the areas of recruitment, selection, compensation, benefits, and career development, the picture has become more complex and challenging as we are now called upon to recruit, train, supervise, and motivate a global workforce consisting of people with widely varying needs, values, and ambitions. As managers we still have a long way to go to catch up.

HOW CAN YOU BECOME A GLOBAL MANAGER?

Many a manager's eyes glaze over as the CEO announces that the initiative for the coming year is "globalization." And virtually all managers are initially at a loss for concepts, methods, and plans when confronted with the task of "making our people and culture more global."

If this describes your current situation, this book is for you. I have updated *A Manager's Guide to Globalization* to be more responsive to the concerns I have heard from dozens of managers who are struggling with what it means to manage in a global setting—questions about authority and decision making within a matrix organization, cross-cultural communications, supervising and coordinating people from different locations and cultures, developing new suppliers from anywhere on the planet, and responding to global rather than local customers.

One assumption behind this book is that you as a manager in a globalizing organization are responsible for more than just your own job and function. More than ever, you are being asked to think about the *total* organization, and increasingly this means an organization that stretches around the world. While you do not have to become a systems theorist, it *is* necessary to think about your organization as a total business, to understand how it achieves its objectives and how you contribute to its success.

Functional managers are increasingly being asked to take the perspective of general managers in dealing with global customers and workforces. And this means thinking more broadly than ever before and moving into areas where you may not have had much experience—areas such as finance, manufacturing, marketing, sales, human resources and engineering. In this book, you will find assistance in understanding the dimensions of this challenge and specific ideas about what you can do to thrive in a global organization.

CHALLENGES OF GLOBAL MANAGEMENT

As a global manager, you are ultimately the facilitator of personal and organizational development on a global scale. You must be attentive to and a developer of organizational culture, values, and beliefs that reach well beyond your own cultural, technical, and managerial background, and you also need to be a consummate "reframer" of the boundaries of your world view, such as

- Boundaries of space, time, scope, structure, geography, and function.
- Boundaries of functional, professional, and technical skills relevant for a past age.
- Boundaries of thinking and classification of rational versus intuitive, national versus foreign, we versus they.
- Boundaries of cultural assumptions, values and beliefs about the world, your relations with others, and your understanding of yourself.

This transition is broad and challenging. But it holds great opportunities and promise. While many of us as individuals and organizations will need to "learn how to learn" again, we have the opportunity to live fuller, more satisfying lives in the process. **In the end, to be competent global**

managers, we must find new perspectives for living and working in global organizations. We must create new technologies for helping ourselves and our colleagues develop a flexible mindset, work with few fixed rules, and become comfortable with the constant readjustment of goals, objectives, and strategies.

Andy Grove, the indefatigable leader of innovative Intel, writes in the September 18, 1995, issue of *Fortune* that

> You have no choice but to operate in a world being shaped by globalization and the information revolution. There are two options: adapt or die. The new environment dictates two rules: First, everything happens faster; and second, anything that can be done will be done, if not by you, then by someone else somewhere. Let there be no misunderstanding. These changes lead to a less kind, less gentle and less predictable workplace.

So this world will be more challenging and less forgiving. Not surprisingly, it pays to do what you are doing now—getting more information about what to expect and how to prepare yourself for this new global future.

Globalization is about changing organizations, but first it is about *open people*. **It is impossible to develop a free-flowing, competitive global organization with structured, inhibited people.** So globalization is largely the business of mindset and behavior change. The human factor appears to be the key to change and development, whether organizational, social, economic, or political. The human factor, as we will see, is also the key to organizational resilience, creativity, and survival.

On a broader, more philosophical scale, the test for all managers today is whether we can achieve the radical transformation necessary in people's thinking and behavior *within the context of democratic ethics,* where people have the right and freedom to choose the form and practice of their own development. This democratic ethical issue lies at the heart of organizational change in a free society. We have seen from Mao-tse-tung, Stalin, and others that vast social, economic, and organizational changes can be achieved through the use of totalitarian terror. We have also seen, at least in the case of the former Soviet Union, that these vast changes can come unraveled in moments, even after 70 years.

The basic dilemma of organizational change is that it must be freely adopted by the people that it affects, who are likely to be against its introduction. In some ways, the entire field of organizational development can be summed up as enabling the people who constitute an organization to identify and become committed to changes that will meet the best long-term interests of their professional lives, their organization, and society as a whole.

I hope that as a result of reading this book, you will become part of the solution, rather than part of the problem, by being more open to the changes that are occurring around you, more understanding of the demands that are being placed upon you, and more able to develop the mindset and skills necessary to make a continuing productive contribution to your organization's success.

BUILDING BLOCKS FOR THIS BOOK

This book is constructed in five parts. **Part One, The Context**, includes Chapters 1 and 2, which provide an overview of the organizational and personal challenges involved in globalization. In Chapter 1, "Going Global," we start by examining the globalization phenomenon for different kinds of companies at various levels of international and global development. Since the ultimate focus of this book is to develop your capacity as a global manager by redirecting your thinking about global organizations, this warm-up chapter initiates some of the themes you will encounter.

Chapter 2, "Global Mindset and Global Management Skills," introduces the general organizational framework within which we will operate, noting the levels of globalization—strategy/structure, corporate culture, and people. These are the fundamental aspects of global organizations that must be aligned to achieve global effectiveness and efficiency. In this chapter, you will also be introduced to six global management skills, each with its own associated mindset attribute, characteristic, and action, around which the rest of the book is organized.

Part Two, Global Strategy and Structure, encompasses Chapters 3 and 4. Here we will deal with the broad organizational challenges of defining global strategy and structure and examine the complexities of balancing global and local interests. In Chapter 3, "Managing Competitiveness," you will explore the world trends that are forcing companies to go global and the ways in which they are responding with new strategies and structures. Through this review, you will also learn some basic terminology if you are approaching international business for the first time. **A major theme of this book, however, is that globalization is *not* just a matter of strategy and structure.** Too often senior executives believe they have a global organization if they operate around the world. You will see that this is far from the whole picture for today's globally competitive organization.

In Chapter 4, "Managing Complexity," we will deal head on with one of the fundamental challenges of global management—how to manage the complexity of a global organization. Questions of centralization versus decentralization, global efficiency versus local responsiveness, and geographic versus functional priorities, all need to be managed simultaneously. We will review how various companies have successfully dealt with these challenges.

Part Three, Global Corporate Culture and Change, will address the challenges of managing a flexible organization that can respond to rapid changes in the world and meet global customer demands for speedy, effective responsiveness. Part Three includes Chapter 5, "Managing Organizational Alignment," and Chapter 6, "Managing Organizational Change."

In "Managing Organizational Alignment," you will discover that in case after case, the reason many corporations do not respond effectively to global competition is that their corporate culture contains prescriptions for success that may have been appropriate in other times but are inappropriate for a more global future. Breaking with past values and behavior and developing new values, mindset attributes, and skill lies at the heart of the ability to be globally competitive. Global organizations maintain their adaptability through their global corporate cultures. Global managers who are constantly monitoring and altering information systems, task forces, and international decision architectures are the ones who best enable their organizations to respond to new demands from competitors, customers, and the marketplace.

In "Managing Change," you will look at the fact that strategies, structures, and corporate cultures are not stable but constantly changing in response to complex changes in the world. As a result, you as a global manager will need to manage continuous change. This is a considerable emotional, as well as technical and professional, challenge. We all need *some time* to rest. But global managers in global companies find that the work is "less kind and less gentle," as Andy Grove has noted. As a result, you will need to find a new rhythm for your life, in which you can live with the pressures of constant change and let go of the past, while simultaneously taking control of the future.

With world change increasing in its speed and complexity, many managers feel they are being overtaken by chaos. It is true that this new world appears to be filled with more uncertainty and that many people are having to adjust to unfamiliar business practices. You must learn to flow with chaos in ways that you probably have not done before. We will provide some guidance for you as you navigate these new waters.

In **Part Four, Global Teams and People,** we examine the people implications of working in a global organization. These two chapters, "Managing Multicultural Teams" and "Managing Learning," address the human resource challenges of operating in a global context.

In Chapter 7, "Managing Multicultural Teams," we probe the power and possibility of multicultural teamwork. Since teams are a fundamental element of organizational life today, a global organization depends on managing and leading multicultural teams. We will look at multicultural teams as a key to managing joint ventures, developing newly emerging markets, and coordinating the best human resources on a worldwide basis.

These five management skills obviously have enormous implications for the development of managers in global enterprises. In Chapter 8, "Managing Learning," we will review some of the best practices that companies have undertaken to help managers develop the mindset, characteristics, skills, and behaviors required for successful global management. We will also examine a strategically linked and integrated approach to human resource development and reflect on HRD challenges for the twenty-first century.

At the end of each chapter dealing with the six management skills, we will suggest actions you can take to develop your capabilities in each area. In a section called "Practices and Tasks," we review specific ways managers have begun to practice each of the new skills they need in order to work in a global organization. This helpful list of "to dos" will give you something on which to focus Monday morning!

Finally, in **Part Five, The Continuation,** we will step back and examine the meaning of all that we have discussed for your future as a global manager. The twenty-first century will challenge each of us to develop our potential if we are to fulfill the promise of the new millennium. My own work in the global arena over the last 35 years has made me realize that ultimately this requires a change not only of mindset, but of philosophy, and perhaps in the end, personal style—if not personality.

We are facing a radical shift in the definition of effective management. Rather than being rewarded for creating order out of chaos, we may be entering an era in which creating chaos out of order is the key to personal and organizational survival. In other words, creative, flexible attitudes and the ability to react quickly to unanticipated events may be the major challenge for many of us in the future.

If this is the case, then I, by management experience and training, am the wrong person for the new world and you may be also. But management experience and training may *no longer* be the guide to the future. We all may need to explore new ways of thinking, based not on our past experience but on our future visions. This is not easy and in many ways constitutes a whole new way of learning. Some people have said that we will need to "learn how to learn" all over again.

After reading this book, you will be on the road to global learning. It is one of the keys to becoming a valued and valuable contributor to your organization's future.

WHO WILL BENEFIT FROM THIS BOOK

Since the publication of the first edition of this book four years ago, I have made presentations on globalization and taught seminars to over 5,000 managers from a wide range of companies throughout the world—in Australia, Hong Kong, Indonesia, Japan, Korea, Singapore, Brazil, Colombia, Belgium, Germany, Italy, The Netherlands, Norway, Russia, Sweden, the United Kingdom, and the United States. *A Manager's Guide to Globalization* has been translated into Japanese, Korean, and Portuguese. But many managers have told me that the book was a challenge to read. They found that my presentations and seminars clarified the issue of globalization for them and suggested I revise the book to make it more "user-friendly." This is what I have attempted to do. I have rewritten the book with a lighter style and taken out many of the conceptual frameworks and models that were somewhat confusing.

The book continues to present some original theory, especially in the areas of global mindset, characteristics, and management skills. I have also tried to integrate much of the current literature to ensure that students, teachers, and consultants would have the latest information about globalization. The bibliography has been expanded and updated with many more articles and books on what companies are doing to effectuate globalization. The bibliography has also been arranged by chapter to make these resources as accessible as possible to you.

In the end, however, this book, as the title indicates, is directed toward managers who are working to define their new roles and responsibilities in organizations that are going global. I have tried to provide a framework within which you can understand the globalization phenomenon and cultivate the mindset and skills you will need to manage competently in the new world of international business. I have included a wealth of examples and practical ideas so that you will be able to blend theory and practice in your own work.

To find success as a global manager, you will no doubt face some fundamental challenges to the way you think about yourself and the world around you. I hope this book will provide a roadmap for you through the maze of globalization.

Stephen H. Rhinesmith
Chatham, Cape Cod,
and Boston, Massachusetts
October 1995

ACKNOWLEDGMENTS

This book, while quickly written in 1992 and revised heavily in 1995, has been more than 30 years in its development, with many people contributing to my understanding of the issues I address. While the list that follows is not exhaustive by any means, I would like to acknowledge my debt to those people and institutions who have contributed to my global education.

To AFS (American Field Service) Intercultural Programs, which gave me my first glimpse of the rest of the world at age 17 as an AFS student to Germany, and which later twice entrusted me with the responsibilities and personal fulfillment of its presidency.

To John Naisbitt, who was there when I needed encouragement and who served as the ideal model of the joys of writing about things you care about.

To W. Warner Burke, who has given me wonderful opportunities to develop my ideas through my work with him and his clients, and Mark Kiefaber, with whom I have shared many training weeks testing and developing my ideas.

To clients at American Express, Arthur Andersen, AT&T, ARCO, Baxter International, Bristol Myers-Squibb, Ford, Intel, Motorola, Samsung, Siemens, Sprint, Volvo Truck, WR Grace, and the World Bank, all of whom gave me the chance to work with their executives and managers in globalization efforts.

To Kate Loitz for her superb and sensitive editing of this edition and to Karen Snow for her comprehensive research and excellent organization of the updated bibliography.

To my wife Kathe and my sons Christopher and Colin, who have supported me and endured my many nights on the road and thousands of miles of travel while I gained the experience and developed the perspectives outlined in this book.

FOREWORD TO THE
SECOND EDITION

This revised edition of Stephen Rhinesmith's superb *Manager's Guide to Globalization* could not have arrived at a better time. Today it is clear that our human resources are the competitive edge in the global economy. For hundreds of years a country's natural resources and capital were the measure of a country's wealth. First Japan and then South Korea and the other three economic tigers proved that you didn't have to have natural resources for economic success, and now capital is a globally traded commodity.

That leaves the quality of a country's human resources as the distinguishing characteristic in global competitiveness. How well a country or a company develops its human resources will be the measure of its participation in the global economy of the 1990s.

But as Dr. Rhinesmith points out, the changes in how we manage have as yet been no match for the technological changes and the geopolitical restructuring of the world in which we must now operate. Dr. Rhinesmith helps us rethink the role of management in this new world and redefine the skills needed by managers of global organizations to be responsive and effective in this new arena. He guides us in the transition from thinking about our jobs in a national context to thinking about our organizations in a global context.

In this second edition of the book, Dr. Rhinesmith has refined his groundbreaking work describing the relationship between a global mindset and effective global management. He provides answers to the questions What is the global mindset needed for this new world? What new skills do managers in global organizations need to have? How can we develop a human resource system that can better prepare managers for the world they will face in the twenty-first century?" These are critical questions for our organizations today, and Dr. Rhinesmith provides intriguing insights based on his years of experience in the international arena.

A Manager's Guide to Globalization is aimed primarily at middle and upper managers of large international, multinational, and globalizing companies who are facing the new complexities and uncertainties of a changing world. It will be supremely useful in helping these managers understand what it *really* means to "go global." There is no other publication to date that comes close to providing as much theory and practice on the issue of the human side of globalization. Dr. Rhinesmith's "six skills for success in a changing world" will help managers understand in a very personal, readable way the highly competitive, complex, multicultural, uncertain, and ever-changing world of global management. These six skills—managing competitiveness, complexity, organizational alignment, change, multicultural teams, and learning—are the gateway to personal and organizational success on a global basis and represent many of the new directions for the manager of the future.

Dr. Rhinesmith's basic message is that we must look toward the broader picture with a more systems view of the world, and, in the process, we must learn to deal with the paradoxes and uncertainty that a broader world view thrusts upon us. Both of these ideas are difficult for many managers. Having been raised in a world of limited functional specialization with a reasonable degree of certainty built into professional expertise, many managers today have lived with a very different paradigm than that described in this book. The challenge raised by Dr. Rhinesmith is for them to develop a broader, more flexible mindset and to back it up with a personal ability to deal with less structure and more openness to the unfolding of complex events, many of which cannot be planned for in advance.

While the subject matter of this book is broad, it has been organized in a way that is very readable and teachable. It can be used by human resource managers to reexamine their performance appraisal systems for global management skills, as well as to develop new management and executive training programs to help managers address the important issues outlined by Dr. Rhinesmith.

Since the first edition of this book was published four years ago, Dr. Rhinesmith has been in increasing demand as a speaker and consultant to globalizing companies throughout the world. In this second edition, he shares the insights he has gained and adds many specific examples of the challenges faced by companies "going global." His suggested solutions based on his experience provide valuable help to managers faced with this new "globalization phenomenon."

Yet this book is not just based on Dr. Rhinesmith's experience. One of the important contributions is its excellent bibliography, which has been updated and located at the end of each chapter for easy accessibility. It is probably the best yet compiled in the field of global management.

Finally, and most important, in this second edition Dr. Rhinesmith has provided a framework within which to understand that globalization requires an integrated, systemic view of organizational life. He has constructed the book around three levels of organizational operation—strategy/structure, corporate culture, and people. He stresses that these three levels are delicately interrelated and that a change in one, especially strategy and structure, must be followed by changes in corporate culture and people or new globalization strategies will not be successful.

Dr. Rhinesmith has given us nothing less than a new paradigm for the future management of global corporations. Any leader interested in articulating a global plan, aligning a global corporate culture to this plan, and mobilizing employees to develop the global mindset and skills necessary for personal and organizational success will find this book a must for his or her business management strategy.

John Naisbitt

CONTENTS

PART TWO

GLOBAL STRATEGY AND STRUCTURE

Chapter 3

Managing Competitiveness 47

Chapter 6

Managing Organizational Change   131

PART ONE

THE CONTEXT

1

CHAPTER

Going Global

Globalization has arrived in the world, but not in most of the world's **organizations**. Yet there is little doubt that to be viable during the next century *all* organizations, whether domestic or international, will need to become more global in their outlook, if not in their operations.

It is somewhat ironic that conventional wisdom about the inability of U.S. firms to compete effectively in the global marketplace usually focuses on inadequate spending in technology, plants, and equipment. There is growing evidence that the real vulnerability may lie in the lack of a "global mindset" in key managers, a mindset that enables them to envision the possibilities of a global marketplace and then execute a global strategy effectively.

SEA CHANGES

Robert Reich, the U.S. Secretary of Labor in the Clinton Administration and a former Harvard professor, notes in his book *The Work of Nations* that "we are living through a transformation that will rearrange the politics and economics of the coming century. There will be no **national** products or technologies, no **national** corporations, no **national** industries. There will

---

* Parts of this chapter have appeared in the *Training and Development Journal,* "Developing Leaders for a Global Enterprise" (April 1989) and "An Agenda for Globalization" (February 1991).

no longer be national economies." Reich also says, "All that will remain rooted within national borders are the people who comprise a nation. 'American' corporations and 'American' industries are ceasing to exist in any form that can meaningfully be distinguished from the rest of the global economy" (Reich 1991, pp. 3 and 77).

As much as 32 percent of the content of a McDonnell Douglas aircraft is of foreign origin and MDC chairman John McDonnell expects a substantial increase in coming years. "Our integrated circuit labels read: 'Made in one or more of the following countries: Korea, Hong Kong, Malaysia, Singapore, Taiwan, Mauritius, Thailand, Indonesia, Mexico, Philippines. The exact country of origin is unknown . . . Our MD-11 has an overwing fuel tank made in Spain; the winglet in Italy; the tailcone in Japan and sections of the fuselage in Korea" (Wolff 1994, p. 438).

With such globalization of manufacturing a reality, Reich argues that a nation's commitment to the development of its **people** is the prime way to ensure global competitiveness. If this is true on a national basis, it is certainly true on an organizational level, and this book examines methods of helping people like you become self-confident, competent global managers. Lee Iacocca has said, "If a guy wants to be a chief executive 25 or 50 years from now he will have to be well-rounded. His education and experience will make him a total entrepreneur in a world that has changed into one huge market . . . He'd better speak Japanese or German and understand history . . . and he'd better know those economies cold." Ed Dunn, vice president of Whirlpool, one of the most aggressive global companies, puts it this way: "The world is going to be so significantly different it will require a completely different kind of CEO (with) multi-environment, multi-country, multi-functional, maybe even multi-company and multi-industry experience." (*Paradigm 2000* April/May 1990, pp. 9–10).

Managers are looking for productivity, growth, and competitive advantage in this new global age. Jack Welch, the transformational leader of General Electric, believes, like Reich, that the appropriate prescription is "people power" in companies where the corporate culture is guided by "speed, simplicity and self-confidence." Frank P. Doyle, senior vice president for corporate relations staff at GE, noted during a recent meeting that "people are becoming the winning edge determining the competitiveness of companies and countries" (*Paradigm* 2000 June/July 1990, p. 6).

As the reality of the sea changes in economic and political history becomes undeniable, you can see the reaction in world business all around you. AT&T has introduced a Language Line that provides 24-hour instantaneous interpretation services by phone in 143 languages and dialects. Someone must be "going global" because there is obviously a business need for interpreters! Just call 1-800-752-6096.

To date globalization has had the greatest impact on the telecommunications, electronics/computer, finance, pharmaceutical, chemical, transportation, and automotive industries. If you are in one of these industries, you know it. If you aren't, get ready. It's just a matter of time before you too will be going global.

WHAT DOES IT MEAN TO BE GLOBAL?

There is a great deal of confusion today about exactly what it means to be global. For most people it means doing business abroad. While doing business abroad is a first step, it is not the complete story. To be global, a company not only must do business internationally but also must have a corporate culture and value system that allow it to move its resources anywhere in the world to achieve the greatest competitive advantage. This is far more than exporting, licensing, and distribution agreements or foreign sourcing of technology, capital, facilities, labor, and material. Being global requires a mindset and skills that extend far beyond the current scope of most organizations.

There are five distinct forms of corporations operating in today's global environment. For some, their current form is a stage in development toward more complex forms. For others, their current form is the most appropriate for their industry or the nature of their business. It is also possible, especially in large, complex organizations like AT&T, GE, and ABB, to have all five organizational forms in one corporation. Different industries, different businesses, and different competitive conditions demand different approaches to doing business internationally. The correct question therefore is not Should we go global? but Which aspects of our company could benefit most from being globalized? You will find more on this in Chapter 3, "Managing Global Competitiveness." For the purposes of orientation, however, let's look briefly at the variety of organizations that are most often referred to when people talk about globalization today.

Domestic Enterprise

A domestic business operates solely within its own country, using domestic suppliers and producing and marketing its services and products to customers at home. But as we have already indicated, a domestic enterprise should not consider itself immune from globalizing forces. International hostile takeovers, cross-border mergers and acquisitions, and new market access by roving global competitors can all intrude upon the market niche and profitability of the most secure domestic enterprise.

Traditional wisdom has held that corporations go offshore for markets or cheap raw materials or manufacturing labor. In reaction to the changes in global business, however, a new form of domestic enterprise has recently become part of the new global economy. These are companies like Kmart, Bloomingdale's, and other retailers in the United States who source globally for domestic production and sales. These enterprises see themselves, and are usually seen by others, as purely domestic corporations, utilizing domestic manufacturing sites to produce products for domestic markets, even though they have gone to Tokyo for financing, India for research scientists, or Germany for technology! Such "global-domestic" enterprises, as they might be called, are created to a large extent by executives and managers who have developed a global mindset but who nonetheless enjoy a good profit margin in their home market and have no incentive to market abroad.

Traditional wisdom for domestic companies is so strong that most CEOs of small- and medium-size companies never think about going abroad for capital. Yet there are increasing advertisements, even on television, for banks in the Middle East and Far East eager to provide financing for U.S. domestic corporate needs. When we think of globalization, therefore, we must increasingly think of opportunities for companies that want to remain purely domestic in their manufacturing and sales but are willing to go global for their sourcing of capital, raw materials, technology, and human resources.

Exporter

The exporter, a category that includes thousands of small- to medium-size businesses in the United States, is a successful national business that sells or markets its products and services in foreign countries but operates primarily from its position of domestic competitiveness and advantage. This firm has little information about marketplace conditions outside its national boundaries and will most often operate through independent agents or distributors. The exporter tends to be opportunistic and transitional in form, changing from country to country as trends and events that it does not anticipate or understand affect its success.

Managers in export organizations need some sophistication about assessing global market opportunities. Obviously, they cannot export to countries where there is no demand for their products. Their strategic business intent therefore must be well developed on a global basis, but their organizational structure and skills need not be globally oriented. With luck they need merely to find the right in-country representative to handle their buying or selling needs.

International Enterprise

The international enterprise many times supplements its international sales and distribution capability with localized manufacturing. At headquarters, international operations are often run by an international division, which allows those not involved in international operations to conduct their domestic business fairly independently of any international perspective. Typically, the parent company operates with a centralized view of strategy, technology, and resource allocation, with technology transfer as a key dynamic in headquarters/field relations. Decision making regarding customer service shifts to the local or national level for marketing, selling, manufacturing, and competitive tactics, but the international activity remains largely isolated from core domestic operations.

The international corporation is international in its operations and its business strategy, but only its international division is international in its structure and operations. Because the core corporate culture of the organization is usually unaffected by the international component, there is little interaction between the international and domestic sides of the business. The worldwide operations of giants like NEC, Fujitsu, Mitsubishi, and Siemens are evidence that international corporate organizations can exist successfully. In these companies, foreign operations are still considered to be foreign subsidiaries and are treated as appendages of the home-country headquarters. The greatest danger encountered by international companies arises from this split between their dominant domestic operations and their international divisions. The largely autonomous country subsidiaries, each of which manages different products or businesses, cannot fulfill their potential when they are controlled by a home headquarters that suffers from a domestic mentality—and this can occur even though its international operations may be quite extensive. Until an international company successfully "internationalizes" its headquarters staff and its career paths, it will have difficulty realizing the full benefits of its international operations.

Multinational Enterprise

The multinational enterprise is committed to its international businesses to such an extent that it has established mini-replicas of its domestic business in many different countries and markets. In the process, such an organization may pride itself on turning the management of its foreign operations over to local employees. Nestlé of Switzerland, for instance, owns and operates the Poland Springs designer water company of Maine as a domestic U.S. business.

One of the objectives of a multinational corporation is to look like a "multidomestic" organization. In this form, it hopes that local regulatory authorities will treat the local entity as a national unit. It can thus gain domestic competitive advantage by supplementing its operations with globally sourced resources, skills, and technology.

Global Enterprise

The global organization is an extension of an international or multinational corporation. Instead of **isolating** the international dimension of business, as happens in an international corporation, or **replicating** it in many countries, as does a multinational corporation, the global organization **shares** resources on a global basis to access the best market with the highest quality product at the lowest cost.

Global organizations like Coca-Cola, Gillette, McDonald's, Ford, Shell, ABB, Sony, and Unilever are working to shed their national identities. They are highly adaptive to changes in the environment and extremely sensitive to all global trends that may affect the future. As you can see, this is a very sophisticated form of organization that demands a sophisticated business strategy. The global organization requires a completely different mindset and very adaptable managers and corporate cultures. The global organization constantly scans, organizes, and reorganizes its resources and capabilities so that national or regional boundaries are not barriers to potential products, markets, or new technologies.

In some cases, global enterprises have headquarters outside of their country of origin and may even have **multiple headquarters** for different functions, different product lines, or different businesses. See Figure 1–1 for a comparison of multinational and global company organizations. Differentiation and integration are used in these complex organizational

FIGURE 1–1

A Comparison of Multinational and Global Company Organization

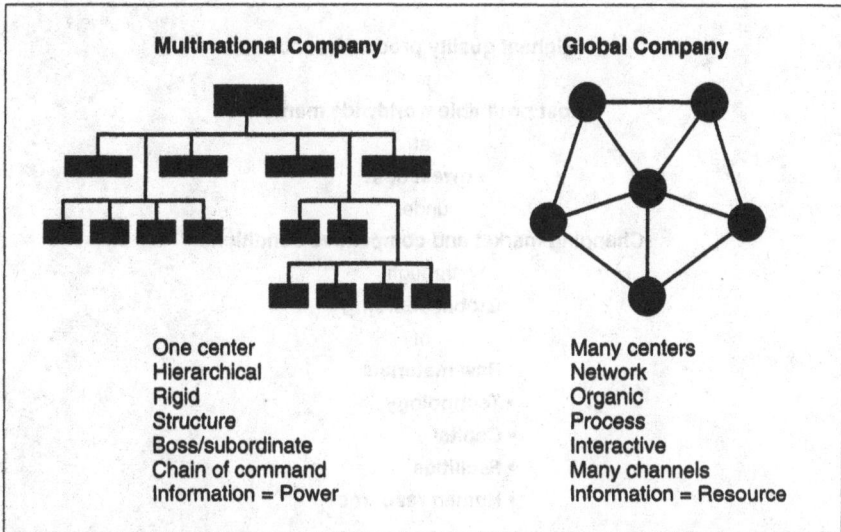

Multinational Company

One center
Hierarchical
Rigid
Structure
Boss/subordinate
Chain of command
Information = Power

Global Company

Many centers
Network
Organic
Process
Interactive
Many channels
Information = Resource

Source: 1992 Training Management Corporation

structures, with heavy emphasis on the simultaneous management of global efficiency, local responsiveness, and global coordination of policy, people, and resources for the greatest competitive advantage and profitability.

A global corporation is always looking for potential products or businesses. As can be seen in Figure 1–2, which represents the components of a global strategy, a global corporation concentrates on delivering the highest quality product to the most profitable markets from the lowest cost positions with the most appropriate management resources, largely without regard to where dollars, people, resources, and technology reside.

To reach and penetrate marketplaces before local or international competitors are equipped to exploit the opportunities, speed, flexibility, and corporate resilience become key factors in the successful management of a global organization. When a corporation moves from an international to a global perspective, an essential shift takes place—a shift from the tight control of a bureaucracy to an entrepreneurial, flexible, rapid-response capability that is totally comfortable with cross-cultural influences and conditions. These are explored in greater detail later in Chapter 5, "Managing Organizational Change."

FIGURE 1–2

The Components of Global Strategy

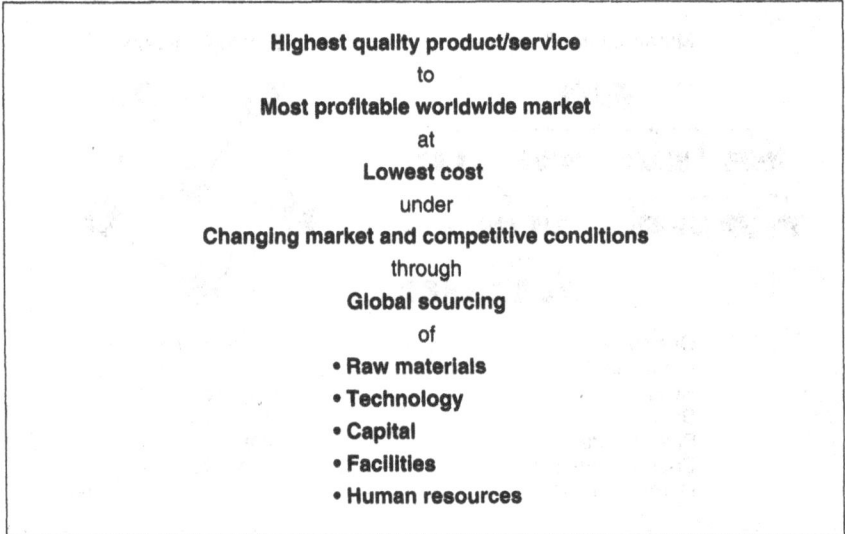

Highest quality product/service
to
Most profitable worldwide market
at
Lowest cost
under
Changing market and competitive conditions
through
Global sourcing
of
- **Raw materials**
- **Technology**
- **Capital**
- **Facilities**
- **Human resources**

Source: Rhinesmith and Associates, Inc., 1992.

Transnational Corporation

Bartlett and Ghoshal (1989) have suggested that there is an additional form in the evolution of the global corporation—the transnational corporation. They believe that the transnational corporation combines the **efficiency** of global structure, the **local responsiveness** of the multinational corporation, and the **technology transfer** capabilities of international enterprises. These three strategic capabilities are blended together into the transnational corporation through its corporate culture and unique integrating and coordinating mechanisms that allow it to simultaneously manage all the advantages of the three earlier developmental stages.

Most global managers do not differentiate between being a global organization and a transnational corporation, but it is important to understand the difference. A *global* corporation concentrates primarily on achieving economies of scale through sharing resources, while a *transnational* organization simultaneously works to meet needs for local responsiveness and global technology transfer while achieving economies of scale and cost efficiencies. To this extent, a transnational corporation is many times more complex and involves some form of matrix organization.

For the purposes of our discussion, the transnational model is a modified global enterprise.

EVOLUTION OF GLOBAL ORGANIZATIONS

While it is not inevitable that an organization should proceed from an international to a multinational to a global structure, the organizational experts Stopford and Wells in 1972 presented a simple diagram (Figure 1–3) that is still relevant to explaining why many companies choose to evolve their international structure. The Stopford and Wells model suggests that at an early stage of foreign expansion, when both foreign sales and the diversity of products sold are limited, worldwide companies typically manage their operations through an international division—an international company. As some companies expand their sales abroad but do not significantly increase their foreign product diversity, they adopt an area or geographical approach—the multinational model. On the other hand, companies that

FIGURE 1–3

Evolution of Global Organizations

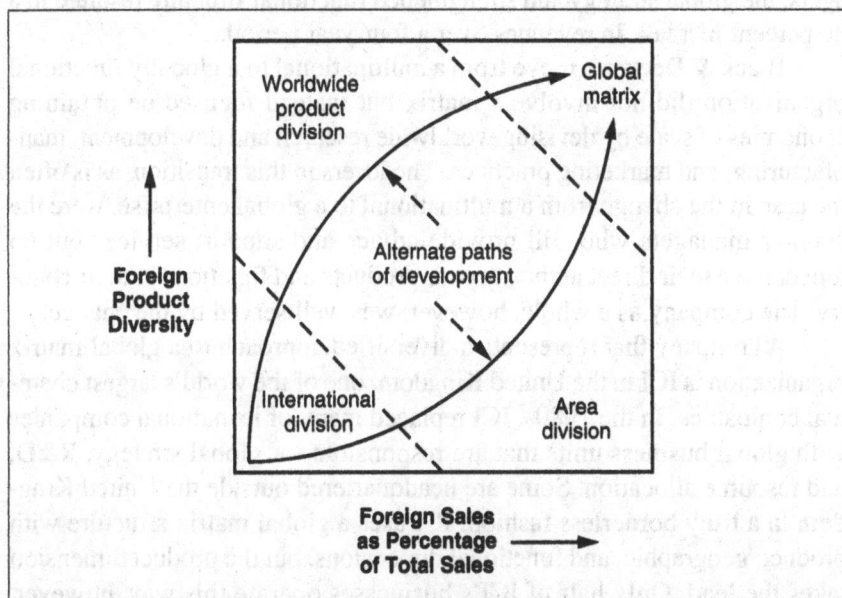

Source: "Evolution of Global Organizations" from *Managing the Multinational Enterprise*, by John M. Stopford and Louis T. Wells, Jr. Copyright © 1972 by Basic Books, a division of HarperCollins Publishers, Inc.

face substantial increases in foreign product diversity tend to adopt a world-wide product division structure—the global approach. When both foreign sales and foreign product diversity are high, companies move to a global matrix structure.

While not by any means prescriptive, this is an interesting way to understand both the evolution of some organizations and the reason why other organizations stop at different levels of development from international to global matrix. A good example is found in Black & Decker, a U.S.-based manufacturer of hand tools that switched from a multinational to a global strategy. In the 1980s, Black & Decker was threatened by a Japanese competitor, Makita, whose strategy to produce and market a wide range of standardized products worldwide made it a low-cost producer that was able to steadily increase its market share. Black & Decker, with its multinational, locally focused structure and products, was unable to respond with adequate cost efficiencies. It embarked on a major program to coordinate new-product development worldwide, resulting in globally standard core products that could be marketed throughout the world. In addition, it consolidated world-wide advertising and gave functional managers authority to coordinate their areas across national borders. While there was resistance from country managers, the global strategy and strengthened functional structure resulted in a 30 percent increase in revenues over a four-year period.

Black & Decker's move from a multinational to a globally functional organization did not involve a matrix but instead focused on obtaining economies of scale by devising worldwide research and development, manufacturing, and marketing practices. The losers in this transition, as is often the case in the change from a multinational to a global enterprise, were the country managers who still provide advice and support services but no longer have their direct authority over products and functions in their country. The company as a whole, however, was well served by the change.

A company that represents a diversified approach to a global matrix organization is ICI in the United Kingdom, one of the world's largest chemical companies. In the 1980s, ICI replaced many of its national companies with global business units that are responsible for global strategy, R&D, and resource allocation. Some are headquartered outside the United Kingdom in a truly borderless fashion. ICI uses a global matrix structure with product, geographic, and functional dimensions, but the product dimension takes the lead. Only half of ICI's businesses operate this way, however, because they represent the best fit between their global structures and their industries. The remaining 50 percent of ICI's businesses are more localized within Europe and many are engaged in exporting to the rest of the world. Thus we see that one company, ICI, can be a domestic, an export, and a global enterprise simultaneously. This is often the case with widely diversified international companies. Clearly, it is not necessary to globalize all product lines of any given business, an idea explored further in Chapter 3, "Managing Competitiveness."

THREE LEVELS OF GLOBALIZATION

Ask Andy Grove, the sage of Silicon Valley and founder of Intel, whether Intel is a global corporation. He will answer emphatically, "Yes." Ask Dov Frohman, director of Intel's Research Center in Israel, the same question and he will just as emphatically answer, "No." Ask Sharon Richards, cross-cultural coordinator for Intel and she will answer, "Yes in strategy, but no in the skills and attitudes of the people and the corporate culture of the company." Who's right? All three are—and that's the first problem with globalization. Nobody, even in the same company, seems to have the total picture of how to make globalization work. In fact, Intel is working conscientiously to integrate and align its global strategy, structure, culture, and people.

There is a great deal of interest today in selecting, training, and preparing managers to work in global organizations. CEOs are defining *globalization* as a major corporate objective of the 1990s, much as *quality* and *customer focus* were driving corporate objectives of the 1980s. But most U.S. firms are confused about how to globalize and particularly about how to instill a global perspective in the human side of an organization. Unlike the 1980s, however, we do not have a Demming, Crosby, or Juran to help us define exactly what global management entails. So how do we make sense of all this? How do we organize the themes and trends of the world into something global managers can deal with on a day-to-day basis?

The first step for any manager, as well as for the organization as a whole, is to develop a **global mindset**—an openness to other cultures that facilitates international dealings and decisions. This is the subject of Chapter 2, "Global Mindset and Global Management Skills." The rest of this book deals with the less theoretical aspects of organizational life, which are divided into three levels of activity: **strategy/structure, corporate culture**, and **people.** (See Figure 1–4.) An integrated approach to managing global organizations addresses all three levels. The problem facing executives, managers, and employees of globalizing corporations is that few people within an organization comprehend all three areas. Senior managers usually

FIGURE 1–4

Levels of Globalization

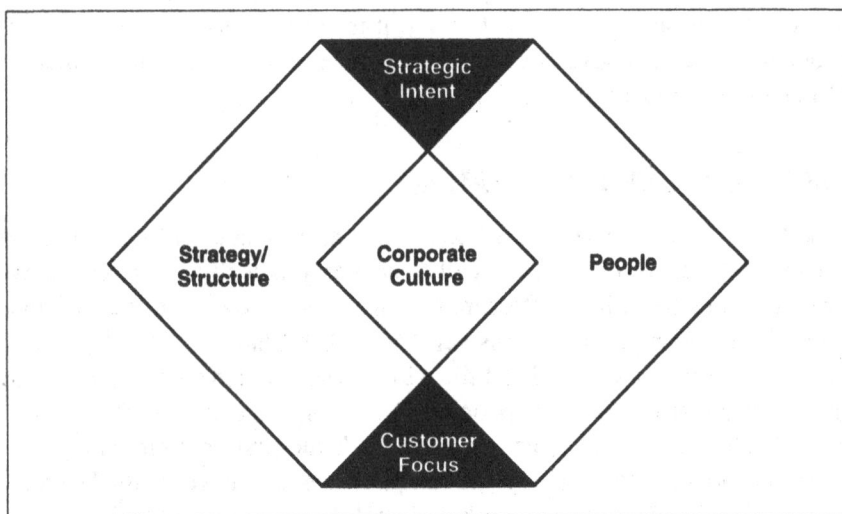

concentrate on global strategy and structure. Middle managers complain that various aspects of the corporate culture prohibit them from acting globally. And human resource people focus on building better interpersonal and cross-cultural skills.

To make matters worse, the situation is no better on the outside. External consultants are biased in one direction or another or have expertise on only one level of managerial activity. Business-school academics are versed in global strategy and structure but not in cross-cultural relations. Cross-cultural experts focus on psychology, with little understanding of strategic business issues. Authors like Bartlett and Ghoshal (1990), who have written about globalization, mention the importance of *administrative heritage* (corporate culture) for globalization but insist that strategy and structure are the determinants of competitive success of a global company. Others, like Copeland and Griggs (1984), convincingly explore cultural factors that affect individuals engaged in global business operations but have not examined these same cultural issues as they apply to a global corporate culture and the problems of managing flexibility and adaptiveness of corporations.

For globalization to be successful, an organization must align its global strategy at all three levels—**strategy/structure, corporate culture, and people**. Failure to do this has been the single most common reason that organizations have failed in their attempts to go global.

Level I: Strategy/Structure

Strategy/structure defines the relatively fixed mix of centralization/decentralization and geographic/functional/business/product structure to be used for best competitive advantage. A global organization must devise a structure that encourages quick decision making. It may relocate some functions to places other than headquarters. A multicentered organization emerges that can serve all parts of the firm anywhere in the world. Philips, for example, is establishing centers of competence in regions where national cultural values and behavior best match the competence. Its long-range technology development center was moved from the United States to the Far East to take advantage of longer-term thinking and reward patterns. IBM and Digital Equipment Corporation have moved their R&D facilities to Italy where intuitive, innovative behavior has been highly successful.

Such structural changes arise from global strategies rooted in straightforward critiques of national and regional cultural standards. The more you know about, and the less you are restrained by, your own cultural attitudes, the more effectively you can contribute to the strategic and structural decisions of a global organization.

Level II: Corporate Culture

Corporate culture encompasses the values, norms of behavior, systems, policies, and procedures through which an organization adapts to the complexity of the global arena. The foremost concern of any global corporation is the speed and agility with which it can respond to new developments anywhere in the world. To achieve this, the corporation must create a common vision and value system that provides guidance for decentralized management. It must also constantly scan the environment for new trends and directions.

Successfully developing a global corporate culture involves not only understanding, skill, and the reallocation of resources but also the ability to deal with issues of identity, power, and psychology that are always difficult to overcome in any organizational change. The quandary has most often been described as the choice between global integration and local responsiveness. The pressures for global integration include the importance of international customers, the presence of multinational competitors, and the investment intensity of new technologies. It is easy to see how each of these areas can take on a global, rather than national, identity and function. The hard part is getting there.

Dow Chemical is a good example of a company that utilizes high-speed information tools to operate integrated global production scheduling. Using a computerized linear programming model, the company weighs everything from currency and tax rates to transportation and local production costs to identify the cheapest maker of each product. In some instances, Dow's computer network chooses among factories on three continents to supply customers throughout the world (Kupfer 1988, p. 48).

Electrolux, the Swedish company that made 100 acquisitions in the 1980s on both sides of the Atlantic, needed to develop conflict resolution tools for management of its highly diverse multinational conglomerate. With a history of extreme decentralization, Electrolux had to move from a company of hundreds of independent villages to a set of flexible networks—with product development, manufacturing, and supply all spanning international borders. Electrolux experienced tension on at least four different levels: between product divisions and marketing companies, between these two types of entities and country managers, between country managers and international product area managers, and between country managers and the international marketing coordinators. To cope with these ongoing issues, the company allocated international responsibility for decisions in a clear and decisive manner to country managers for sales activities and to central departments for other activities. They also co-opted the country managers into a new forum, "The 1992 Group," to oversee the development of all aspects of product-line strategy.

Recent research in Europe has identified five distinct elements critical to building a global corporate culture (Evans, Doz, and Laurent 1990, p. 118):

1. **A clear and simple mission statement**, such as IBM's four goals: profit, quality, efficiency, and growth; and its three values: attract, motivate, and retain.

2. **The vision of the chief executive officer**, such as that of GE's Jack Welch who wants the company to be number one or two in all GE's businesses.

3. **Company-controlled management education**, such as Ericsson and Olivetti's global management development centers in Britain—not Sweden or Italy, their home countries.

4. **Project-oriented management training program**, such as the one-week seminar ICL, the British computer company, put its top 2,000 managers through in order to change its corporate culture.

5. **Emphasis on the processes of global corporate culture**, such as the board-level involvement at ICI, BP, and Philips in all appointments of the top 100 managers.

Developing a global corporate culture with appropriate management practices depends heavily on molding the institutional attitudes and skills of executives, managers, and employees throughout the organization. Without a global corporate culture, the best vision or global strategy will never get off the ground.

Level III: People

The people level of our model involves the development of human resources to manage teams, uncertainty, and personal and organizational learning in a way that enables the organization to continuously improve in spite of constant global, market, and competitive change.

In the end, a global organization's people, and especially its global managers, constitute *the most critical factor* in the organization's ability to survive and grow. People represent an organization's purpose, mission, values, and mindset, which are the generative juices that enable it to respond creatively to the unanticipated. Thus, in a global organization, the human resource challenge is the traditional one of recruitment, selection, training, and succession planning, but on a global scale from global sources. Global and cross-cultural training and career-path planning are fundamental for all global managers, regardless of their domestic or international assignments.

GLOBALIZATION LEVELS AND CORPORATE OBJECTIVES

Now you must examine how these various levels of globalization fit with your company's objectives. Figure 1–5 provides an overview of globalization levels and corporate objectives. Each level of globalization has its own drivers that set corporate objectives.

At Level I: Strategy/Structure, the drivers are the nature of the business and the environment in which your company is operating. The business objective, *profitability,* is achieved through strategy and structure that enable your business to respond effectively on a global basis. Note that the drivers of a global company's strategy and structure are not just technology, competition, and customers. Many companies are finding that they need to be more global not only to serve global customers but also to more effectively utilize the advantages offered by global suppliers.

FIGURE 1–5

Globalization Levels and Corporate Objectives

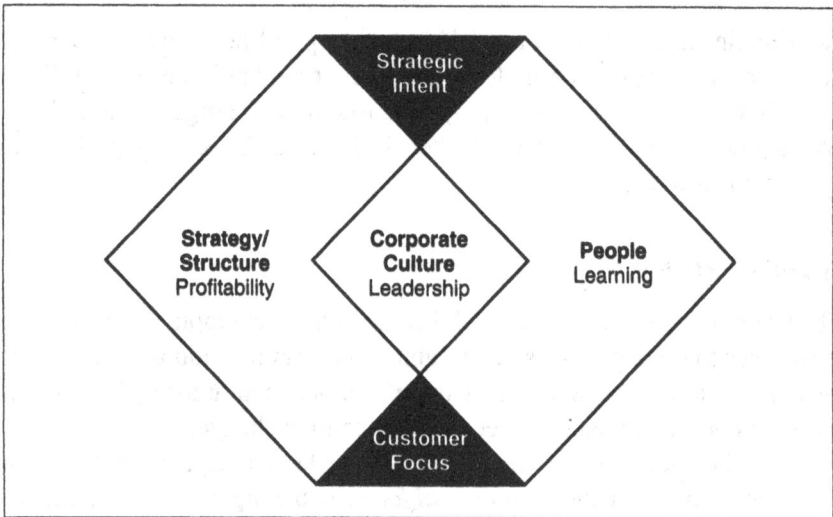

At Level II: Corporate Culture, the driving forces are the interest, perceptions, and values of *leadership*. It is fairly clear that leaders set the priorities, perceptions, values, and interests of corporations and establish the recognition and reward systems that encourage behavior the leaders feel is critical for the corporation to achieve its strategic objectives. The resulting corporate culture allows the organization to be resilient and adaptable to changes in the environment.

Global leaders are responsible for **articulation** of the global business strategy and structure, **alignment** of the corporate culture to support this strategy and structure, and **mobilization** of the people to execute these strategies. Managers in a global organization support these activities and ensure that the organization operates in such a manner that these activities are efficiently and effectively carried out.

At Level III: People, the driving force should be *human resource professionals*, who in partnership with line management provide a human resource system that stimulates individual and organizational learning. Too often in the past, HRD professionals have lagged behind in their capacities to develop people with the appropriate mindsets and skills for the future. In a successful global organization, however, you will find the HRD function is increasingly sophisticated and a major partner with line management in achieving all levels of global success.

ALIGNING STRATEGY/STRUCTURE, CORPORATE CULTURE, AND PEOPLE

Perhaps the most fundamental challenge global companies face is aligning their corporate culture and people with their new global strategies and structures. In company after company, managers are finding that it is far easier to develop a new strategy and to change a company's structure than it is to make the new strategy and structure work. For this, people must broaden their mindset, learn new skills, and make a commitment to an innovative way of working, always the most difficult task.

As a result, globalization implies a major human resource challenge. Meeting this global management challenge will be expensive in both time and resources. U.S. firms need to get on with the task of building a new model for leadership development in a global community—a model that derives not from the traditional management skill base of planning, staffing, and control, but rather from a recognition of a whole new array of leadership requirements.

The challenge for all of us involved in management, as well in the development of management, is to change the context in which we think about our human development responsibilities. We clearly need to discard traditional models and views and begin to think from a global rather than a domestic paradigm. In the process, we must challenge and change many of our views about hiring, training, controlling, motivating, and measuring our managers. This change will require a long-term commitment, probably three to five years for most large enterprises simply to get moving. In all likelihood, it will take a full generation to implement the approach. By that time, the world will have changed again, and we will have a whole new game to worry about!

Before you move on, think about a question raised by Robert Reich in *The Harvard Business Review*: "Who Is Them?" and "Who Is Us?"

Mazda's new sportscar was designed in California, financed in Tokyo and New York, its prototype was created in Worthing, England, and it was assembled in Michigan and Mexico using advanced electronic components invented in New Jersey and fabricated in Japan. (Reich 1991, p. 79.)

Now, who is "us"?

What are the mindset and skills you will need to execute global strategies? How do you develop an integrated approach to globalization that allows global strategy and structure to be supported by a global corporate culture and a globally aware workforce? These are some of the issues you will explore in the next chapter, "Global Mindset and Global Management Skills."

SELECTED BIBLIOGRAPHY

Adler, Nancy. *International Dimensions of Organizational Behavior.* Boston: Kent Publishing, 1986.

Adler, Nancy, and Dafina N. Izraeli, eds. *Women in Management Worldwide.* Armonk, N.Y.: M.E. Sharpe, 1988.

Bartlett, Christopher A., and Sumantra Ghoshal. *Managing Across Borders: The Transnational Solution.* Cambridge: Harvard Business School Press, 1989.

————. "Matrix Management: Not a Structure, a Frame of Mind." *Harvard Business Review,* July–August 1990, pp. 138–45.

Copeland, Lennie, and Lewis Griggs. *Going International: How to Make Friends and Deal Effectively in the International Marketplace.* New York: Random House, 1985.

Coulson-Thomas, Colin. *Creating the Global Company.* New York: McGraw-Hill, 1992.

Davis, Stanley M. *Future Perfect.* Reading, Mass.: Addison-Wesley, 1987.

Drucker, Peter F. *The Changing World of the Executive.* New York: Times Books, 1985.

————. *The New Realities.* New York: Harper & Row, 1989.

————. "The New World According to Peter Drucker." *Business Month,* May 1989, pp. 48–59.

Evans, Paul, Yves Doz, and Andre Laurent, eds. *Human Resource Management in International Firms: Change, Globalization, Innovation.* New York: St. Martin's Press, 1990.

Ghoshal, Sumantra, and Nitin Nohria. "Horses for Courses: Organizational Forms of Multinational Corporations." *Sloan Management Review,* Winter 1993, pp. 23–35.

Grove, Andrew S. "A High-Tech CEO Updates His Views on Managing and Careers." *Fortune,* September 18, 1995, pp. 229–30.

Hampden-Turner, Charles, and Alfons Trompenaars. *The Seven Cultures of Capitalism: Value Systems for Creating Wealth in the United States, Japan, Germany, France, Britain, Sweden and the Netherlands.* New York: Doubleday, 1993.

Heenan, David A, and Howard Perlmutter. *Multinational Organization Development.* Reading, Mass.: Addison-Wesley, 1979.

Johnston, William B. "Global Workforce 2000: The New World Labor Market." *Harvard Business Review,* March–April 1991, pp. 115–27.

Kupfer, Andrew. "How to Be a Global Manager." *Fortune,* March 14, 1988, pp. 43–48.

Lussler, Robert N., Robert W. Baeder, and Joel Carman. "Measuring Global Practices: Global Strategic Planning through Company Situational Analysis." *Business Horizons,* September–October 1994, pp. 56–63.

Mitroff, Ian. *Business Not as Usual.* San Francisco: Jossey-Bass, 1987.

Moran, Robert T., and John R. Riesenberger. *The Global Challenge: Building the New Worldwide Enterprise.* London: McGraw-Hill Book Company, 1994.

Naisbitt, John. *Megatrends: Ten New Directions Transforming Our Lives.* New York: Warner Communications, 1982.

————.*Global Paradox: The Bigger the World Economy, the More Powerful the Smallest Players.* New York: William Morrow & Company, 1994.

Nelson, Carl A. *Managing Globally: A Complete Guide to Competing Worldwide.* Burr Ridge, Ill.: Irwin Professional Publishing, 1994.

O'Hara-Devereaux, Mary, and Robert Johansen. *Global Work: Bridging Distance, Culture and Time.* San Francisco, Calif.: Jossey-Bass, 1994.

Overman, Stephanie. "Shaping the Global Workplace." *Personnel Administrator,* October 1989, pp. 41–44 and 101.

Paradigm 2000 Newsletter 1, no. 1, (April/May) 1990.

———, no. 2, June/July 1990.

Reich, Robert B. "Who Is Us?" *Harvard Business Review,* January–February 1990, pp. 53–64.

———. "Who Is Them?" *Harvard Business Review,* March–April 1991, pp. 77–88.

———. *The Work of Nations: Preparing Ourselves for 21st Century Capitalism.* New York: Alfred A. Knopf, 1991.

Rhinesmith, Stephen H. "An Agenda for Globalization." *Training and Development Journal,* February 1991, pp. 22–29.

Sherman, Stratford. "Are You as Good as the Best in the World?" *Fortune,* December 13, 1993, pp. 95–96.

Steingraber, Fred G. "Managing in the 1990s." *Business Horizons,* January–February 1990, pp. 49–61.

Stopford, J.M., and L.T. Wells, Jr. *Managing the Multinational Enterprise.* New York: Basic Books, 1972.

Thurow, Lester. *Head to Head: The Coming Economic Battle among Japan, Europe and America.* New York: William Morrow and Company, 1992.

Toffler, Alvin. *Powershift: Knowledge, Wealth and Violence at the Edge of the 21st Century.* New York: Bantam, 1990.

Wolff, John. "The Ancient Art of Globalization: We Truly Will Be a Global Industry Only When We Produce Globally." *Vital Speeches of the Day,* 1994, pp. 437–40.

2

CHAPTER

Global Mindset and Global Management Skills

Whirlpool's CEO, David Whitwam, believes that the key to globalization is getting your organization—and not just top management—to think globally.

> For a company to become a truly global enterprise, employees have to change the way they think and act, taking on progressively more responsibility and initiative until the company behaves globally in all of its parts—without the CEO cracking the whip (Maruca 1994).

Success requires both thinking and acting.

But how can you as a manager develop a global mindset and the global management skills you need to meet the changing, emerging, increasingly complex conditions we have been describing?

THE GLOBAL MINDSET

First, of course, we must agree on what a mindset is. For our purposes, a mindset is a predisposition to see the world in a particular way, a filter through which you look at the world. In order to become an effective global

---

* Parts of this chapter have appeared in the *Training and Development Journal* in "Global Mindsets for Global Managers" (October 1992).

manager, you must examine and modify your existing mindset, essentially to broaden your perspective.

A mindset is a *way of being* more than a set of skills, an orientation to the world that allows you to see certain things that others do not see. People with an optimistic mindset tend to see the glass as half full rather than half empty. People with an entrepreneurial mindset see opportunities to open new business areas in ways that translate into success. And people with a global mindset look at the world as an arena in which to express their talents, maximize their success, and influence others. Most important, **a global mindset is something you can develop.** And it is not as tedious as it may sound. The global mind sees the world as a playground as well as a school.

The global mindset you should be aiming for helps you scan the world from a broad perspective, always looking for unexpected trends and opportunities that may constitute a threat or an opportunity to achieve your personal, professional, and organizational objectives. People with a global mindset tend to approach the world in six specific ways. By understanding and cultivating these attitudes, you can move toward the global perspective that underlies the six skills for success as a global manager. These mindset attributes are aligned with the three levels of globalization—strategy/structure, corporate culture, and people.

Mindset Attributes for Managing Strategy and Structure

To manage strategy and structure, you must be concerned about how your function and organization fit into your industry, how to create competitive advantage, and how to prepare yourself to meet the increasing demands of a complex world. We will discuss this in more detail in Chapters 3 and 4. Two mindset attributes provide the foundation for your ability to manage structure and strategy in a global organization.

People with a global mindset drive for the broader picture A global manager is constantly looking for *context,* concerned about the backdrop against which current events are happening. This backdrop may include some history, but it is more concerned with broad current and future trends. A global mind is never content with a simple explanation of an event, never satisfied with one task when it can manage a project, never happy with a project when it can manage an organization. People with a global mindset are constantly scanning the horizon of their profession, business, and industry to learn more about potential markets and competitors, new technology, and new suppliers.

Even if you are in a company that has not taken the decision to go global, be aware that there is a great need today for managers with a global mindset in companies that view themselves as domestic. Many people argue that there is no longer any such thing as a domestic organization of any consequence because if you are successful domestically, there is an increasing probability that a foreign competitor will enter your market to challenge your position. As we will see in the next chapter, many organizations that market to domestic customers must also be more globally oriented to source materials, technology, capital, and even people that can help them provide the best product at the highest quality and lowest cost.

Global scanning of information about your business, therefore, is an important skill for *any* manager of *any* organization, domestic, international, or global.

People with a global mindset balance contradiction inherent in the many demands placed on them by the competition, marketplace, stakeholders, and environment The concept of *balance* is central for a global mindset because it entails the simultaneous appreciation of contradictory ideas. As a global manager, you may find yourself in a global matrix organization with many competing demands by functional, geographic, and various business units that are often in conflict. You are asked by your country manager to be responsive to a local customer, an alteration that may in turn undercut your ability to be responsive to a global customer or to reduce costs on a regional level to meet the incursion of a global competitor. A traditional manager may spend many hours trying to prioritize the demands, seeking an optimal resolution of the conflicts, but a global manager recognizes that another demand will surface tomorrow. The global manager learns to *live* with conflict rather than to try to *resolve* the conflict inherent in a global matrix organization. One day, the answer will flow in one direction, and the next day it will tilt toward another solution. This means that you will need to hone your analytical, negotiating, and influencing skills if you are to survive in the constant push and pull of global management. This is easier said than done, but you must develop balance to thrive in a global organization.

Mindset Attributes for Managing Corporate Culture

In addition to mindset attributes for managing strategy and structure, the successful global manager must align corporate culture and have a mindset that balances the contradictory forces of control and flexibility.

People with a global mindset engage process first by learning to trust process over structure, then by aligning it to ensure consistency of execution of global strategies and the effective deployment of global policies Most of us have spent our careers in organizations that solve problems by changing structure. We have also reported through functional lines that identify us with a particular organizational unit rather than with the customer or a process, like total quality. Global organizations today, however, find that to be successful they must stress cross-functional process more than hierarchical structure. As a result, managers are learning to look at core competencies, value-chain management, total quality management, and many other processes that are geared to marshaling the resources of the total organization to achieve business objectives.

A global mindset is therefore oriented toward process over structure. It is that simple—and that difficult. Managers with a global mindset are willing to sometimes make the tradeoff of their own interests or the interests of their unit for actions that will enhance the business as a whole. To do this, however, the managers and the business must be focused on integrating processes, not establishing fiefdoms. People with a global mindset recognize and acknowledge that process is more powerful than structure—indeed, that process is the key to organizational adaptability, resilience, and survival.

People with a global mindset flow with change and manage their organization's ability to respond to surprise and ambiguity as opportunities for new initiatives A global mindset is comfortable with surprise, ambiguity, and change, having experienced enough of the world to know that events are unpredictable for many reasons. Sometimes we are surprised because global circumstances are too complex; sometimes we are surprised because they are simple, but outside our experience; sometimes we are surprised for reasons that are simply unknowable. Feeling comfortable with ambiguity, accepting surprises, and seeing change as opportunity are all part of the global mindset you must develop if you are to succeed in a rapidly evolving business world.

Mindset Attributes for Managing People

The ability to develop an effective global strategy and structure, then align and execute it through the proper corporate culture, ultimately depends on your people skills. How well do you manage multicultural teams and how well do you learn the new ideas, attitudes, and behavior necessary to work in a constantly changing world?

People with a global mindset *value diversity* and work well with multicultural teams as a basic way to accomplish their professional and organizational objectives Multicultural teamwork is a fundamental filter for a global mindset. Global organizations cannot be successful without teamwork among many different regions, product lines, and functions. Without question, managers with a global mindset cannot conceive of operating successfully by themselves because the challenges are too great, too diverse, and too geographically spread out to be dealt with by any one person. Teamwork and interdependence must replace the Superman management style.

In the process of global teamwork, managers find tremendous diversity of backgrounds, cultures, values, beliefs, and behavior. Multicultural team members have a wide range of expectations concerning how they work together. As part of developing a global mindset, you must acquire the sensitivity and flexibility to meet the needs of diverse people while attaining project and organizational objectives.

People with a global mindset continuously seek to *learn globally* by rethinking boundaries and trying to be the best in the world at what they do   People with a global mindset are constantly searching for improvement in their professional and private lives by opening themselves to surprise, not insulating themselves from the unexpected. It has been observed that there is a difference between being trained and being educated: To be trained is to be prepared *against* surprises; to be educated is to be prepared *for* surprises. Not a bad definition. As a global manager, you must be educated rather than trained because global management is *full* of surprises.

Successful global managers also realize they will be involved in *lifelong learning*. There is no end to the knowledge and experience a global manager needs. To be a fully effective manager in a global organization, you must challenge yourself to learn about ever-broader regions of the world, to become acquainted with international trade, currency, and government regulations, and to learn how to manage people from many cultures and organizational backgrounds. This is *in addition* to your technical and professional expertise and your knowledge of your company and industry.

These six aspects of a global mindset form the foundation for our six key global management skills. You can tell as much by the verbs used to describe the global mindset as by the nouns. The *verbs* indicate that people with a global mindset

> *Drive*
>> *Balance*
>>> *Engage*
>>>> *Value*
>>>>> *Flow*
>>>>>> *Learn*

These actions represent a tremendous range of abilities. As a global manager, you must be a doer yet be willing to occasionally step back and "go with the flow." You must align process and ensure that your decisions are coordinated with the overall strategy of your company while at the same time you must be open to the changes that will surprise you in a complex, competitive world. And you must value teams and teamwork while continuously seeking to improve the quality and rewards of professional life for yourself.

The global mindset can be compared with the more traditional managerial mindset that may be perfectly legitimate for some domestic organizations but in a global context requires *additional* perspectives. Note that the global perspective is not *instead of* the traditional mindset, but *in addition to*. Such complexity is characteristic of the modern world. We are never allowed to replace the old with the new, we just add more requirements that make life more complex. You will see this in particular in the next chapter's discussion of the forces pushing organizations to go global. The contrast between the traditional management mindset and the global mindset is illustrated in Figure 2–1.

FIGURE 2–1

Comparison of Traditional and Global Mindsets

	Traditional Mindset	**Global Mindset**
Strategy/Structure	Specialize	Drive for broader picture
	Prioritize	Balance contradictions
Corporate Culture	Manage job	Engage process
	Control results	Flow with change
People	Manage self	Value diversity
	Learn domestically	Learn globally

Moving managers from a domestic to a global profile is not an either/or process; it is a both/and process. In other words, you do not give up your functional perspective and skills when you drive for the bigger, broader picture. You *add* the bigger, broader picture to the functional skills you already have. This often depends on the degree to which an organization rewards behavior in the second column versus the first.

THE GLOBAL MINDSET AND PERSONAL CHARACTERISTICS

There is a definite connection between a global mindset and personal qualities or characteristics. It is possible that you will adopt an attribute of the global mindset more easily *because* of a personality trait you already have. For example, you may value cross-cultural diversity (a mindset attribute) because you are a person who is sensitive to interpersonal differences (a characteristic). On the other hand, modifying your mindset may enhance a certain characteristic. To follow the above example, valuing cross-cultural diversity may lead you to become a person who is more interpersonally sensitive to cross-cultural differences.

Human resource managers have spent years trying to develop screening and selection procedures for identifying global managers. Most of these screening mechanisms have used personal characteristics as the basis for testing, because it is difficult to test a candidate's mindset. Obviously, the best test of a global manager is behavior, not mindset or characteristics, but this is nearly impossible to measure in advance unless the person has been with an organization for a long time. Perhaps the best approach is to use what screening tools are available for hiring, but to rely more on developing global mindset attributes and skills within the organization. (For more on this issue, see Chapter 8, "Managing Learning.")

Figure 2–2, outlines the relationships between the six defining attributes of the global mindset and the personal characteristics associated with these attributes. Competent global managers are described as

Knowledgeable

    Analytical

        Strategic

            Flexible

                Sensitive

                    Open

FIGURE 2–2

Global Mindset and Personal Characteristics

	Global Mindset	Personal Characteristic
Strategy/Structure	Drive for broader picture Balance contradictions	Knowledgeable Analytical
Corporate Culture	Engage process Flow with change	Strategic Flexible
People	Value diversity Learn globally	Sensitive Open

The most effective global managers also display a good mix of self-confidence and humility. People who adapt best cross-culturally are those who feel relatively secure with themselves. You will always encounter some form of challenge in cross-cultural interactions, and often this challenge is directed at questions of who you are and what you believe in. When faced with such issues, the most successful people are those who have a reasonably well-clarified philosophy and approach to life that is inclusive, rather than exclusive, of others. They are experienced enough to be confident in their judgments, but also know that there is rarely one right answer to any issue of importance and that every major decision requires a certain amount of circumspection, questioning, and listening for new viewpoints.

Imagine how difficult it is for an engineer, trained to expect that there are correct answers for many technical problems, when he or she faces the challenge of becoming a global manager where decisions must be made with a lack of information, doubts about expertise to make proper judgments, and time pressure that will not allow adequate analysis. The interpretation of ethical dilemmas from a cross-cultural perspective, for example, is one of many challenges you will face.

Again, let's look at the characteristics you should cultivate as they align with the three levels of global management that all managers need to attend to: strategy/structure, corporate culture, and people.

Characteristics for Managing Strategy and Structure

Knowledgeable

Constantly driving for the broader picture will necessarily make you more *knowledgeable*. As a global manager, your technical, business, and industry insight is the fundamental quality that allows you to successfully manage the competitive process, both domestic and foreign. Your knowledge must be broad as well as deep and must have a well-developed international dimension that includes constant scanning of information and competitive and market conditions on a global basis.

Analytical

You must have highly developed *analytical* ability to deal with the complexity of global operations and the contradictions of global matrix organizations. Let's face it. Managing in a global matrix organization in 75 countries is more complex than managing in a small- or medium-size functional business in one country. To be able to operate successfully in a global organization, you must be able to take a broad view of the world and view the business as a system. As Peter Senge has eloquently noted in *The Fifth Discipline* (1990), managers need to have a "systems view" of the world as well as "personal mastery" of their function. A systems view requires the ability to understand different levels of business vision, mission, and strategy and to grasp their implications for global structure, culture, and people.

Characteristics for Managing Corporate Culture

Strategic

We have noted that a global manager is constantly challenged to align process across the organization rather than to manage in functional, geographic, or product silos. While this is not easy for someone who has become used to one way of life, one world view, and one comfortable skill set, the demands for a new strategic vision are undeniable. The management of a global corporate culture that is adaptable and capable of dealing with rapid change in the environment requires that you hone your strategic skills. Being strategically aligned will allow you to focus on the right issues and add value to the *horizontal* processes that form the core competitive competencies for your organization.

Flexible

The speed and constancy of change, as well as the complexity of many global organizations, leads many managers who have gained a reputation for technical expertise to feel overwhelmed by the lack of certainty they encounter. This is not uncommon and may be one of the reasons you are reading this book. Uncertainty requires new capacities to see change as opportunity, not threat, and to be flexible enough to respond quickly. As a global manager, you will find that more and more of your decisions must be made with inadequate information, or at least less information than you are used to having. You must therefore be willing to make decisions based on your experience, rather than on refined empirical data. For this reason, most competent global managers have rather broad experience and a demonstrated ability to operate under many different managerial, organizational, and international circumstances.

Characteristics for Managing People

Sensitive

Since a global organization conducts the majority of its creative and operational work in multicultural teams, global managers must have a sensitivity to cultural diversity that few people possess naturally. Learning to be cross-culturally sensitive is a formidable challenge. It requires not only a sensitivity to others, which is so often stressed, but also a fairly well-developed ego and self-concept, which is often not stressed.

The ability to operate cross-culturally comes more naturally to some than to others, but in any case, it demands unending adjustments. With the wide range of cultures and people in the world, you will find some more difficult to deal with than others. Those who work internationally must, therefore, be constantly attentive to increasing the range of their skills and abilities to work constructively with the broadest range of people and cultures.

Open

Finally, all successful global organizations are seeking continuous improvement. Continuous improvement, in turn, does not happen unless you are willing to constantly reexamine your own and your organization's performance. And this improvement cannot be achieved without a capacity for reflection.

Your ability to reflect on recent and current events will equip you for dealing with the next round of challenges. It will also enable you to weave some sense of development and progress into the fabric of your professional life and the lives of the organization and people with which you work. Most successful global managers are driven by life-long learning because they recognize that they can never know too much about the world around them.

These are the six personal characteristics behind the six attributes of the global mindset. As you strive to cultivate them, be aware of how readily they cross-fertilize. Your increased flexibility will quite naturally increase your confidence to deal with process over structure, which in turn will allow you to become even more flexible. All of these mindset attributes and personal characteristics underpin the six global management skills that form the keys to success.

GLOBAL MANAGEMENT SKILLS

If the global mindset and personal characteristics are the *being* side of global management, then management skills are the *doing* side. A management skill is the capacity to execute specific action at a level sufficient to achieve a desired effect, and it arises from your cultivation of mindset attributes and personal characteristics. You can see in Figure 2–3 how the six mindset attributes provide a fertile field for development of the six skills required of a successful global manager. As Figure 2–3 illustrates, the global management skills are again aligned with the three levels of organizational activity.

FIGURE 2–3

Global Mindset and Management Skills

	Global Mindset	Management Skill
Strategy/Structure	Drive for broader picture	Managing competition
	Balance contradiction	Managing complexity
Corporate Culture	Engage process	Managing alignment
	Flow with change	Managing change
People	Value diversity	Managing teams
	Learn globally	Managing learning

Management Skills for Strategy and Structure

Managing competition You must constantly scan your environment for changes in customer, market, competitive, and supplier conditions, as well as socioeconomic and political trends that may affect your organization and its strategic intent. Then you must determine your global strategy and the kind of organizational structure you will use to execute this strategy. This is the subject of Chapter 3.

Managing complexity When you begin to operate in a global organization, you must learn to manage the tradeoffs among many competing interests, as well as deal with the inherent contradiction and conflict that exist in all global organizations. You will need to understand what should be centralized and what should be decentralized, where country managers should have power and authority and in what areas global product managers must have the final authority. You may also have to learn to manage from three or four different perspectives as you find yourself on different coordinating councils and task forces. This is the subject of Chapter 4.

Management Skills for Corporate Culture

Managing alignment You must strive for a global corporate culture with the values, beliefs, systems, and norms of behavior that allow you to implement decisions in a way that is speedy and responsive to your customers and preemptive to your competitors. Many globalization efforts fail because managers do not pay enough attention to aligning their corporate culture with their new strategic directions. As part of this alignment, information systems, financial systems, and performance appraisal and reward systems, to name a few, must be altered to reflect the globalization of the organization and to reinforce the new behavior that you and your employees will need to operate in the new environment. This is the subject of Chapter 5.

Managing change You must accept and manage the ever-present chaos of your environment in a way that provides for continuous improvement, while providing structure and taking advantage of opportunities that can arise from the lack of structure. Global organizations operate in a more complex environment, one in which the "best laid plans" will never be enough. One in which there will always be surprises and sometimes there may be chaos. Accepting this as the normal state of affairs is difficult for many managers who over the years have learned to be (or present themselves as being) on top of things. When you move into a global world, there is too much to be on top of. So you should think about allowing yourself times when things are a little out of control. Without such interludes, creativity and innovation will be stifled. This is the subject of Chapter 6.

Management Skills for People

Managing multicultural teams   You must develop the sensitivity and managerial skills demanded by a multicultural environment in order to lead, understand, manage, and supervise people from a wide range of cultures in a broad range of situations. A newly global business environment draws in many new people from a wide variety of backgrounds. Unless you have spent time overseas or had some frequent interaction with people from other cultures, you will be startled by the differences that exist in management style, decision making, the management of meetings, and the ways people are motivated and supervised. This area of cross-cultural management is one of the most daunting for many people assigned to global management for the first time. It can also be one of the most rewarding as you work with and get to know people from all over the world. This is the subject of Chapter 7.

Managing learning   You must not only continuously learn about yourself but also train and develop others in effective global management. By facilitating constant organizational learning, you will make your business responsive and adaptive to global change and challenge. An important part of global management, learning must be both personal and professional and eventually must extend to the degree to which you are able to develop learning in others and in your organization. It is clear that the people and organizations that will survive in the future will be those for whom learning is a primary activity. You may need to look at your career differently, consider an overseas assignment, and attend training programs that you previously felt were outside your scope of work or interest. This is the subject of Chapter 8.

A MANAGER'S GUIDE TO ACTION

Let's pull all of this together into a framework that illustrates the relationships among skills, characteristics, actions, and attributes of the global mindset.

FIGURE 2-4

A Global Manager's Guide to Action

Strategy/Structure

1. Manage **competitiveness** by being *knowledgeable* and *driving* for the broader *picture*.
2. Manage **complexity** by being *analytical* and *balancing* contradiction.

Corporate Culture

3. Manage **alignment** by being *strategic* and *engaging* process.
4. Manage **change** by being *flexible* and *flowing with change*.

People

5. Manage **teams** by being *sensitive* and *valuing diversity*.
6. Manage **learning** by being *open* and *learning globally*.

In Figure 2–4, A Global Manager's Guide to Action, you can see how the six skills relate to each of their associated variables. As you work on developing various skills, mindset attributes, and characteristics, be aware of how they interact. As we have noted, you can start at any point. By concentrating on the **actions,** you can develop the skills and characteristics of a global manager and the attributes of a global mindset. You will gain an understanding of how they affect your ability to manage in a global organization and what other managers and companies have done to apply each skill to compete in the global marketplace. Each of the following chapters ends with a list of specific actions you can take to enhance your progress as a successful global manager.

Figure 2–5 shows another way for you to visualize the relationships among the skills, characteristics, actions and attributes of the global mindset. In this fan diagram, each area away from the core represents one of the six global management skills. At the same time, the diagram provides a list of the characteristics, actions, and global mindset attributes that success demands.

DIFFERENT NEEDS FOR GLOBAL MANAGEMENT SKILLS

Not *all* managers in a global organization may need the full arsenal of global mindset attributes, characteristics, and skills. Percy Barnevik, the head of ABB has said

FIGURE 2–5

Global Skills, Characteristics, Actions, and Mindset Attributes

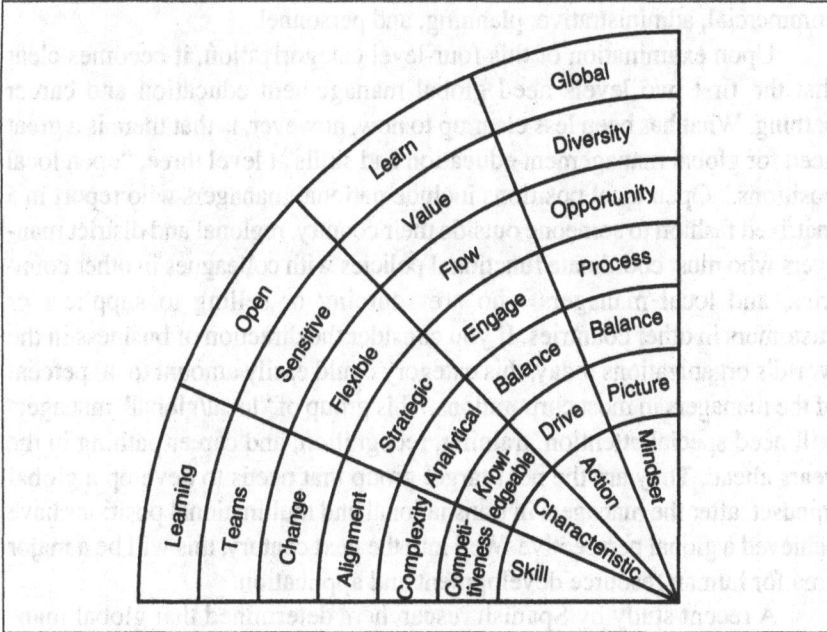

A global company does not need thousands of global managers. We need maybe 500 or so out of 15,000 managers to make ABB work well—not more. I have no interest in making managers more "global" than they have to be. We can't have people abdicating their nationalities, saying "I am no longer German, I am international." The world doesn't work like that. If you are selling products and services in Germany, you'd better be German! (Taylor 1991, p. 94)

One useful way of looking at different managers in a global organization has been suggested by Enrico Auteri and Vittorio Tesio of Fiat (1991, p. 10). They have developed four categories of positions operating at different levels in a global organization. **Transnational positions** operate over the whole geographic area pertaining to the business without segmentation or limitations. **Multinational positions** operate in the context of several countries defined by specific limitations. **Open local positions** operate within the context of a single nation, with significant links, reference points, and dependence on elements outside the country. **Local positions** operate within the context of a single nation on the basis of locally determined variables, without significant interaction with other countries. Within these definitions, Autero and Tesio found that more than 40 percent of the managerial positions of Fiat worked with international interaction. The most exposed areas were commercial, administrative, planning, and personnel.

Upon examination of this four-level categorization, it becomes clear that the first two levels need global management education and career pathing. What has been less clear up to now, however, is that there is a great need for global management education and skills at level three, "open local positions." Open local positions include national managers who report in a matrixed fashion to someone outside their country, regional and district managers who must coordinate functional policies with colleagues in other countries, and local managers who are sourcing or selling to suppliers or customers in other countries. If you consider the direction of business in the world's organizations today, this category could easily amount to 40 percent of the managers in most corporations. This group of "local/global" managers will need special attention, training, recognition, and career pathing in the years ahead. They are the next target group that needs to develop a global mindset, after the managers in transnational and multinational positions have achieved a global perspective. Well into the next century, this will be a major area for human resource development and application.

A recent study by Spanish researchers determined that global managers are less in evidence than is commonly believed and that, in fact, regional management is more widespread than global management (Roure et al., 1993). Local and regional managers need to operate more narrowly within a local culture and many times must have relationships with people throughout the society that will help them with their management responsibilities. This is one reason that many international corporations prefer to have local managers handle local affairs.

It may be true that few industries, if any, require global managers at every level. Managers at different levels have widely varying responsibilities and perspectives, and few managers have jobs that are globally integrative in nature. For most managers, "managing internationally" means managing regionally, rather than globally. Operating on a regional basis, however, requires the same mindset and skills we have outlined for the global manager. A regional or local manager operating within a regional framework must balance multiple objectives, meet conflicting interests of marketing, labor, product, and financial pressures, and justify results to management.

Local country managers are the people most affected when a company decides to change from a geographic to a regional or global product structure.

For "Mr. American Express" in the local country, who under a multinational management structure was responsible for profit and loss as well as all product initiatives, it is a massive shock to become a "liaison" who is only consulted when regional or global product managers decide that they will introduce a product into his local market to gain regional or global competitive advantage or meet the needs of a regional or global customer. In essence, the local country manager moves from a line to a staff position. **This shift of local country management from line to staff responsibilities is consistently one of the greatest human resource challenges of globalization.**

Moran and Riesenberger differentiate between the mindset and skills needed by a corporate CEO, corporate staff, subsidiary general manager and staff, and all employees. They discuss 12 global competencies, outlined below, and attempt to differentiate the degree to which each of these four groups needs to possess each competency.

Moran and Riesenberger's 12 Global Competencies

1. Possesses a global mindset.
2. Works as an equal with persons from diverse backgrounds.
3. Has long-term orientation.
4. Facilitates organizational change.
5. Creates learning systems.
6. Motivates employees to excellence.
7. Negotiates and approaches conflicts in a collaborative mode.
8. Manages skillfully the foreign deployment of expatriates.
9. Leads and participates effectively in multicultural teams.
10. Understands his or her own culture, values, and assumptions.
11. Accurately profiles the organizational culture and national culture of others.
12. Avoids cultural mistakes and behaviors in a manner that demonstrates knowledge and respect for other countries.

These 12 competencies are substantially incorporated in the six mindset attributes, characteristics, and skills defined above. While it seems clear that not *all* managers in global organizations need all six attributes, characteristics, and skills, all managers who have responsibilities that interface with managers in other countries, regions, or product lines will need to have most of them. Drawing too fine a separation among the globalization needs for different categories of management works against developing a truly global corporate culture that encourages participation by all of the management team.

INTEGRATION OF GLOBAL MANAGEMENT SKILLS WITH LEVELS OF GLOBALIZATION

The relationships among the skills of the global manager and the levels of globalization are illustrated in Figure 2–6. It demonstrates how the six skills apply to the three organizational levels: strategy/structure, corporate culture, and people.

To deal effectively with organizational **strategy and structure**, you must learn to manage the **competitive process** and **organizational complexity**.

Managing a global **culture** requires the ability to simultaneously **align** organizational **process** *and* flow with **change**.

To ensure that global strategy is *fully* implemented, however, requires alignment not only of the corporate culture, but also the **people** in the organization. Aligning people requires the ability to manage multicultural **teams** and **personal learning**.

FIGURE 2–6

Framework for an Integrated Approach to Globalization

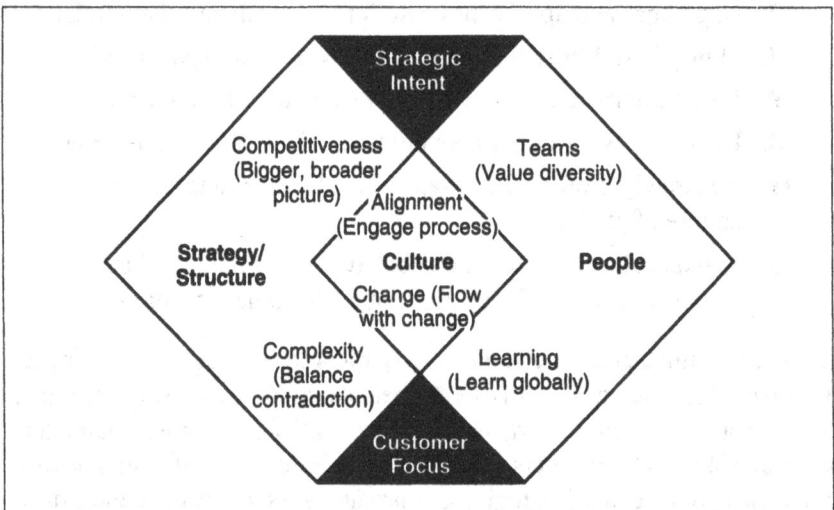

This integrated approach to globalization combines well-known theories of organizational change concerning alignment with the specific skills that global managers must master. In general, these skills will be needed at least by the top three to four levels of most large global companies, or about 10 percent of the total workforce. For an organization of 50,000 people, therefore, you could expect about 5,000 people to have developed many of the skills, characteristics, and mindset attributes outlined in this chapter.

GLOBAL SKILLS, PRACTICES, AND TASKS

One of the most important pieces of this framework involves the translation of a *skill* into specific practices and tasks that will enable you to impact others in your organization. This is the *operational* level, where your actual success will be measured. Remember that a skill is a specific capacity to execute action at a level sufficient to achieve a desired effect. Each skill requires *practices* that are distinctive and contribute to the skill. These practices, in turn, translate into a series of *tasks* that you must execute to be effective. For example, to be successful at managing the competitive process (**skill**), you must constantly scan the global environment for potential competitors (**practice**). To accomplish this, you must read a wide assortment of publications and perhaps take out a subscription to the *Asian Wall Street Journal* or *The Economist* to supplement your current reading of the local or even national newspaper (**task**).

In another instance, to manage complexity successfully (**skill**), you may have to manage relationships that are simultaneously cooperative and competitive, such as a strategic alliance with a foreign competitor (**practice**). To do this well requires analytical skills (**characteristic**) to determine which aspects of the relationship are cooperative and which competitive, and to compartmentalize information, decision making, and operations accordingly (**task**).

GLOBAL COMPETENCY LEARNING CYCLE

The last link in this framework for the global manager's six skills for success is an analysis of how all of these variables relate to one another in a way that enables you to understand and develop the mindset attributes, personal characteristics, and managerial skills to perform the necessary practices and tasks. A manager is *globally competent* when he or she has the six mindset attributes, personal characteristics, and management skills

to perform the necessary tasks and practices of successfully operating
in a global environment.

Figure 2–7 diagrams the relationships among these in the global competency learning cycle. In this process, a skill is developed by the constant
flow of mindset attribute to practice to task to mindset attribute. In the application of mindset to behavior, you develop a skill. But remember that a
global mindset and its attributes are not in themselves skills. You can have
a skill only when your expanded global mindset is applied to your behavior.

Likewise, a characteristic is not a skill. You may be flexible by nature
but not apply that flexibility to working with organizational change. Flexibility becomes a global managerial skill when you use your natural flexibility to adjust to changes in the organization and to adjust the organization
to changes in the environment. A personal characteristic, however, is not
a part of the formal learning process. It exists either as a contributing factor to the original mindset or as a result of the learning process. It is therefore diagramed outside the global competency learning cycle.

These six development clusters represent the essence and focus of
the leadership development and training necessary to support the global
enterprise. In this chapter, you have studied an integrated framework for
globalization that encompasses both *organizational* analysis of

FIGURE 2–7

Global Competency Learning Cycle

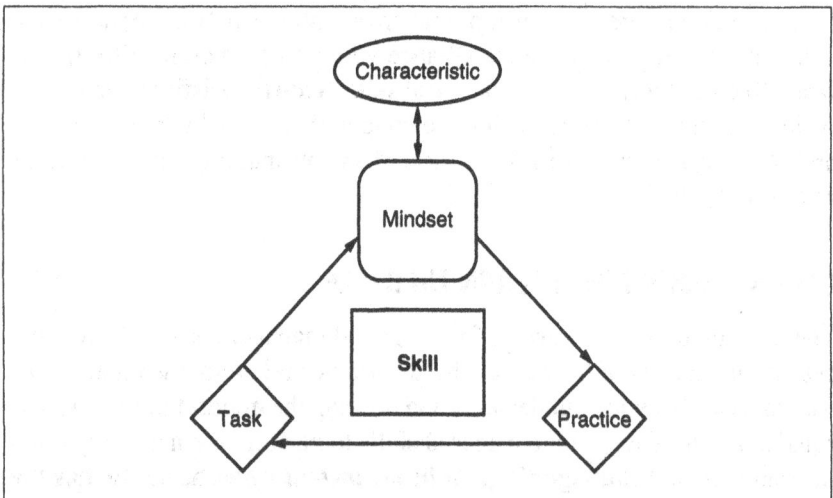

strategy/structure, corporate culture, and people and *managerial* mindset attributes, characteristics, and skills. In the following chapters, you will explore the context within which these competencies operate and examine specific practices and tasks that you as a global manager can undertake to improve your ability to make a meaningful and significant contribution to your organization's globalization process.

SELECTED BIBLIOGRAPHY

Auteri, Enrico, and Vittorio Tesio. "The Internationalization of Management at Fiat." *Journal of Management Development*, February 1991, pp. 26–27.

Barker, Joel Arthur. *Discovering the Future: The Business of Paradigms*. St. Paul, Minn: ILI Press, 1989.

Bartlett, Christopher A., and Sumantra Ghoshal. "Matrix Management: Not a Structure, a Frame of Mind." *Harvard Business Review*, July–August 1990, pp. 138–45.

———."What Is a Global Manager?" *Harvard Business Review*, September–October 1992, pp. 124–32.

Boyatzis, Richard E. *The Competent Manager: A Model for Effective Performance*. New York: John Wiley, 1982.

Chesanow, Neil. *The World-Class Executive*. New York: Rawson Associates, 1985.

Cleveland, Harlan. *The Future Executive*. New York: Harper & Row, 1972.

Copeland, Lennie, and Lewis Griggs. *Going International: How to Make Friends and Deal Effectively in the International Marketplace*. New York: Random House, 1985.

Ferguson, Henry. *Tomorrow's Global Executive*. Homewood, Ill.: Dow Jones-Irwin, 1988.

Fisher, Glen. *Mindsets: The Role of Culture and Perception in International Relations*. Yarmouth, Me.: Intercultural Press, 1988.

Kupfer, Andrew. "How to be a Global Manager." *Fortune*, March 14, 1988, pp. 43–48.

Lane, Henry W., and Joseph J. DiStefano. *International Management Behavior*. Scarborough, Ontario: Nelson Canada, 1988.

Maruca, Regina Fazro. "The Right Way to Go Global: An Interview with Whirlpool CEO David Whitwam." *Harvard Business Review*, March–April 1994, pp. 135–45.

Moran, Robert T.; Philip R. Harris; and William G. Stripp. *Developing the Global Organization: Strategies for Human Resource Professionals*. Houston: Gulf Publishing, 1993.

Moran, Robert T., and John R. Riesenberger. *The Global Challenge: Building the New Worldwide Enterprise*. London: McGraw-Hill Book Company, 1994.

Peak, Martha H. "Developing an International Management Style." *Management Review*, February 1991, pp. 32–35.

Rhinesmith, Stephen H. "Global Mindsets for Global Managers." *Training and Development Journal*, October 1992, pp. 63–68.

Rhinesmith, Stephen H.; John N. Williamson; David M. Ehlen; and Denise S. Maxwell. "Developing Leaders for a Global Enterprise." *Training and Development Journal*, April 1989, pp. 24–34.

Rossman, Marlene L. *The International Businesswoman: A Guide to Success in the Global Marketplace*. New York: Praeger, 1986.

Roure, Juan; Jose Luis Alvarez; Carlos Garcia-Pont; and Jose Nueno. "Managing Internationally: International Dimensions of the Managerial Task." *European Management Journal* 11, no. 4 (December 1993): pp. 485–92.

Senge, Peter. *The Fifth Discipline: The Art and Practice of the Learning Organization*. New York: Doubleday, 1990.

Stewart, Edward C. and Milton J. Bennett. *American Cultural Patterns: A Cross-Cultural Perspective*. rev. ed. Yarmouth, Me.: Intercultural Press, 1991.

Taylor, William. "The Logic of Global Business: An Interview with ABB's Percy Barnevik." *Harvard Business Review,* March–April 1991, pp. 91–105.

Tichy, Noel, and Mary Anne Devanna. *The Transformational Leader*. New York: John Wiley & Sons, 1986.

PART TWO

STRATEGY/STRUCTURE

3

CHAPTER

Managing Competitiveness

In 1987 when David Whitwam took over Whirlpool as CEO, it was mired in an unwinnable war in the North American appliances market. Seeing growth opportunities outside the United States, Whitwam led Whirlpool to its daring $1 billion purchase of N.V. Philip's European appliance business, which was itself in trouble. This move catapulted Whirlpool overnight into

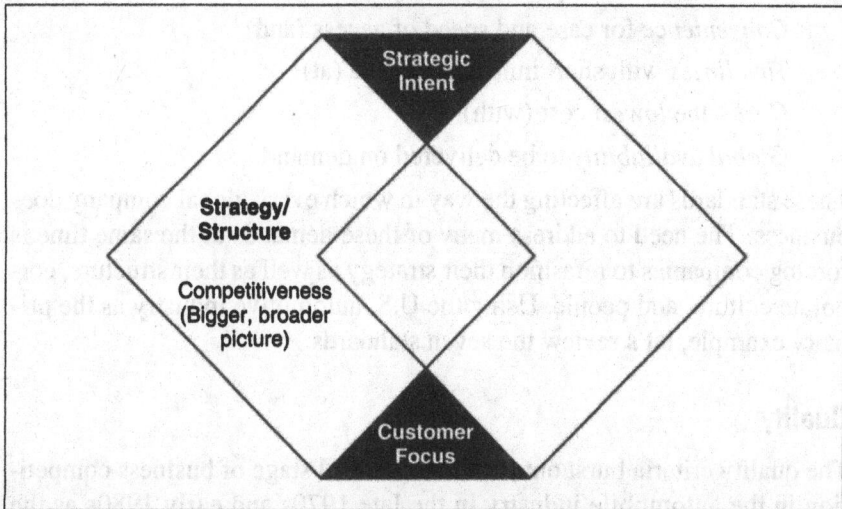

the number one position in the worldwide appliance business. In the ensuing years, however, Whitwam spent a great deal of time and money molding once parochial organizational values, systems, and methods of
operation, and unifying them into a consumer-focused global organization
that uses its talents to achieve breakthrough market performance around the
world. In 1987 Whirlpool was primarily a North American company. Today
it manufactures in 11 countries and markets products in 120 locations as
diverse as Thailand, Hungary, and Argentina. A new era is underway for
Whirlpool and for the appliance industry as a whole.

NEW STANDARDS OF GLOBAL COMPETITIVENESS

Whirlpool went global to access new markets and develop new strength
through acquisition. It was also responding to a changing world in which
competitive and customer pressures demand that companies compete on
many more fronts than ever before. While there are many factors contributing to the complexity of the current global marketplace, seven standards of competitiveness have emerged in the 1990s as critical to a
company's success. Even more important, many of these standards must be
met *simultaneously* if a company is to be successful against a wide range
of competitors. The seven standards are

> *Quality* of product and process (with)
>
> *Variety* for maximum choice (and)
>
> *Customization* for specific tastes (provided with)
>
> *Convenience* for ease and speed of access (and)
>
> *Timeliness* with short innovation cycle (at)
>
> *Cost*—the *lowest* cost (with)
>
> *Global availability* to be delivered on demand.

These standards are affecting the way in which every global company does
business. The need to address many of these demands at the same time is
forcing companies to refashion their strategy as well as their structure, corporate culture, and people. Using the U.S. automotive industry as the primary example, let's review the seven standards.

Quality

The quality criteria burst onto the international stage of business competition in the automobile industry in the late 1970s and early 1980s as the

Japanese invaded the United States with quality cars that outshone the Big Three American car manufacturers. The new product quality raised intense interest among American auto manufacturers (and many others) in how the Japanese attained their superior products. Upon closer examination, they recognized that this new level of product quality could not be achieved without totally new quality processes.

The Americans' first response was to try to duplicate some of the Japanese process through quality circles. While a first step, quality circles were difficult to implement because they were part of a larger cultural and organizational system that was more team oriented in Japan than in the individualistic United States. It took the Americans some years before they realized that quality was not just a manufacturing process, but a total management process. As Total Quality Management (TQM) became understood and utilized in the United States, organization after organization started to change not just its process but its strategy, structure, culture, and people to achieve the new quality standards.

In June 1980, a fortuitous event put the American automobile industry on the path to its new competitiveness. A Ford manager was watching a late-night television program about W. W. Demming. He decided to invite him to assist Ford in the redesign of automobiles to compete with the Japanese. The result—the Ford Taurus—changed the face of competition not only with the Japanese, but also among the Big Three, as Taurus has become the best-selling car in the United States.

Quality of product, process, and, eventually, service has increasingly become the focus for many organizations to enhance their competitive position. But in the 1990s, a dramatic shift has taken place: **Quality is becoming commoditized**. Quality is no longer a means of gaining global competitive advantage. It is now a minimum entry point into global competition. You simply cannot compete globally if you do not have high-quality products and services.

As consumer demand for high quality intensifies, many companies and many countries have been left behind. The commoditization of quality will also have a strong effect on the capacity of many of the newly emerging economies to compete on a global basis, and it will enhance the importance of regional and other trade associations where countries can be protected from global competitive forces. Russia, for example, will find it very difficult to compete in finished goods on a global basis. Most of Russia's international economic activity of the 1990s has been developed in commodities—oil, gas, cotton, timber, diamonds, and other materials—

that condemn it to operate as a developing country, dependent on the supply and demand cycles of a commodity market. While this is one way for Russia to become integrated into the global economy after years of "self-management," it will be a long time before Russian manufacturing will produce goods for export at the quality level demanded by the global marketplace.

Variety

Not only are global companies faced with world-class quality competition, but new customers are demanding that quality products and services be delivered in increasing variety. At the 1995 auto show in Detroit, there were 671 different types of motor vehicles, including cars, trucks, and vans. There is no reason why anyone needs this kind of choice. But the demand for variety is the result of changing social tastes, the desire to be identified with new socioeconomic-ethnic groups, and the increasing wealth and education of the middle class throughout the world.

All consumer products are facing this dilemma. The supermarkets of the United States now have an incredible 217 breakfast cereals from which to choose! The increasing sophistication of the choices desired by newly emerging consumer groups, combined with the technological capacity to produce variety in an abundance unknown in the past, mean that to be globally competitive corporations must be prepared to offer much greater variety in their products and services.

Customization

The desire for variety at the extreme raises demands for customization. The Japanese responded with the Lexus push-button seat control that allows you to establish settings for two drivers. Prior to entering the car, you push a button that adjusts the wheel, seat, mirrors, and other interior features to your preferred settings. Thus ends the feud between large and small people over who left the seat forward.

To meet demands for variety, companies are turning to new manufacturing, assembly, and marketing processes. For example, Mazda's newest sports car was designed in California and financed in Tokyo and New York; its prototype was created in Worthing, England; and it was assembled in Michigan and Mexico using advanced electronic components invented in New Jersey and fabricated in Japan.

Convenience

On January 17, 1995, Chrysler Corporation announced that beginning in July 1995, customers could special-order certain models of cars and have them delivered 16 days after the order date. The same process in 1994 took 36 days. In 1993, 73 days. Ford immediately countered with a goal to deliver certain models in 15 days.

This kind of speed to market is increasing in numerous industries. The banking industry started some years ago with its initiation of automatic teller machines. The advent of the ATM allows people to have access to money at *their* convenience—anytime, 24 hours a day. Banking service has been revolutionized from the sleepy model of the 1960s and 70s to the aggressive computer- and telephone-based banking that allows people to do all their banking from home or across the country.

Another form of convenience is the miniaturization accomplished by Sony. Starting with portable radios and tape players, Sony has cultivated portability and miniaturization as a core competence to enabling it to capture market share not solely by manufacturing a high-quality product, but by making it convenient to access and use anywhere at any time.

Timeliness

New product innovation cycles are also rapidly speeding up. With fast-changing technological advantages and increasing market segmentation around the world, companies that are able to develop new products on a rolling basis will gain greater market share. They will be able to respond to the latest demands from the most up-to-date technological base.

The most heralded company in this regard is 3M, which five years ago set a target of obtaining 20 percent of its revenues from products that had not existed five years earlier. Today, its target is to earn 35 percent of its revenues from products that did not exist three years ago. 3M has made timeliness and innovation part of its corporate culture. Apple Computer reported that for the year ending September 30, 1993, it derived 75 percent of its revenues from products that didn't exist *one year* before! The lesson is that someone, somewhere, is thinking the impossible, or at least what might appear to be the impossible.

Dow Chemical is the sixth-largest chemical company in the world, but it is aiming to take on the characteristics of a small company in order to preserve its capacity to respond quickly to demands in the marketplace.

As a result, it has broken down a $19 billion company (as of 1993) into 32 business centers to foster entrepreneurial initiative. Many companies are following Dow's lead and organizing themselves to be simultaneously large and small, thereby gaining the efficiencies of a large business, while retaining the flexibility and responsiveness of small businesses.

Cost

Most global business people will agree that cost has replaced quality as the main competitive pressure of the 1990s. Not that quality is not important; it remains critical. But many customers are now demanding that the highest-quality product be delivered at the lowest possible price. The days of premium prices for higher quality are gone in many industries, and driving costs out of product processes has become a major objective of the 1990s for almost all companies. Business, management, and consulting activities are focused on re-engineering of product, process, support, and management with an unprecedented intensity.

Ford is engaged in its largest reorganization since Henry founded the company—and it is driven by the need to drive costs out of the product development process to remain competitive with Toyota and others. Alex Trotman, Ford CEO, wants to pull together Ford's scattered operations around the world to create an integrated company that will serve the market in India as well as the one next door in Indiana. This massive effort, known at the company as "Ford 2000," means that dozens of engineering centers around the world will be merged into five new ones, and 25,000 salaried employees will move to new locations, or at least report to new bosses. Ford will revolutionize the way it designs and develops the 70 or so lines of cars and trucks that it sells in over 200 markets. Volume purchases and reduced duplication of effort are expected to save more than $4 billion a year. If these savings are realized, Ford will more than double the $3.8 billion profit that its automotive operations made in 1994.

The cost focus has also had international implications. Cheap labor, as one means of reducing costs, is changing. With advanced technology, unskilled labor is becoming a smaller and smaller component of globally manufactured goods. As a result, developing countries that used to have a global competitive advantage from low-cost labor are finding that competitive advantage eroding. Instead, skilled labor is at a premium and developed regions like the United States, Western Europe, and Japan are now going to India and Russia for computer software programmers who will work at a fraction of the cost of their home-market skilled labor force. Skilled jobs are being exported, not unskilled, and this is having a dramatic effect on the global talent pool.

Other economic and social dislocations are being created by the cost-consciousness of the 1990s. Not only are skilled labor positions going off-shore, but value-chain management is resulting in new attention to suppliers. Ford, in its Ford 2000 globalization effort, will be reducing its suppliers by 90 percent, from 50,000 to 5,000! The only suppliers who will survive the Ford cut will be those who can deliver their products on time to vehicle design centers and manufacturing and assembly plants throughout the world.

Global Availability

This focuses attention on the last standard of global competitiveness—global availability of products and services. Many global service businesses in consulting, telecommunications, banking, and other industries are discovering that their clients are going global and in the process, expect global services that are consistent around the world, available in every country, and consolidated, billed, and reported through a central product manager.

For many service industries, this entails a restructuring of operations from country to regional or global product managers, reconfiguring their financial and information systems and reorganizing their personnel to operate on a global, as well as local, basis. The demands are simply creating havoc in some organizations. But those who are successful will have acquired a major competitive advantage.

New demands for quality, constantly changing tastes, global fads, and short product life cycles are all pushing enterprises to seek global partnerships and alliances to gain access to new markets, or to defend markets that are currently held. If you ask most major American corporations that have ambitious global expansion plans what is driving their interest, they will respond that their U.S. market is mature and that the newly emerging markets of Eastern Europe, Western European integration, and the rapidly developing markets of the Far East and Latin America provide new profit opportunities that have to be exploited. To gain access to these markets, however, companies are developing local joint ventures and interregional strategic alliances at an explosive rate.

These emerging markets are attracting American companies from aerospace to telecommunications and consumer products. Coca-Cola estimates that by the end of the 1990s, the United States may account for no more than *10 percent* of its profits. It already makes 80 percent of its profits from operations outside the United States. Robert Keough, the president of Coca-Cola, has said, "When I think of Indonesia—a country on the Equator with 180 million people, a median age of 18, and a Moslem ban on alcohol—I feel I know what heaven looks like!" (Cohen 1991)

THINKING OUTSIDE WHOSE BOX?

On each of these seven dimensions there has been a company or a country that thought "outside the box" to develop a competitive advantage. You can assume that there are leaders, managers, and companies somewhere in the world who are thinking the impossible with regard to your business. What is perceived to be possible and what is perceived to be impossible in today's world appear to be a function of two major factors in most companies.

The first factor affecting the possible is the vision of leadership. I have been in meetings with senior managers who have told employees that they were setting not just "stretch" targets, but "irrational" targets, for revenues or cost reductions. A senior vice president of exploration and production of a Texas oil company congratulated his senior managers on having cut 25 percent of their cost base the year before. He acknowledged that it had been a difficult and excruciating job for everyone and that he appreciated all the efforts because it had moved the company from number 15 to number 9 in the per-barrel cost of oil production. He congratulated them on this major achievement. But he went on to say that for the coming year, he expected another 25 percent cut in the production price. His managers were wide-eyed. They argued that this was impossible. They reminded him of how difficult it had been to take out the first 25 percent and said that it would be impossible to take out another 25 percent and still do business the way they had been. He agreed and responded that that was just the point. They would now need to do business *completely differently* in order to reduce costs by another 25 percent. When his managers asked how they could do that, he responded, "I don't know, I just know you have to do it."

Irrational targets force people to think outside the box. They must reinvent processes and methods to find ways to meet the new targets. In many companies today in many parts of the world, there are people setting targets that you and your company would never consider because you think it is impossible. **To succeed in today's global business environment, competing with the best in the world, you have to think the impossible and demand the irrational.**

A second source of thinking outside the box is in the synergy available from the representation of many cultures. Samsung's President Lee has announced a corporate goal of becoming a $200 billion company early in the twenty-first century; it is currently a $60 billion company. When asked how this will be achieved, he said he did not know but that it is important for Samsung to be the world's largest manufacturing company. Korean culture and its attendant visioning process will gain commitment and support from a Korean workforce, a very different and more powerful effect than the same process will have in the United States. This is due in large measure to cultural differences. Because thoughts and actions are so heavily culture-dependent, what is rational for one culture may be irrational for another. For large Japanese corporations, the kind of downsizing being undertaken in many large U.S. businesses in the 1990s is unthinkable because their culture endorses lifelong employment. The Japanese are worried that their inability to shed costs through personnel reduction may put them at a disadvantage in the race to be the low-cost producer. In this case, Americans have the cultural advantage in what is "thinkable."

As a global manager, do not hesitate to reexamine what's in the box and what's outside the box. The exercise will broaden your thinking and may engender some surprising solutions to the problems you confront.

FUNDAMENTALS OF INTERNATIONAL STRATEGY

How are companies responding to these global competitive changes? What impact do these trends have on international strategy? George Yip (1992) has identified three elements that impact a global strategy—globalization drivers, global strategy levers, and global organization and leadership.

Globalization Drivers

Globalization drivers are primarily outside the control of a business. They include market, cost, government, and competitive factors that affect a company's ability to be competitive in different areas of the world. **Each industry has its own level of globalization potential that is determined by external drivers.** For example, common customer needs and tastes may result in customers in different countries having similar demands. Many factors affect whether needs and tastes are similar or dissimilar, including differences in economic development, climate, physical environment, culture, and political structure. These factors are *outside the control* of a company, and if they change, the business will have to change.

A recent survey of 3,000 technology companies in the global electronics and computer industry revealed 10 major drivers of globalization of an industry that has rapidly gone global in the 1990s (Baatz 1993). These 10 drivers and the percentage of companies responding that each is an important reason for going global are

1. Speeding up delivery to customer (45%).
2. Improving ties with strategic partners abroad (42%).
3. Supporting domestic customers' international operations (34%).
4. Meeting cultural needs of foreign customers (31%).
5. Accessing new technologies (25%).
6. Avoiding overseas protectionism (25%).
7. Finding lower taxes and government benefits (23%).
8. Accessing foreign technical and management talent (22%).
9. Accessing low-cost labor (10%).
10. Avoiding domestic regulatory constraints (9%).

Note that the biggest drivers have to do with customer-driven delivery and support. Of the top four drivers, three are related to providing better service. Most of the remainder have to do with governmental matters, either domestic or foreign.

Globalization Levers

Globalization levers are the means that companies have to respond to changes in their environment. According to Yip, four specific levers, and the degree to which they affect a company, determine whether it pursues a global strategy, which seeks to maximize worldwide cost efficiencies and performance through *global* resource sharing and integration, or a multinational strategy, which seeks to improve worldwide performance by maximizing *local* competitive advantage, revenues, and profits. These are (1) the extent to which the business offers the same or different products or services around the world; (2) the location of value-adding activities from research to production to after-sales service; (3) the degree to which a worldwide business uses the same brand names, advertising, and other marketing elements in different countries; and (4) the nature of global competitors and the degree to which competitive advantage can be gained by playing one country or regional market against another.

You can quickly see that different industries and companies would pursue different strategies depending on the nature of their business. Whirlpool CEO Whitwam says:

> The only way to gain lasting competitive advantage is to leverage your capabilities around the world so that the company as a whole is greater than the sum of its parts. Being an international company—selling globally, having global brands or operations in different countries—isn't enough . . . To me, "competitive advantage" means having the best technologies and processes for designing, manufacturing, selling and servicing your products at the lowest possible costs. Our vision at Whirlpool is to integrate our geographical business wherever possible, so that our most advanced expertise in any given area—whether it's refrigeration technology, financial reporting systems or distribution strategy—isn't confined to one location or one division. We want to be able to take the best capabilities we have and leverage them in all of our operations worldwide. (Maruca 1994, p. 140)

Whitwam is working to create a truly global organization, not a multinational company operating in different countries.

Unilever, on the other hand, takes a more multinational approach. The Unilever Group includes Unilever PLC, a British company, and Unilever NV, a Dutch company. Operating in the health, household, and food industries, the two companies operate as one and own 500 independent companies worldwide with approximately 300,000 employees. Unilever thinks globally and acts locally with control based in geography rather than in a global product structure. Unilever uses its geographical structure for cost savings in local functions such as advertising, where a 30-second commercial may market several of its products rather than just one. Unilever also finds the geographical organization allows it to focus on cultural differences and the effect they have on consumer tastes and marketing. The company enhances managerial competencies by giving managers cross-cultural training before sending them abroad. Its key is attention to product and geographic diversity.

Nestlé pursues a different strategy. Nestlé is a 125-year-old company based in Switzerland with 197,000 employees and 421 factories in 61 countries. It is one of the dominant players in the coffee and food industries. Operating with a very lean staff, Nestlé pushes decisions down to the operating level and has reduced reporting to one page. In marketing, Nestlé manages its brands so well it owns rights to several of the most recognized brands in the world today. In designer bottled waters, for example, Nestlé ownership includes Perrier, San Pellegrino, Poland Spring, and Calistoga. Brand management is one of the keys to its success globally. Management's strategy is to build a strong brand image through expansion of current brands or acquisition of already well-known brands.

Businesses that pursue different global strategies will have unique answers to globalization. Some common strategies are (1) building major share in strategic countries; (2) global product standardization; (3) global activity concentration such as building a global value chain; (4) globally uniform marketing such as global brand names and advertising; and (5) globally integrated competitive moves to gain advantage in one country or another. Each of these strategies calls for a particular approach to the business and tailored formulae for a global organization.

All of these strategies eventually confront global managers with a series of differentiation and integration challenges. On one hand, the company has a clear need for a global strategic intent and for broad-based resource, technology, and marketing schemes. At the same time, it needs a focus on competitiveness that deals with regional or local conditions, as well as local culture, behavior, and values. For many international organizations, a central executive-suite issue is how to organize, integrate, and manage activities to become global players. This is particularly important for large U.S. firms that are just now beginning to understand that an export mentality—or having offshore divisions or businesses in an international structure—does not mean they are equipped to compete effectively on a global basis.

A recent study of nine international service organizations (Citicorp Banking and American Express in financial services; McKinsey, Towers Perrin, Arthur Andersen, and Ernst and Young in management consulting; Four Seasons and Sheraton hotels; and National Data Corporation) revealed significant differences between the way service and manufacturing organizations structure their international operations (Campbell and Verbeke 1994). While manufacturing organizations tended to globalize and centralize many of their operations to achieve better economies of scale, service organizations tended to decentralize their operations in order to be responsive to local demands for customer service. The firms clustered in two groups. The first group (Ernst and Young, McKinsey, Citicorp, and Towers Perrin) emphasizes high national responsiveness and decentralized transfer of learning across national borders. In these firms, the parent companies manage a portfolio of multiple national businesses, each characterized by a strong local presence with products customized to local markets.

This was done, however, within a strong global corporate culture that promotes teamwork to support the diffusion of organizational learning. These companies follow a fundamentally multinational organizational model. The second group (American Express, Arthur Andersen, Four Seasons, Sheraton, and National Data Corporation) stresses the centralization of innovation and expects their subsidiaries to operate according to guidelines and directions from the parent companies. Quality control and service consistency are paramount, and any new knowledge or expertise is first developed by the parent company and then transferred to overseas subsidiaries. These companies follow an international organizational model.

In all nine companies, economies of scale were less a strategic driver than was customer responsiveness. These service firms were intent on leveraging their core competencies either through centralized innovation and low national responsiveness or through high national responsiveness and decentralized innovation.

Global Organization and Leadership

You will deal with issues of organization and leadership throughout this book, but at this point note that no global strategy can be achieved without its translation into the policies and procedures of the organization. This achievement is dependent on the nature and quality of leadership. George Yip agrees that the ability of an organization to achieve its global strategy is dependent upon its organizational structure, management processes such as planning and budgeting, and information systems. He adds that the "people and culture" are ultimately the most important decision factors. Each of these factors reinforces the others. **Global strategy is a** *system* **that requires systems thinking. The environment, the business, the organization, the corporate culture, and the people are all critical elements of a global strategy, which must be managed as an integrated set of activities to achieve business competitiveness.**

The single greatest challenge in global organization is the struggle to achieve a globally integrated organization that achieves economies of scale and responsiveness to global customers, while *simultaneously* retaining local flexibility for multiple customers throughout the world. No company has achieved a totally satisfactory solution, but there are many good examples, some of which are examined in the next chapter. The slogan "Think global, act local," says Yip, is wrong. It should read instead, "Think and act global and local."

This review of the basic elements of international business strategy introduces you to current thinking in this area. (For further reading, refer to the bibliography at the end of this chapter.) In the end, internationalization flows through products/services, markets, functions (finance, etc.), and technology. To understand the degree of globalization in your own organization, you need to review the strategy drivers and levers for your industry and the globalization potential for your organization.

It is important to note that **not all companies should be global in their operations**. The relative importance of overseas production, for example, varies greatly by industry. Aerospace has traditionally been a largely domestic business, part of the nation's military-industrial complex. Oil, tobacco, drugs, rubber, and chemicals, on the other hand, have long been international in production and operations.

If your choice is to make direct investment, then assembly and manufacturing facilities are often a likely target, although R&D, financial sourcing, suppliers, and facilities may all be objectives for international operations. Different industries exhibit different preferences for internationalization. Contract manufacturing works best with electronics, clothing, and automobiles, while equity joint ventures and wholly owned subsidiaries are best in R&D-intensive and advertising-intensive sectors. Licensing is best in chemicals, pharmaceutical, and other processing industries such as plastics and electronics. Franchising works most advantageously in soft drinks, fast foods, car rental, hotels, and personal and business services. Turnkey operations are best in heavy industry and will increasingly be used in Eastern Europe and the former Soviet Union because these areas need completely integrated technological systems to ensure that new technology will operate. This is due as much to the lack of suppliers as to the lack of spare parts, maintenance, and other factors normally available in the infrastructure of more industrialized countries.

This is just a peek at the many factors a company needs to consider in developing its international business strategies, the kinds of business issues with which you as a global manager need to be familiar if you are going to understand the constraints and opportunities available in a global organization.

FUNDAMENTALS OF INTERNATIONAL STRUCTURE

Whatever international strategy a business chooses, it must be supported by appropriate structure and culture and by the human talent to implement the strategy. Many executives mistakenly believe that structure is not just one piece of successful globalization, but the critical element. You can refuse to accept this extreme position without discounting the importance of a rational international structure. The correct structure is a necessary aspect of corporate globalization, albeit insufficient to support globalization alone.

One study conducted a thorough analysis of what it calls *diversified multinational corporations,* or multinational corporations that are in many different businesses (Prahalad and Doz 1989). It determined that specific industries profit from varying combinations of global integration and local responsiveness, as illustrated in Figure 3–1, which shows the integration-responsiveness grid for Corning.

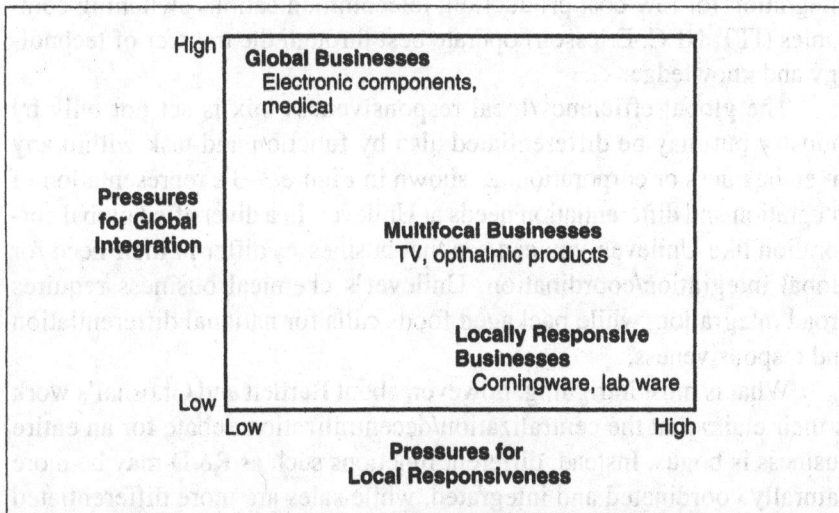

The position of various industries on this type of grid will vary over time. International economic, social, consumer, competitive, and technological forces will push one industry or another into assorted points on the grid. For this reason, constant global scanning of the best international position and structure for various industries emerges again as an important strategy/structure consideration for all global managers.

Figure 3–2 shows the results of Bartlett and Ghoshal's study of structure in nine different corporations. Branded packaged product producers (Unilever, Kao, Procter & Gamble) require a strategy and structure that

FIGURE 3–1

Integration-Responsiveness Grid for Corning

FIGURE 3–2

Industry Requirements and Company Capabilities

	Dominant Strategic Capability of Company		
	Responsiveness (multinational)	Efficiency (global)	Transfer of Knowledge and Competencies (International)
Dominant Strategic Requirements of Industry			
Responsiveness (branded packaged products)	Unilever	Kao	Procter & Gamble
Efficiency (consumer electronics)	Philips	Matsushita	General Electric
Transfer of Knowledge (telecommunications switching)	ITT	NEC	Ericsson

Reprinted by permission of Harvard Business School Press from *Managing Across Borders: The Transnational-Solution* by Christoper A. Bartlett and Sumantra Ghoschal. Boston: 1989 p. 21. Copyright © 1989 by the President and Fellows of Harvard College.

allow for maximum responsiveness to local consumers; consumer electronics companies (Philips, Matsushita, GE) require the efficiency of global integration for low-cost production; telecommunications switching companies (ITT, NEC, Ericsson) operate best through the transfer of technology and knowledge.

The global efficiency/local responsiveness mix is set not only by industry but may be differentiated also by function and task within any given business or corporation, as shown in Figure 3–3's representation of integration and differentiation needs at Unilever. In a diversified global corporation like Unilever, you can see that businesses differ in their need for global integration/coordination. Unilever's chemical business requires broad integration, while packaged foods calls for national differentiation and responsiveness.

What is most intriguing, however, about Bartlett and Ghoshal's work is their claim that the centralization/decentralization debate for an entire business is bogus. Instead, different functions such as R&D may be more naturally coordinated and integrated, while sales are more differentiated and responsive. This is one way of overcoming classic interfunctional rivalries within global organizations.

FIGURE 3–3

Integration and Differentiation Needs at Unilever

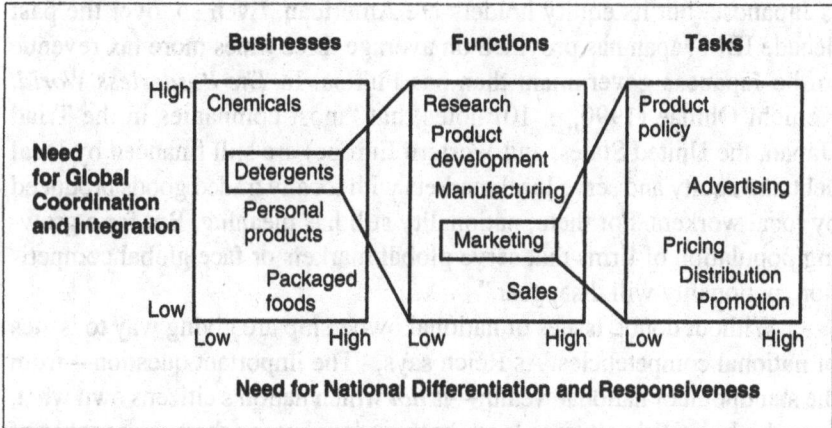

	Businesses	Functions	Tasks
Need for Global Coordination and Integration (High → Low)	Chemicals / Detergents / Personal products / Packaged foods	Research / Product development / Manufacturing / Marketing / Sales	Product policy / Advertising / Pricing / Distribution / Promotion
	Low — High	Low — High	Low — High

Need for National Differentiation and Responsiveness

Reprinted by permission of Harvard Business School Press from *Managing Across Borders: The Transnational-Solution* by Christoper A. Bartlett and Sumantra Ghoschal. Boston: 1989 p 97. Copyright © 1989 by the President and Fellows of Harvard College.

3M is another good example of their theory on the unique requirements of individual businesses. The 3M corporation, headquartered in Minneapolis, Minnesota, offers 60,000 products in 23 major businesses, based on more than 100 technologies, with operations in 55 countries employing 89,000 people. 3M has been described as a flotilla of 23 distinct ships with particular ranges, serving multiple purposes. Some are globe-trotting vessels, others are more like smaller, faster ships that work close to shore. Some turn slowly and others are very nimble. Planning and executing strategies for these companies will therefore vary enormously depending on the nature of the business and the strategic advantages of integration and differentiation in different aspects of each business.

Finally, Bartlett and Ghoshal note that within functions, it is also possible to spread out various tasks. Product policy is more globally centralized and coordinated, while pricing, distribution, and promotion decisions are more decentralized for national differentiation and local responsiveness. In general, there is a definite trend toward centralizing for economies of scale and coordination of innovation, while simultaneously decentralizing for local responsiveness. The manner and degree to which companies deal with these issues, as Bartlett and Ghoshal have pointed out, usually depends on the nature of the business. But the drama is ultimately played out by function and task.

NATION-LESS CORPORATIONS

Is IBM Japan an American or a Japanese company? Its workforce of 20,000 is Japanese, but its equity holders are American. Even so, over the past decade IBM Japan has provided on average three times more tax revenue to the Japanese government than has Fujitsu. In *The Borderless World*, Kenichi Ohmae (1990, p. 10) notes that "most companies in the Triad (Japan, the United States, and Western Europe) are still financed by local debt and equity and serve local markets with locally traded goods produced by local workers. For them, nationality still has meaning. But for a growing population of firms that serve global markets or face global competition, nationality will disappear."

Without doubt, issues of national ownership are giving way to issues of national competencies. As Reich says, "The important question—from the standpoint of national wealth—is *not* which nation's citizens own what, but which nation's citizens learn how to do what, so they are capable of adding value to the world economy and therefore increasing their own potential worth" (1991).

In the end, global companies are recognizing the advantages of multicentered headquarters for various businesses and functions around the world. Geographic location of activities is subject to where in the world each function can best be accomplished. National borders do not matter, only infrastructure that is compatible or incompatible with global business objectives. Hewlett-Packard, for example, has moved the R&D, production, and marketing of its large-format plotters from San Diego to Barcelona, supplying not only Europe, but also the United States and other world markets. Whenever Hewlett-Packard makes such a decision, management asks four questions: How has the facility functioned in the past? Does the local government provide a favorable environment? Are locally produced parts readily available? Can this be a "center of excellence for the world"? ("H-P . . . " 1993)

The objective for all of us during the years ahead is to know that we are a center of excellence for the world, both organizationally and personally.

PRACTICES AND TASKS FOR MANAGING COMPETITIVENESS

Managing competitiveness requires you to be curious and constantly attentive to the world and its changing social, economic, and political conditions. It is an engagement with life that can be vibrant and exciting. This outline presents practices and tasks you can undertake to develop your competency in managing competitiveness, the first of the six skills for success as a global manager.

Skill 1: Managing Competitiveness

Key Question	How do you define critical success factors?
Definition	Ability to gather information on a global basis concerning global sourcing of capital, technology, suppliers, facilities, market opportunities, and human resources and the capacity to utilize the information to develop a global strategy and structure that increase the competitive advantage and profitability of your organization.
Action and Mindset	Driving for the broader picture
Personal Characteristic	Knowledgeable

Key Practices and Tasks

As you can see from this definition, managing competitiveness fundamentally requires "driving for the broader picture." To be a successful global manager, you must constantly expand your vision to look at the seven global forces driving you and your competitors as well as your customers. You will need to scan the world for information about your customers, your products, your competitors, and political, social, and economic trends that may affect you and your work. Global managers never stop learning, never feel they have all possible information, are never satisfied with the limitations of the scope of their knowledge. They are always looking beyond the horizon, not only for competitors, but also for opportunities. Here is a list of things you can begin doing immediately to increase your ability to manage competition globally.

1. Outline the *critical success factors* that will make or break your organization and department's ability to be globally competitive and use these as a framework to filter global information for key trends.

    1.1 Determine the most important industry drivers and levers that affect your organization and your job to ensure that you are focusing in on the right issues. Issues might include

developing speed of responsiveness to global as well as local
customers, gaining economies of scale, and/or transferring
best practices to various sites around the world.

1.2 Use critical success factors as a framework to search for and
filter information on a global basis that will affect your
ability to be successful in the execution of your job
responsibilities. Search the Internet for the latest
breakthroughs in your critical success factor areas.

2. Develop a capacity for *systems thinking* at every level of
personal and organizational functioning, searching for contexts
and broader influences on a global basis that may affect personal
or organizational success. You can begin by analyzing how your
job and function are dependent on other jobs or functions within
your organization and by developing annual goals to anticipate
how changes in these areas may affect your work.

3. Establish *personal and organizational information systems* that
can scan globally for trends, best practices, and resources that
provide new opportunities for increased competitive advantage
and profit.

3.1 Read professional and commercial publications that track
your function and industry trends and practices
internationally, in addition to the national publications you
probably read now. *The Economist* is a good weekly
publication with a European perspective; *The World Monitor*
is a good view of the world from the American side; *World
Press Review* will give you a summary of world events from
different viewpoints of publications around the world; *The
Financial Times* provides an excellent daily overview of
world events from a European perspective; and *The Japan
Times* fills in the Asian viewpoint. This assumes, of course,
that you are reading a national newspaper like the *New York
Times* or *Le Monde* each day.

3.2 Join international professional associations and attend
meetings and conferences that stress the global aspects of
your job responsibilities.

4. Establish information processing systems that *deliver the right
level of information to the right people at the right time* for the
most effective and timely decision making on a worldwide basis.

4.1 Share information you gain that is relevant to increasing
your productivity or effectiveness with others in your
organization throughout the world who could benefit from it.

4.2 Ensure that the people you manage or with whom you work
abroad have the information they need to make as many
decisions locally as possible to increase the quality of their
decisions and their speed of response to local customer needs.

5. Conduct and update your *competitive analysis* on an ongoing
basis to ensure that you are aware of what your key competitors
are doing worldwide, even if some activities seem to be
irrelevant to your current interests or priorities.

5.1 Track global merger and acquisition activity and foreign
investment patterns of competitors and potential competitors.

5.2 Continually scan the global environment for potential
competition that could come from suppliers or customers
who might want to vertically integrate, as well as diversified
multinational corporations that might wish to expand
through merger and acquisition in your industry.

6. Monitor *international trade, tariff, economic, social, and
political changes* that may affect local, regional, or international
competitiveness.

6.1 Read broadly in your industry and professional press and in
popular literature about international social, political, and
economic megatrends.

6.2 Subscribe to the State Department information service or
join an international society or forum.

Many of these practices and tasks have been used by people throughout the world as they begin to operate more globally. Some may constitute
a starting point for you as you reexamine the way you are managing within
this new global environment.

SELECTED BIBLIOGRAPHY

"AT&T Global Service." *New York Times,* March 11, 1992, p. D4.

Baatz, E. B. "Fourth Annual CEO Survey." *Electronics Business,* April 1993, pp. 38–44.

Bartlett, Christopher A., and Sumantra Ghoshal. *Managing across Borders: The Transnational Solution.* Cambridge: Harvard Business School Press, 1989.

————."Organizing for Worldwide Effectiveness: The Transnational Solution." *California
Management Review* 31, no. 1, (1988).

Birkinshaw, Julian. "Encouraging Entrepreneurial Activity in Multinational Corporations." *Business Horizons*, May–June 1995, pp. 32–38.

Campbell, Alexandra J., and Alan Verbeke. "The Globalization of Service Multinationals." *Long Range Planning* 27, no. 2 (1994): pp. 95–102.

Carnevale, Anthony Patrick. *America and the New Economy: How New Competitive Standards Are Radically Changing the American Workplace.* San Francisco: Jossey-Bass, 1991.

Cohen, Roger. "For Coke, World its Oyster." *New York Times,* November 21, 1991, p. D1.

Doz, Yves. *Strategic Management in International Companies.* New York: Pergamon Press, 1986.

Dreifus, Shirley B. (ed.). *Global Management Desk Reference: 151 Strategies, Ideas and Checklists from the World's Most Successful International Companies.* New York: McGraw-Hill, 1992.

Garland, John, and Richard Farmer. *International Dimensions of Business Policy and Strategy.* Boston: Kent Publishing, 1986.

Goold, Michael; Andrew Campbell; and Marcus Alexander. *Corporate-Level Strategy: Creating Value in the Multibusiness Company.* New York: John Wiley & Sons, 1994.

Hamel, Gary, and C.K. Prahalad. *Competing for the Future: Breakthrough Strategies for Seizing Control of Your Industry and Creating the Markets of Tomorrow.* Boston: Harvard Business School Press, 1994.

Hammerly, Harry. "Matching Global Strategies with National Responses." *Journal of Business Strategy,* March/April 1992, pp. 8–12.

Hewitt Associates. "Case Studies: Whirlpool, Nike, Salomon and PSEG." *Compensation & Benefits Review,* January–February 1995, pp. 71–74.

"H-P Gives Spain a Global Unit." *Business Europe,* March 15–21, 1993, pp. 7–8.

Levitt, Theodore. "The Globalization of Markets." *Harvard Business Review,* May–June 1983, pp. 92–102.

Maruca, Regina Fazro. "The Right Way to Go Global: An Interview with Whirlpool CEO David Whitwam." *Harvard Business Review,* March–April 1994, pp. 135–45.

Naisbitt, John, and Patricia Aburdene. *Megatrends 2000: Ten New Directions for the 1990s.* New York: William Morrow and Company, 1990.

Nguyen, Andrea, and Brian H. Kleiner. "Quality Management: How Four European Companies Succeed." *Business Credit,* November/December 1994, pp. 32–34.

Ohmae, Kenichi. *The Mind of the Strategist.* New York: Penguin Books, 1983.

———. *The Borderless World.* New York: Harper Business Press, 1990.

Porter, Michael (ed.). *Competition in Global Business.* Cambridge, Ma: Harvard Business School Press, 1986.

Prahalad, C.K., and Yves Doz. *The Multinational Mission: Balancing Local Demands and Global Vision.* New York: Free Press, 1987.

Pucik, Vladimir; Noel M. Tichy; and Carole K. Barnett (eds). *Globalizing Management: Creating and Leading the Competitive Organization.* New York: John Wiley & Sons, 1992.

Reich, Robert B. *The Work of Nations: Preparing Ourselves for 21st Century Capitalism.* New York: Alfred A. Knopf, 1991.

Smith, David C. "Going Global: Restructuring Aims to Boost Efficiency." *WARD'S Auto World,* December 1994, pp. 39–45.

Taylor, William. "The Logic of Global Business: An Interview with ABB's Percy Barnevik."
    Harvard Business Review, March–April 1991, pp. 91–105.
Tichy, Noel M., and Stratford Sherman. *Control Your Own Destiny or Someone Else Will:
    How Jack Welch Is Making General Electric the World's Most Competitive Company.*
    New York: Doubleday, 1993.
Treacy, Michael, and Fred Wiersema. *Discipline of Market Leaders: Choose Your Customers,
    Narrow Your Focus, Dominate Your Market.* Reading, Mass.: Addison-Wesley, 1995.
Yip, George S. *Total Global Strategy: Managing for Worldwide Competitive Advantage.*
    Englewood Cliffs, N.J.: Prentice-Hall, 1992.

4

CHAPTER

Managing Complexity

The best global organizations deliver the complexity of the world into the hands of their managers. If consumers in different regions of the world demand variety in their products, that need is represented. If global competitors are achieving better cost efficiencies through off-shore sourcing

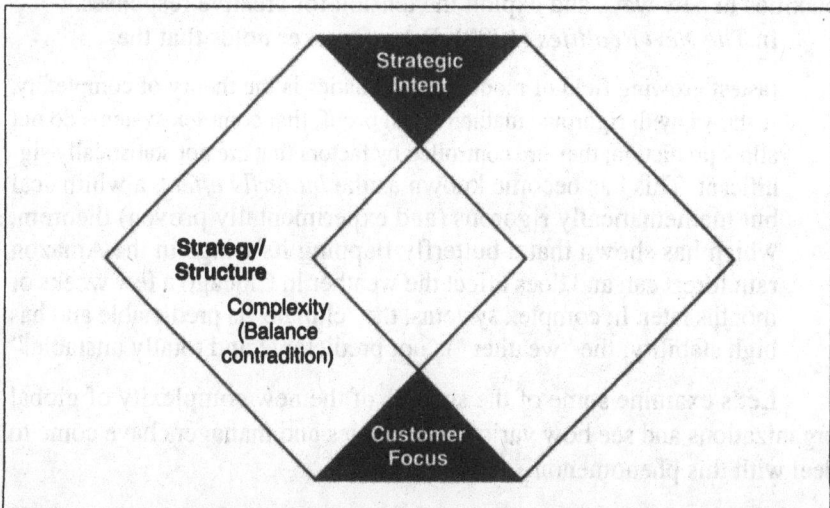

71

of raw materials, that fact is known. If the latest manufacturing process has been discovered in Korea and is being used to gain competitive advantage in Brazil, a successful global organization knows about it and informs its managers. Successful global organizations make details of the world's complexity known to their managers, but how do managers cope with this information?

Most managers in organizations that have recently globalized complain about the complexity and difficulty of working with so many new perspectives and demands. They feel they cannot get the job done the way they used to without consulting all sorts of people and dealing with a wide range of viewpoints and opinions. Some blame the new organizational structure or senior management for not clarifying priorities and delineating clear methods of operation. These complaints would be natural and normal in the old order. But in the new world of global change, the ability to manage paradoxical or contradictory demands at the same time is a key organizational and managerial challenge that must be met to be successful. Achieving a balance will simplify your world and thereby reduce one of the dimensions on which you may be vulnerable—a customer who demands product variety that you cannot give, a competitor who is finding better economies of scale, or a new technology that you are not aware of that could change your industry.

Simply put, experienced global managers understand that complexity and contradiction are inherent in any global organization. Your task is not to eliminate the tension this creates, but to learn to manage these complexities in new ways and exploit the tension for creative responses.

In *The New Realities* (1989), Peter Drucker notes that the

> fastest growing field of modern mathematics is the theory of complexity. It shows, with rigorous, mathematical proof, that complex systems do not allow prediction; they are controlled by factors that are not statistically significant. This has become known as the *butterfly effect*, a whimsical but mathematically rigorous (and experimentally proven) theorem, which has shown that a butterfly flapping its wings in the Amazon rain forest can and does affect the weather in Chicago a few weeks or months later. In complex systems, the "climate" is predictable and has high stability; the "weather" is not predictable and totally unstable."

Let's examine some of the sources of the new complexity of global organizations and see how various companies and managers have come to deal with this phenomenon.

SOURCES AND METHODS OF MANAGING COMPLEXITY

The increased complexity that you and other global managers face has three sources:

1. Multiple objectives.
2. Increased geographic scope.
3. Conflicting interests of multiple stakeholders.

Let's take a look at each to understand the challenge it presents within the context of a global organization.

Balancing Multiple Objectives

First, global management is complex because it involves the *simultaneous management of multiple objectives*. All global organizations must manage three conflicting needs:

1. The need for *efficiency* to lower costs.
2. The need for *responsiveness* to meet a variety of customer demands.
3. The need for *best practices* to be shared on a global basis.

Traditionally, the need for efficiency has been met through *centralization*. The need for responsiveness has been met through *decentralization*. And the need for best-practice sharing has been met through *coordination*. In a global organization, all three must be done simultaneously, but as you can see they require three actions that pull in different and sometimes contradictory directions. This requires that you become comfortable managing complexity—the second skill of a global manager.

Cultural Approaches to Managing Complexity

American, European, and Japanese organizations have traditionally approached the complexity problem in three different ways.

   Americans have tended to use **formalization,** through which they have established structures and impersonal systems and procedures to determine priorities among competing objectives. This has led to highly defined guidelines for managing worldwide decision making under conditions of multiple objectives and maximum complexity. ITT established its worldwide preeminence through the development of a wide-ranging set of management systems. Harold Geneen's management review meetings became legendary as formalized procedures established to determine the best decisions. Geneen's philosophy was to make careful and logical decisions on the basis of unshakable facts, then force the logic out into the open. Forcing the logic out into the open may be less simple now than it appeared to be in the past. While different cultural thought patterns have always been present, the degree to which they have been considered important has never been as strong as it is today. Again, one person's logic is another's irrationality. When you run a more interdependent system, the "logic" that is forced into the open can be widely varying, based in part on differences in cultural perceptions and values.

The *Europeans* have taken a second approach to the simultaneous management of multiple objectives, depending less on formalization than on **socialization**. Large multinational European-based companies like Shell, ICI, Philips, Unilever, and van Houten have over the years developed a global mindset in their managers through an extensive global socialization process of recruitment, selection, training, rotation, and development of a cadre of key international managers. Each manager becomes versed in the corporate culture and is known and trusted by senior management. Eventually the cadre becomes the glue that holds the organization together. While this an expensive process, it is increasingly being recognized as central to managing a global corporate culture. Even American organizations are using their senior management development seminars to develop cadres of managers from around the world who become acquainted across functional, geographic, and product lines through executive development seminars. American companies that have relied on this process include Ford, WR Grace, GE, Pepsi, and 3M.

A third method of managing multiple objectives has been used by the *Japanese*, who rely on **centralization** of decision making. But centralization in the Japanese company has been highly dependent on the Japanese *ringi* decision-making process in which consensus is built from diversity. This approach has a number of weaknesses. First, Japanese decision making, while inclusive of Japanese, tends to be exclusive of those who are not Japanese. While this centralized approach works well for companies managed totally by Japanese staff, it is one of the reasons Japanese have had difficulty in comanaging international operations. A second problem with the centralized approach is that it usually is expensive. Managers at the center are constantly juggling many different requests for information, guidance, support, and decisions. This results in a build-up of centralized staff resources, which can become burdensome and costly. A final problem with the centralized approach is that it creates an unavoidable schism between the headquarters and the field. Subsidiaries, or even more independent operations, chafe at the thought of having all important decisions centralized, feeling that their viewpoints are many times not considered in global decisions. This leads to frustration that can eventually affect international morale, productivity, and effectiveness.

Percy Barnevik, the maverick CEO of ABB, has apparently found ways to ameliorate some of these dilemmas by combining a centralized reporting system that still allows for considerable local autonomy. A global organization with sales of $35 billion, ABB is not a small organization. Yet the corporate headquarters in Zurich has only 140 people, 5 of whom constitute the global personnel department for a workforce of 220,000 people spread through 20 countries! Part of the reason Barnevik has been able to achieve this unusual corporate culture is that ABB is a recent combination of two corporations: Asea of Sweden and Brown-Boveri of Switzerland. As a result, the company has little entrenched culture, a short history, and no nationalist allegiances—three rare aids to forming a global corporation with which most organizations are not blessed. In his international acquisitions, Barnevik has applied the same philosophy of small corporate headquarters staff and tight, compact "multidomestic" operating units. When ABB purchased Combustion Engineering in Stamford, Connecticut, for example, he reduced the staff in the head office from 900 to 68 and cut the workforce in half.

Barnevik says, "You optimize globally, you call the shots globally and you have no national allegiances." Yet he has created 1,300 legal entities and 5,000 profit centers in 65 small business areas combined into eight larger business groups of $1 billion to $7 billion in annual sales. This decentralization has obvious payoffs in local responsiveness, but it is an extreme form.

It seems apparent that none of the three approaches to managing multiple objectives—formalization, socialization, or centralization—is the total answer. Instead, like Barnevik, you must formulate a unique combination of the three for each business, location, and function.

Balancing Increased Geographic Scope

A second source of complexity in global management is the *geographic scope* of operations for which a global manager is responsible. As soon as you open an office or a manufacturing or distribution center in another geographic location, you have increased the complexity of your business.

When you do this in foreign locations, with cultural, legal, and time differences, you have exponentially increased the number and range of challenges you face in accomplishing tasks that at home would be routine.

It is a tenet of faith with most global managers that you cannot manage local decisions centrally. While this was more possible in the past, the speed of today's changing markets and competitive conditions, combined with new consumer demands for speed and responsiveness, is forcing organizations to decentralize decision making. The key decision for you as a global manager, as explored in the Unilever example in Chapter 1, is *what* decisions will be decentralized in *which* functional areas and within *what* kind of business structure. To assist in this, I have used a functional integration exercise with a number of companies to help them decide at what level different functions should be coordinated. In this framework, there are eight levels of functional integration you can use:

1. Globally across regions and product lines.
2. Globally across regions within product lines.
3. Internationally (international division only) across regions and product lines.
4. Internationally within product lines.
5. Regionally across product lines.
6. Regionally within product lines.
7. Locally across product lines.
8. Locally within product lines.

Level 1 is the most global and level 8 is the most local option for each function. For example, you may decide, as American Express has, that your *brand* will be managed at level 1—globally across all regions and product lines. In other words, all American Express products and services are now marketed under the same name anywhere in the world.

By comparison, at level 8 many global consumer product companies may manage their R&D locally. A company like Coca-Cola varies the taste of its syrup to suit local preferences for sweetness. Many Asian countries prefer soft drinks that are sweeter than those Europeans prefer. As a result, the same brand-name Coca-Cola has a different taste in India than it does in Germany. A certain amount of R&D on the composition of the syrup to meet a local need would therefore be done for that product in each country.

The determination of what functions should be coordinated at what level is the essence of global organization. This will depend on the nature of your business and whether you have chosen to organize as internationally, multinationally, or globally. But within each of these basic structures, corporations will vary the way functions are organized. Many today are gravitating toward a regional model.

Linear Responsibility Charting

Another method global and regional organizations use to clarify decision-making responsibilities is a *linear responsibility chart*. In most reorganizations, a fundamental problem is clarification of roles and responsibilities in the new structure. When organizations move from a multinational to a global matrix organization, the shift from clarity to confusion in roles and responsibilities could not be more dramatic. A multinational organization, as we have seen, is the most decentralized and in many ways the simplest form of international organization. All responsibilities are decentralized to regional and country managers and there is little concern about coordination across countries, functions, or product lines. In a global matrix organization, on the other hand, managers are suddenly faced with coordinating across countries and regions, as well as across functions and product lines at all levels (local, regional, and global) of the organization. **The shift from a multinational to a global organization is not just a shift in structure; it is a major reorganization of decision-making processes, which in turn requires a change in corporate culture, systems, and the mindset and skills of managers throughout the organization.** While ultimately such a shift requires a different corporate culture, values, and skills, in the short run a new global matrix organization requires some way to determine who is in charge. With shared responsibilities across functions, regions, and products, many managers become confused about what they can do and what they are responsible for.

Linear responsibility charting, which was developed in project management organizations like the aerospace industry in the 1950s, has become a useful tool. As you can see in Figure 4–1, a linear responsibility chart helps managers determine answers to three basic questions: Who has the final authority to make a decision on any given issue? Who must be consulted prior to the decision? Who must be informed after the decision has been made?

Once these practices are clarified, global matrix decision making depends on the collaborative skills of managers to operate effectively. To achieve this, Ford recently ran a series of training programs on collaborative decision making for its top 3,000 managers; the series was conducted by

FIGURE 4-1

Linear Responsibility Chart

Key responsible person	Participating Groups							
	Ex Comm.	MSC	GSM's	MSU Team	CSF Team	Product Manager	Project Team	Other Functions: Manufacturing; R&D; G&A
	EVP	Ex Dir Sales	Ex Dir Sales	Leader	Leader	Ex Dir	Leader	Ex Dir
Business Process								
Write market strategy	A	A	I	R*	C	I		I
Identify CSF's		A	I	R*	C	I		I
Complete one page summary			I	A	R*	I		I
Write TR				A	R	R*		
Write BPI			A (Sales)	A	R*			A
Write project				A	R		*	
Complete resource plan by CSF			C	A	I		R*	I
Complete overall resource plan market	A		R*	R				R
Complete overall resource plan location	A		R*	R				
Verify resource plan with timing			R	R*				R
Identify "must delivers" year 1	C	R*	C	I	I	I	I	I
European pricing policy	I		C	R		R*		
Market segmentation		A	I	R*		C		
Product offer	A			C		R*		
Local pricing policy			R*	C				
Resource deployment plan locations	A		R*	R				
Promotion			C	C		R*		A
Distribution			C	R*		R		C

Legend: R = Responsible; I = Must be informed; C = Must be consulted; A = Approval; * = Decision maker

William Ury, the coauthor of *Getting to Yes* (Fisher and Ury 1985) and Stan Davis, the coauthor of *Matrix* (Davis and Lawrence 1977). This program introduced Ford managers to the challenges of matrix management and endeavored to provide them with a skill (collaborative decision making) that would enable them to negotiate across multiple stakeholder interests. I conducted a third day of training on cross-cultural management, which built on the first two days and introduced managers to matrix collaborative decision making needs across cultures. The three-day package was developed for Ford 2000 as a means of orienting managers to the new matrix organization Ford adopted on January 1, 1995.

Balancing Conflicting Interests of Multiple Stakeholders

All general managers have struggled with the constant balancing of production versus sales or finance versus research. In global management, these functional interests are compounded by national economic, social, and political interests that are often divergent from the primary concerns of the corporation. Governments, labor movements, social activists, and international regulatory agencies all have interests in the operations of a global corporation. In addition, global customers, investors, financial markets, employees, and competitors are constantly scanning global business strategies and tactics to assess whether their policies and practices meet local priorities, values, and needs.

Global managers are beginning to understand that there is no easy *structural* way to overcome the complexity of global organizations. Instead, you must accept that the only successful approach is *in your own mind*. To overcome complexity, you must seek to understand the perspectives and objectives of all the people with whom you work within a global organization. This may encompass people from other countries, other functions, and other product lines. It will also certainly involve your customers, suppliers, and perhaps government officials and others outside the organization. You must develop a *matrix mind* that can see the world from different perspectives and understand multiple viewpoints and needs.

During my years in global management, I spent as much as 50 percent of my time either on the road or in face-to-face consultation with people from field operations. I spent another 10 to 15 percent reflecting on these discussions and writing "think pieces" that explored the implications of what I had heard for company policy. In the end, decisions were made. And while not everyone was happy, it was not possible for anyone to say that he had not had a chance to state his views. My own thinking was enormously influenced when I attempted to consolidate and balance very different and sometimes contradictory needs, feelings, and philosophies into a coherent policy. At the least, it was a good exercise in developing a more globally matrixed mind.

So the complexities of multiple objectives, increased geographic scope, and conflicting interests of multiple stakeholders have three solutions:

1. Balancing multiple objectives through some combination of formalization, socialization, and decentralization.
2. Balancing geographic scope through functional, geographic, and product coordination, integration, and delegation.
3. Balancing conflicting interests through mind matrixing.

These, however, are more directions than answers. As you appreciate by now, the complexities of global management have no absolute solutions, only *processes* to deal with change.

WAYS TO MANAGE GLOBAL ORGANIZATIONAL CONTRADICTION

We have already discussed several ways to manage global organizational contradiction that arises from complex matrix structures. Some coordination challenges, however, require people to share information and develop a common vision about the new global organization they are sharing. The management of such organizational paradox also demands organizational processes and corporate cultural changes to deal with these conflicts. Let us look at several methods used to manage organizational complexity from a *process*, rather than a *structural*, perspective .

It is hard to think of *balance* when so many conflicting needs are hitting you at once. In fact, you will need to make some prioritizing decisions, merely to keep your sanity. The trick, of course, is determining which decisions can and should be made quickly and which ones should be allowed to "flow" toward their own, more creative solutions.

There are three different ways to manage the organizational contradiction that confronts every global manager. These are global norming, policy flexibility, and collective decision processes.

Global Norming

Many traditional European multinational corporations, as we have noted earlier, have managed global contradiction by establishing strong organizational norms of behavior—a strong corporate culture, through which they have attempted to supersede national differences, and set a pattern for resolving contradiction in global organizational life. But the latest thinking about national cultural differences, discussed by Nancy Adler in *International Dimensions of Organizational Behavior* (1986), is that differences should be managed for synergy rather than homogenized into a global corporate culture based on one national perspective.

The national motto of Indonesia is "Unity though diversity." This is truly a paradox, but one that is seen as an increasingly popular objective in our new multicultural world. Global norming within this context may appear to be out of line with this trend unless you focus on global norming not in terms of content, but in terms of process.

The norms set by a global corporation to manage complexity and diversity should not address differences *per se* but *the way* in which differences are considered and managed. In other words, new methods of conflict management, new forums for expression of diverse perspectives, and new ways for self-managing teams to come to consensus all contribute to global norming without overriding individual cultural values. They provide forms and methods for conflicting values to be debated, considered, and agreed upon.

This is far from easy. As you can see in Figure 4–2, which lists the advantages and disadvantages of diversity, you have to learn to *balance* the gains and losses from managing multiple perspectives in an open way. As Adler points out, however, diversity expands ambiguity, complexity, and confusion, which you must manage effectively. This is one reason that managing complexity is a key skill for global managers to master *and* one reason you need to develop your multicultural skills if you are to engender creative solutions from a multicultural workforce.

Policy Flexibility

Global policies should be flexible, and that flexibility should be in the nature of the policies themselves, as well as in their interpretation and application. For example, according to Barnevik, ABB has three internal contradictions: It wants to be global and local, big and small, and decentralized with centralized reporting. Barnevik states that the "only way to structure a complex, global organization is to make it as simple and local as possible" (Taylor 1991).

To achieve policy flexibility, Dan Simpson, director of strategy and planning for the Clorox Company, notes that his company has achieved a

FIGURE 4–2

Advantages and Disadvantages of Diversity

Advantages	Disadvantages
Diversity permits increased creativity	*Diversity causes lack of cohesion*
Wider range of perspectives	Mistrust
More and better ideas	Lower interpersonal attractiveness
Less "groupthink"	Stereotyping
	More within-culture conversations
Diversity forces enhanced concentration	Miscommunication
Ideas	Slower speech: non-native speakers
Meanings	and translation problems
Arguments	Less accurate
	Stress
Increased creativity can lead to	More counterproductive behavior
Better problem definitions	Less agreement on content
More alternatives	Tension
Better solutions	
Better decisions	*Lack of cohesion causes inability to*
	Validate ideas and people
Groups can become	Agree when agreement is needed
More effective	Gain consensus on decisions
More productive	Take concerted action
	Groups can become
	Less efficient
	Less effective
	Less productive

delicate balance between responding to the local business environment and acting in accordance with global corporate economies and competencies (1995). He believes that control of some elements of the business, such as labor relations, must be local to permit quick, precise responses to changes in local employee morale and work conditions. Other elements of the business, such as sourcing of raw materials, must be handled more globally to allow for economies of scale.

In IBM, according to Peter Schavoir, the former director of strategy, research, architecture, and manufacturing must be managed globally because they are key strategic competencies. In addition, corporate image, brands, and most alliances involving research, development and manufacturing must be managed globally. IBM operates in more than 140 countries, however. It must operate local products, software, and documentation in the first language of its customers, and so IBM manages its sales, human resources, and government relations locally.

Gordon Saw, 3M executive director of international planning, says 3M stresses regional management as a way to provide policy flexibility between global and local priorities. Regional management, he claims, gives balance to a global corporation, because it produces managing directors who are concerned with each country and know the situations there, but who at the same time understand the global views of the corporations. Ford calls these people "Node" managers because they must manage the interface between operations and strategy on a global basis.

Owens Corning, on the other hand, takes a different slant. Paula Cholmondeley, vice president, business development and global sourcing, explains that one side of Owens Corning's business is very global and the other side very local. Fiberglass insulation, it turns out, is a local operation. Since Owens Corning is committed to global coordination of its operations, it has required its local managers to understand their industry or their segment as it relates to the global business, while giving them the authority to make decisions locally.

Collective Decision Processes

Global organizations can establish forums in which differing perspectives can be thrashed out. A company with one of the best collective decision processes is Procter & Gamble. P&G works to ensure that emerging interests gain legitimacy within the organization through global councils and other forums in which divergent opinions are aired. If there are differences between countries in the allocation of resources, they are dealt with in regional meetings in which what is best for the region is considered by local and regional managers.

Another approach is to require people to wear multiple hats. One manager in AT&T is responsible for engineering in his local plant. At the same time, he sits on a North American coordinating council that decides on the allocation of resources across plants within the region. Finally, he chairs a global engineering council that ensures that best practices are shared across the organization around the world. In this multiplicity of roles, he sometimes finds himself in conflict with himself! He has to wear multiple hats and represent multiple viewpoints in different forums. While these myriad responsibilities are at times overwhelming, he has become a much better manager with a much broader understanding of the company than if he had remained only a manager of engineering in his local plant. You might want to investigate other roles you can play on a regional or global level to broaden your perspective of your function and be able to participate more fully in the tradeoff decisions that are inevitable in any global organization.

CONFLICT MANAGEMENT AS A KEY TO MANAGING COMPLEXITY AND CONTRADICTION

Conflict is as unavoidable in your organization as it is in any other global organization. The way in which you manage the many specialized interests and the conflict that ultimately ensues will be a crucial factor in your business's global success. Evans and Doz (1990) report that in 60 global companies they studied, the number-one top management task was "maintaining a dynamic balance between key opposites." They note that in these organizations "dualities should be viewed not as threats to consistency and coherence, but as opportunities for creative organizational development, for gaining competitive advantage, for organizational learning and renewal."

All observers agree that reorganization to avoid conflict is not the answer. It is also clear that with increasing complexity and trade-offs, it is naive to think that global norming can establish a global approach to problem solving and conflict management.

If conflict cannot be reorganized away and cannot be avoided through socialization, formalization, or centralization, how then do corporations deal with the problem? There are four basic methods: **legitimizing conflict, creating company integrators, using temporary coalition management,** and **holding global forums.**

Legitimizing Conflict

A real challenge for any global corporation is to find a means of legitimizing conflict as a positive part of its culture.

Intel has its "push back" norm, in which everyone is encouraged to push back against any new idea until it has proven its reliability, consistency, and relevance. In this model, people are rewarded for constructively challenging old and new ideas in ways that improve them. This requires a delicate balance, obviously, between testing new ideas and creating an adversarial atmosphere that demotivates people from raising new initiatives.

Rewards have to be offered both for putting new ideas forward and for pushing back and testing the assumptions and validity of new thinking.

Other companies legitimize conflict by encouraging diversity in policy development. Some require more than one option for all decisions. Others structure decision-making procedures so that all relevant units, businesses, or functions must voice an opinion on given issues.

Whatever the method, every successful global company must create a cultural norm that legitimizes conflict; views it as a creative dynamic necessary for organizational innovation, change, and learning; and rewards people who not only raise conflicting views, but work to find viable, successful responses to competing interests that move the organization to new levels of success.

Creating Company Integrators

When the frequency of complex decisions reaches the point where it strains normal decision-making channels, top managers often delegate responsibility to specific levels of management who become responsible for decision arbitration. Ericsson, the Swedish manufacturer of telecommunications equipment, has used this approach extensively through marketing vice presidents who, located in each of the 40 countries in which Ericsson has operations, arbitrate issues between local country interests and centralized product divisions, all of which are located in Sweden.

These integrators have "matrixed minds" and are sensitive to the needs of the business from various viewpoints. They are able to be multifocal in their approach and are committed to ensuring that both points of strategic advantage—local responsiveness and global integration—are explicitly examined and balanced.

Ideally, these people have interpersonal, cross-cultural, and group skills that enable them to facilitate decision making among conflicting positions. In the end, however, they must have the necessary clout, supported by senior management, to implement decisions if they are unable to reach an arbitrated solution.

Using Temporary Coalition Management

Perhaps the most favored approach to managing contradiction is through temporary coalition management (Prahalad and Doz 1989). In this approach, *ad hoc* teams are created to conduct studies and make recommendations on key issues when there are contradictory organizational needs.

Task forces, committees, project teams, working parties, and study groups are common methods of achieving recommendations on difficult issues. Ultimately, however, these groups will make little headway if the members are not supported by a corporate culture that values diversity of thinking and explicit management of conflicting ideas. Sweeping conflict under the rug will neither forward the company's goals nor, in the long run, accrue to your favor as a manager.

Holding Global Forums

The last method used by many companies to manage debate and conflict is some form of annual or semiannual global planning retreat where the key stakeholders from throughout the business come together to examine the organization's directions, policies, and priorities. These geographically representative forums, with accompanying product and functional representation, are the arenas in which major business issues are aired and all competing viewpoints are heard. The way in which final decisions are made varies from one company to another. Some use such forums for making decisions, others use them as a means of presenting a variety of ideas to senior management before a decision is taken at the top.

The AFS International Student Exchange Program, when I was president, had three regional meetings each year leading up to the annual board meeting. With 60 countries and their constituencies involved, gaining some semblance of agreement on organizational directions and priorities was a daunting task. The three meetings, held in Europe in September, the Americas in October, and Asia in November, for one week each, gave those of us from the international headquarters a chance to discuss and debate the policies and directions of the organization prior to the board meeting. After the meetings, we prepared policy papers for board members, who themselves represented 20 countries. These policy papers were circulated in December and January to participants from all countries, who had an opportunity to comment on them either directly by writing to headquarters or indirectly through any of the board members. The board then met at the end of January to deliberate the directions and goals for the organization. Every third year, AFS held a World Congress with representatives from every country to discuss the plans and priorities of the organization.

These global forums were held in a not-for-profit organization, but similar forums are used in for-profit corporations. Grace Cocoa, a global specialized food company that produces 10 percent of the world's cocoa powder for industrial uses, in 1991 brought its top 50 managers from around the world together in Holland for a week in order to build their common corporate culture and determine priorities and directions for the future.

The four conflict management methods we have discussed are a few of the ways in which global corporations are today trying to deal with the challenges of complexity and contradiction. There will be many more approaches created in the future.

The following lessons emerge from our discussion:

1. Conflict and debate can be healthy and lead to better solutions.

2. Conflict has to be managed or it becomes unhealthy and destructive.

3. One of the best uses of senior management's time is to establish a pattern for conflict management that ensures that the best decisions are made by the best people at the right levels.

AMERICAN RESISTANCE TO COMPLEXITY, CONTRADICTION, AND CONFLICT

Despite recent controversies ranging from Waco to the Los Angeles Police Department, North Americans have never been much for conspiracy theories. Latin cultures and some of the cultures of Western and Central Europe, like France and Russia, have always attributed life's events to some dark set of conspiratorial forces that needs to be unraveled from an exceedingly complex explanation of how the world works. Americans, on the other hand, value simplicity and straightforwardness. "What you see is what you get." An open, "tell-it-like-it-is" culture does not spend a great deal of time mired in complexity.

Likewise, it has been important in the United States to be pragmatic and concrete. Emphasis upon *doing* rather than *being* was one of the earliest observations made by anthropologists about modern American culture. Americans are action-oriented people and do not enjoy the intrigue of examining complex motives and situations the way Russians do. And they certainly do not relish philosophical speculations about the world and the nature of life the way the French do.

Complexity

When, on the other hand, American managers face the competing interests found in global operations and the complexity of their expression in a range of cultures, their first reaction is to try to find ways in which "we can all cooperate together." Americans have an inherent belief in cooperation and fair play as the basic spirit of organizational life. Much of the world, however, has developed in societies where families and fiefdoms fought to gain as much of the wealth of a society as possible. Sharing this wealth outside one's own family is a foreign concept, just as it is foreign to think that one should be concerned about protecting the interests of outsiders.

This intrigue affects global business practices. It is often difficult to know exactly who makes decisions in Japan or the former Soviet Union. It is equally difficult to know what the criteria for decisions are. This, in turn, creates problems in trying to negotiate or solve problems that may arise in business transactions. The Japanese, for example, have a process they call *haragei,* or "stomach art," which is the skill of building or changing a consensus by unspoken communication. The Japanese stomach artist's first priority is to keep his group together and functioning, often by proclaiming the old policy; then, very quietly, he introduces the new one. If there is conflict, it may never be resolved. But if a new consensus emerges from hints and private talks, the master of stomach art graciously pretends to give way to the new consensus and abandons the old one. No one needs to admit to a change of mind, and everyone saves face.

Figuring out the complexity of global operations is a little like solving a crossword puzzle. You look for clues and sometimes run into blind alleys. This is a blow to many American managers who have climbed the corporate ladder demonstrating their ability to finish all puzzles—on time, correctly, and with a profit!

Contradiction

Americans also do not deal well with contradiction. Their whole thought pattern goes against holding two contradictory ideas at once. Since they are action oriented, Americans seek to prioritize contradictory choices in order to determine how the business can move forward. The emphasis here is not necessarily on determining what is *right* in a philosophical sense, but what is manageable and possible in terms of getting something done and perceiving progress. If forced to, Americans can accept that contradictions exist in life, but they are not anxious to dwell on them.

On the other hand, the exploration of basic contradiction lies at the foundation of Eastern thinking. The Chinese philosophers saw life as two archetypal poles—yin and yang—between which there was continuous fluctuation creating a rhythm in the universe. Reality, whose essence they called Tao, was seen as a process of continual flow and change. Eastern thinking is oriented toward flow and change rather than stability. In the Chinese view, change is expected as part of the natural dynamic of the Tao. When one extreme, the yin, has been reached, the flow starts back toward the other extreme, the yang. Nothing, however, is ever just pure yin or pure yang. There is always some combination of the two and there is *always movement,* because life's activities create new demands that swing the momentum back toward the end of the spectrum that is not in vogue.

This may sound familiar, because it is a pattern that also takes place in organizational life. How many times have you heard someone say after a reorganization to decentralize staff functions, "Don't worry, just wait five years until we have a new CEO and the staff functions will be re-centralized again"? Little did you know that they were just expressing ancient Chinese philosophy!

Paul Evans and Yves Doz, call the contradictions in global organizations "dualities," and they have devised this list of contradictory demands on global managers:

Efficiency	Responsiveness
Centralization	Decentralization
Competitiveness	Partnership
Differentiation	Integration
Comprehensiveness	Applicability
Control	Entrepreneurial chaos
Hierarchy	Network
Analysis	Judgment/Intuition
Cost	Quality
Individualism	Teamwork

They believe that to manage global operations successfully, you need to understand the dynamic balance between these conflicting demands and the fact that neither column is inherently correct. Certainly in the United States there is an increasing emphasis on more cooperative, organic team-oriented values, and the tough-guy, male-dominant, pistol-packing lone problem solver is becoming a metaphor for a mechanistic past!

As pragmatists and problem solvers, Americans prefer to develop a plan to overcome obstacles so that they can move forward with the work that has to be done. They are increasingly encouraged to do this with the cooperation of others to ensure that their interests are included and that they feel represented in the final decision.

At the same time, Americans do not dwell easily or happily on the inherent contradiction in society, since they believe that personal, organizational, and social change are subject to human action. They tend to believe that all they have to do is "get organized and get going."

Conflict

As a culture, America has used much of twentieth-century applied social science theory to develop means of conflict resolution on international, national, intergroup, group, interpersonal, and personal levels. Conflict is seen by most Americans as inherently bad, destructive of a society in which great emphasis is placed on being a good neighbor, a cooperative team player, and a responsive colleague. They have not had much experience in the synergy of diversity or the management of inherently incompatible forces that cannot be resolved. Americans have historically believed in a perfectible world, in which stasis is ultimately reached and nothing further need change.

In the *international* arena, Americans have put forward ways to ensure prolonged peace between nations through turning win–lose situations into win–win strategies. They have developed a range of cross-cultural theories and methods to help people carry on work and play across cultures in the belief that cross-cultural understanding is the key to many of the world's problems. Yet Americans become quite uncomfortable when someone suggests that the problem may not be cross-cultural but an inherent conflict of interest that must be constantly renegotiated in a way that acknowledges the reality of continuing conflict and tension. They accepted this as a fact of life for many years between the United States and the Soviet Union, but it did not affect their everyday lives the way other conflict might. They were not prone to debating the philosophical underpinnings of centrally planned communism and free-market democracy; America knew the right answer.

In the *national* arena, Americans have accepted some small differences between Democrats and Republicans, but nothing like the national differences between Britain's Tory and Labor parties. They believe in harmony in spite of differences and view British MPs shouting one another down as an unseemly spectacle compared with the restrained protocol of American congressional debates, even though Parliament and Congress are dealing with the same fundamental paradoxes of social, economic, and political life.

From an *intergroup* perspective, American social psychologists and sociologists have studied interracial and interethnic relations for more than a century. The professions of social worker, labor negotiator, and diversity trainer have emerged to ensure that when contradiction and conflict appear, there are ways to alleviate the tension and bring people back to the "normal" state of cooperation and harmony within which institutions and fellow managers are expected to perform. Americans are facing an increasing awareness today, however, that the melting-pot approach to cultural diversity will have to give way to the multicultural group. This means acknowledging and managing differences as they never had to in the old days, when everyone else adjusted to the "American way" as the price of being part of the most prosperous and successful nation in the world. This mindset transition will not be simple, and Americans will need to learn a great deal more about cultural differences to become skilled in multicultural group management. (Many of these issues are discussed further in Chapter 7, "Managing Multicultural Teams.")

On the *group* level, American companies judge managers by their ability to get things done, to move forward, to obtain results. Furthermore, they are supposed to do all of this without any surprises for the boss. At the same time, managers are expected to provide security and comfort for their employees so that everyone can feel that stasis, rather than chaos, is the natural state of organizational life. When contradictions arise in groups, they are expected to use the latest problem-solving methods to prioritize alternatives and move ahead. If problems become too complex, they move to computer simulations, computer-assisted decision making, computer-assisted design, and computer-assisted manufacturing. Americans have faith that some technology will bring clarity to complexity, resolution to contradiction, and harmony to conflict.

In the *interpersonal* arena, Americans' fundamental focus is on communication, with the goal of overcoming differences. There is a sense that people have failed if they accept the idea that there is some inherent contradiction in their interests that leads to ongoing conflict and stress in their relationships with others. Tension, after all, is not the "normal" state of affairs; stasis is. Or so they say.

Finally, on a *personal* level, the American penchant for self-examination may be equaled by none. The French may be introspective philosophically, but Americans are introspective about action. They are constantly engaged in performance reviews, values clarification, leadership training, life planning, goal setting, and myriad other activities with the intent of refining both their activities and their ability to get along peacefully with others. The typical American businessman wants to be seen as mature, self-confident, and dependable, moving swiftly and with assurance through a complex and contradictory world. He does not slip, does not let others down, and does not allow himself to contemplate that there are some things "beyond him."

To ensure that they are able to work on all these levels in controllable ways that help them achieve the results they want, American businesses call on a wide range of helping professions: international mediators and cross-cultural training experts, national lobbyists and public relations gurus, company strategic planners and human resource consultants, management development trainers, social workers, psychologists, and psychiatrists. All these people are there to guarantee that managers can sort through these complexities and see the world as it should be—a place that can be "overcome"—that is, rationalized, understood, and acted upon with only the slightest hesitation because, after all, time is money.

AMERICAN PREFERENCES FOR PRAGMATISM, ACTION, AND COOPERATION

At the root of Americans' aversion to complexity, contradiction, and conflict is a preference for pragmatic individualism, action orientation, and cooperation. These three cultural values affect assumptions about what is good and preferred in their lives and also what is the normal state of life versus periods of aberration.

Favoring Pragmatism over Complexity

From the earliest days, Americans have seen themselves as rugged individualists. While they have banded together in towns, villages, communities, and cities for the purpose of preserving or furthering the common good, each individual has retained a unique identity and the right to be his or her own person. Emile Durkheim, writing in 1897, described this American predisposition for individualism as "the cult of individual personality." He noted that in such societies, the high value placed on the development of the individual personality results in people who see themselves as independent and autonomous, rather than a reflection of external pressures.

As a result, Americans abhor complexity because at the most fundamental level it limits their independence and sense of autonomy. Things that are complex are also confining and, ultimately, psychologically debilitating. Complexity imposes on us social obligations, political choices, economic systems, ethical dilemmas, and interpersonal and intrapsychic limitations. It must therefore be avoided, defeated, or muddled through. In any case, one should not dwell on it too long or things will not get done.

More group-oriented cultures do not have such difficulty with obligations and confinements. In Japan, for example, one is rich when one has developed a web of obligations by which one is bound to others. The concept of *amae* means peace and harmony in interpersonal relationships composed of a set of mutual interpendencies that, from the Japanese perspective, is the normal state of human existence.

In the United States, however, people are obsessed with paying one another back as soon as possible in order to be sure they do not have any debts to others that may be called in. After all, the call might come at an inconvenient time, preventing them from absolute control over their lives and how they spend their time. Americans drive toward pragmatism as an extension of personal control and mastery of their environment. They are engaged in a continuous search for freedom to do and be what they want. This self-concept drives Americans away from complexity. If you are an American manager, to become comfortable with complexity, you are going to have to take a deep breath and find ways to first acknowledge and then accept that you may become more confined, that your choices may be limited, and that you may have to trade off what you would *like to do*, if the world were simple, against what you will *have to do* because it is complex.

Favoring Action over Reflection

Not only are they protective of individual freedom, Americans are also obsessed with action. David C. McClelland, the noted Harvard psychologist who first described Americans' drive for achievement, identified it as the "need for constant improvement." Many years of research revealed that an achievement-motivated person takes responsibility for his or her own behavior, is constantly setting challenging but realistic goals, anticipates obstacles to achievement of these goals, and does things in a unique and creative manner to overcome obstacles that may stand in the way.

This is also the classic profile of entrepreneurial behavior and one reason Americans have been very successful in economic affairs, as well as social and political life. The American concern for action was valuable in the industrial age, when straight-line thinking was necessary to get from here to there. The idea of "balanced integration" may be more to the point, however, in a post-industrial, globalized business environment. Instead of rushing to action, American managers may need to learn to sit back, hold contradictory trends in a balanced perspective and do nothing while they wait for the natural forces and rhythms of the universe to play themselves out. The Chinese call this *wu wei*, which literally means *nonaction*. You will learn more about this in the next few chapters, where "engaging process" is discussed as a fundamental principle of the global mind.

Favoring Problem Solving over Systems Thinking

One of the least studied and most important aspects of culture is the affect that it has on one's thought pattern. As we have discussed, Americans like to take complex problems, analyze them through the application of various models and methods, and reduce them to "manageable priorities." These tasks are then assigned to people for action that can be monitored and measured for success.

This reductionist thought pattern has its roots in Cartesian logic. Descartes, the nineteenth century French philosopher, was the philosophical father of the rise of the individual with his pronouncement "*Cogito, ergo sum*"—"I think, therefore I am." Analysis and analytical reasoning became watchwords of the Enlightenment. The ability to analyze and reduce complexities to manageable parts was an inherent part of the scientific era and the basis of the new age of industrial development.

John Naisbitt and Patricia Aburdene, in *Megatrends 2000* (1990), describe what they see as a shift from the mechanistic to the biological metaphor for the most effectual thought pattern in the future. This means a fundamental shift from causal, linear, reductionist thinking to holistic, contextual, integrative thinking. It also means developing the ability to think about complexity as it exists. It means holding contradictory ideas simultaneously. It means managing, rather than resolving, conflict.

This is a new cultural paradigm for the Western world—but not for the East. Eastern cultures, especially the Japanese, have always emphasized holistic, contextual thinking and have seen the management of contradictory ideas and forces as part of a total system that makes room for tension, energy, and creativity. They have pioneered the application of "continuous improvement" as constant tension in the system, and have also pioneered the *ringi decision-making process,* which establishes processes to arbitrate complex decisions and conflicts.

One of many American complaints about Japanese decision making is that it is too slow. The Japanese take a long time to decide their direction because they try to incorporate all contradictory views and dimensions in the decision process. As a result, while they are slow in deciding, they are fast in implementation. Americans, by contrast, are fast in decision making, but slow in implementation. When they begin to put policy into practice, they run into all the resistance that was not co-opted in advance. If we are now approaching a world in which complexity and contradictions are the fundamental new realities, **we may be headed into an information age in which the Japanese hold the same cultural advantage of thought pattern that Americans have had during the industrial age.**

The answer to American global competitiveness of the twenty-first century, therefore, may not lie principally in a new global strategy and structure, or even in developing a global corporate culture or internationally minded managers. American business may literally need to develop managers with globally matrixed minds that can think about the complexity of the new information age in a holistic way. This will involve new skills of balancing contradiction and managing the tension of diversity for creativity and innovation, rather than prioritizing diversity away in the name of fast, actionable results.

DUE PROCESS AS A KEY TO MANAGING COMPLEXITY WITH SUBSIDIARIES

We have discussed many different aspects of organizational complexity in this chapter and have suggested a number of ways to deal with them. We have also examined Americans' predisposition for simple, straightforward, and pragmatic action that involves cooperation. A recent study involved extensive research with 63 subsidiary presidents to understand how global organizations can successfully implement global strategies. The authors discovered that top subsidiary managers at the regional and local level are the key catalyst for, or obstacles preventing, global strategy execution (Kim and Mauborgne 1993). The study determined that the most important factor in obtaining the support of regional and local managers in global decision making is their perception of the degree to which decisions have been reached fairly.

In practical terms, fair decision making seems to be a function of what the authors call *due process*. Due process is the degree to which the following five conditions are met:

1. The head office is *familiar* with subsidiaries' local situations.
2. *Two-way communication* exists in the global strategy-making process.
3. The head office is relatively *consistent* in making decisions across subsidiary units.
4. Subsidiary units can *legitimately challenge* the head office's strategic views and decisions.
5. The subsidiary units receive an *explanation* of final strategic decisions.

Let's examine each of these factors in light of the foregoing discussion of managing complexity in a global organization.

The diagram in Figure 4–3 graphically presents the five different criteria involved in due-process decision making.

The only way that a head office can demonstrate *familiarity* with local conditions is to get on the road. It is impossible to manage subsidiary operations from the 42nd floor of a corporate headquarters in your home country. Managers with global responsibilities must travel globally, and continuously. Receiving reports back home from foreign operations may provide an adequate amount of *information* for you to make decisions, but it does not provide a *feeling* for the people, their concerns, and their perspectives and, more important, it does not allow them to see that you understand their concerns.

Ensuring that *two-way communication* exists in the global decision-making process is, again, a matter of face-to-face time in the field, as well as a proper planning and budgeting process. The sense that policies are developed together, rather than at headquarters, is critical for global management. One Ford manager told me that it was important for senior managers from Dearborn to come to the regions and spend a day "talking with us about our business" without any formal agenda. During the implementation of Ford 2000, senior executives in Dearborn discovered that people in other regions of the world complained that they were not involved in

FIGURE 4-3

Due Process in Global Decision Making

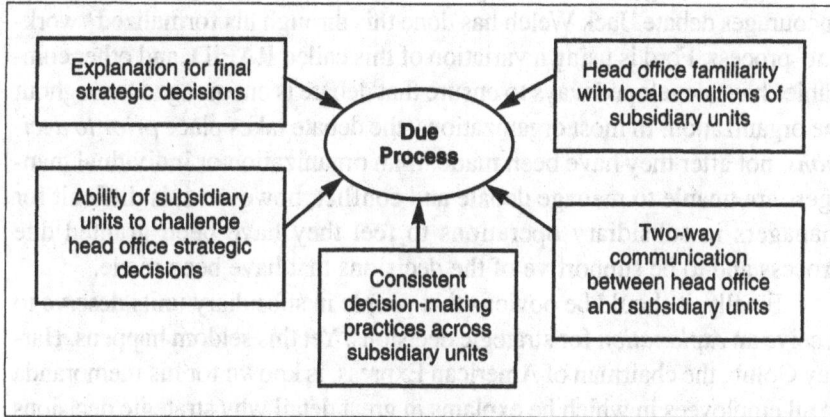

decision making, even though there had been greater discussion and consultation internationally than ever before in the history of the organization. Upon further investigation, it was determined that people do not feel involved unless they are actually sitting face to face in debating policy and strategy. Ford tried other forms of communication, such as information sharing across the world, representation of foreign managers in headquarters, and consultation with foreign managers about key decisions, but none of these was seen as real participation. Only when foreign managers felt part of the process with some common authority and responsibility did they consider themselves true participants in legitimate two-way communication. That may not be reasonable, but it is realistic.

Consistency in head-office decisions across subsidiary units is also a hard standard to reach. Every global manager knows that varying political, social, economic, and regulatory circumstances in different countries around the world may require an exception to any policy. At the same time, too much flexibility in the implementation of global policies will result in perceived favoritism and discrimination, which ultimately will undermine the ability of a global organization to have its policies supported by regional and local managers. The only way to avoid this is to ensure that as a global manager you are clear about the basis for your decision making and the criteria you are using in applying principles across various regions in the world.

The opportunity to *legitimately challenge* the head office's strategic views and decisions is perhaps one of the most difficult processes to build into a global organization. Organizations must develop a culture that encourages debate. Jack Welch has done this through his formalized "work-out" process. Ford is using a variation of this called RAPID, and other companies have developed ways to ensure that debate is encouraged throughout the organization. In most organizations, the debate takes place *prior to decisions,* not after they have been made. If an organization or individual managers are unable to manage debate and conflict, however, it is difficult for managers in subsidiary operations to feel they have been granted due process and to be supportive of the decisions that have been made.

Finally, it should be obvious that people in subsidiary units deserve to receive an *explanation* for strategic decisions. Yet this seldom happens. Harvey Golub, the chairman of American Express, is known for his memoranda to all employees in which he explains in great detail why strategic decisions have been made and why changes in organizational structure and management responsibility have taken place. If you have ever seen a Golub memorandum, you *know* what is meant by a full explanation—and you know that not many senior managers take the time and effort to explain their decisions so thoroughly. The evidence indicates, however, that the clearer senior managers are about the reasons for their decisions and the better they explain them, the greater will be the support they receive for global implementation.

Due process then is a critical element of managing organizational complexity. These five steps are not natural to all managerial styles or all national cultures. Nevertheless, as a competent global manager, these five steps will greatly enhance your ability to have the decisions you so painfully make implemented by the senior subsidiary managers throughout the world on whom you ultimately depend for your success.

PRACTICES AND TASKS FOR MANAGING COMPLEXITY

These suggested tasks and behaviors will help you determine what you can do to manage complexity in your day-to-day management role and to support your company's efforts to deal with the complexity of its global operations.

Skill 2: Managing Complexity

Key Question   How do you structure and allocate resources?

Definition	Ability to identify, analyze, and manage complex global relationships that affect personal and organizational effectiveness.
Action and Mindset Attribute	Balance contradiction
Personal Characteristic	Analytical

Key Practices and Tasks

1. Look for balance and due process in finding the right responses to your global management challenges. Develop means of consulting with your country and regional managers or with headquarters that allow people to feel they are intimately involved in decision making.

   1.1 Establish quarterly reviews in which you can review strategic directions, as well as tactical coordination of customers, competitors, research, and product development, and other basic aspects of your business.

   1.2 Even when something seems straightforward and clear, examine the opposite perspective to see whether it has any merit or provides an opportunity to do something innovative and unexpected that could provide competitive advantage.

2. Determine *which decisions should be centralized* for coherency and efficiency and *which decisions should be decentralized* for local responsiveness by business, function, and task.

   2.1 Research practices in your industry and function concerning centralization and decentralization of various policies, practices, and tasks.

   2.2 Analyze your managerial area to decentralize as many marketing, sales, and customer-oriented operational decisions as possible, while retaining central control over general policies and operational areas such as finance and research where technology or practices can provide policy coherence and/or cost efficiency.

3. Look for *contradiction* and *paradox* in your work and determine how they can be exploited for richer decisions.

   3.1 In situations of generic conflict between functions or interests, use the conflicting positions as a check and balance system to ensure the best decisions.

3.2 Learn to manage and feel comfortable with conflict in order to ensure that you do not prematurely close off deliberation that could lead to better responses because of anxiety over complexity.

3.3 Go to a course on conflict management. Read *Getting to Yes* by Roger Fisher and William Ury. If you have someone who really doesn't want to cooperate with you, read *Getting Past No* by William Ury.

4. Use *intuitive* as well as analytical skills to assess the "feel" for the information gathered and the direction in which the business and the world are going.

4.1 Be willing to make decisions with less than total information.

4.2 Learn to trust your sense of things rather than wait for all the facts to make a decision for you.

4.3 If your intuitive skills are not strong, find people who have strong skills and build them into your decision-making process.

5. Review the *allocation of responsibilities* in your department or organization at global, regional, and local levels. Are tasks as decentralized as possible to allow for local customer responsiveness? Are you coordinating best practices on a regional or global level? Are you working through the value chain to obtain economies of scale and cost reductions wherever possible on a regional or global basis?

5.1 Create a linear responsibility chart for your department or business that allows people to be clear about their responsibilities in complex matrix decision making.

5.2 Ensure that you have explained to your managers and employees the nature of globalization and what your vision of a global organization is.

Managing complexity requires broadened thought patterns and conflict management skills on both conceptual and interpersonal levels. Global organizations are more complex than domestic organizations, and they experience much more conflict as a result of the diversity of views and perspectives that must be brought to bear in decision making.

SELECTED BIBLIOGRAPHY

Adler, Nancy. *International Dimensions of Organizational Behavior.* Boston: Kent Publishing, 1986.

Davidow, William H.; and Michael S. Malone. *The Virtual Corporation: Structuring and Revitalizing the Corporation for the 21st Century.* New York: Harper Business, 1992.

Davis, Stan, and Paul Lawrence. *Matrix.* Reading, Mass.: Addison-Wesley, 1987.

Drucker, Peter F. *The New Realities.* New York: Harper & Row, 1989.

Elliot, Jacques, and Stephen D. Clement. *Executive Leadership: A Practical Guide to Managing Complexity.* Arlington, Va.: Cason Hall & Co., 1994.

Evans, Paul, and Yves Doz. "The Dualistic Organization." In Evans, Paul; Yves Doz and Andre Laurent, eds. *Human Resource Management in International Firms: Change, Globalization, Innovation.* New York: St. Martin's Press, 1990.

Evans, Paul; Yves Doz; and Andre Laurent, eds. *Human Resource Management in International Firms: Change, Globalization, Innovation.* New York: St. Martin's Press, 1990.

Fisher, Roger, and William Ury. *Getting to Yes.* Cambridge: Harvard Negotiation Project, 1985.

Hampden-Turner, Charles. *Charting the Corporate Mind: Graphic Solutions to Business Conflicts.* New York: The Free Press, 1990.

Hungenberg, Harold. "How to Ensure That Headquarters Add Value." *Long Range Planning* 26, no. 6 (1993): pp. 62–73.

Johnson, Barry. *Polarity Management: Identifying and Managing Unsolvable Problems.* Amherst, Ma: HRD Press, 1992.

Kim, W. Chan, and Renee A. Mauborgne. "Making Global Strategies Work." *Sloan Management Review,* Spring 1993, pp. 11–27.

———."Effectively Conceiving and Executing Multinationals' Worldwide Strategies." *Journal of International Business Studies,* Third Quarter 1993, pp. 419–48.

Naisbitt, John, and Patricia Aburdene. *Megatrends 2000: Ten New Directions for the 1990s.* New York: William Morrow and Company, 1990.

Pascale, Richard Tanner. *Managing on the Edge: How the Smartest Companies Use Conflict to Stay Ahead.* New York: Touchstone, 1990.

Prahalad, C. K., and Yves Doz. *The Multinational Mission: Balancing Local Demands and Global Vision.* New York: Free Press, 1987.

Quinn, Robert E. *Beyond Rational Management: Mastering the Paradoxes and Competing Demands of High Performance.* San Francisco: Jossey-Bass, 1988.

Rhinesmith, Stephen H. "Americans in the Global Learning Process." *The Annals of the American Academy of Political and Social Science* 442 (March 1979): pp. 98–108.

Simpson, Daniel. "Planning in a Global Business." *Planning Review,* March/April 1995, pp. 25–27.

Taylor, William. "The Logic of Global Business: An Interview with ABB's Percy Barnevik." *Harvard Business Review,* March–April 1991, pp. 91–105.

Ury, William. *Getting Past No: Negotiating Your Way from Confrontation to Cooperation.* New York: Bantam Books, 1993.

PART THREE

GLOBAL CORPORATE CULTURE AND CHANGE

5

CHAPTER *

Managing Organizational Alignment

Global organizations don't work as matrix *structures*. They work as *people* and *processes* coming together with a common vision, values, and work practices that allow them to operate across cultural, functional,

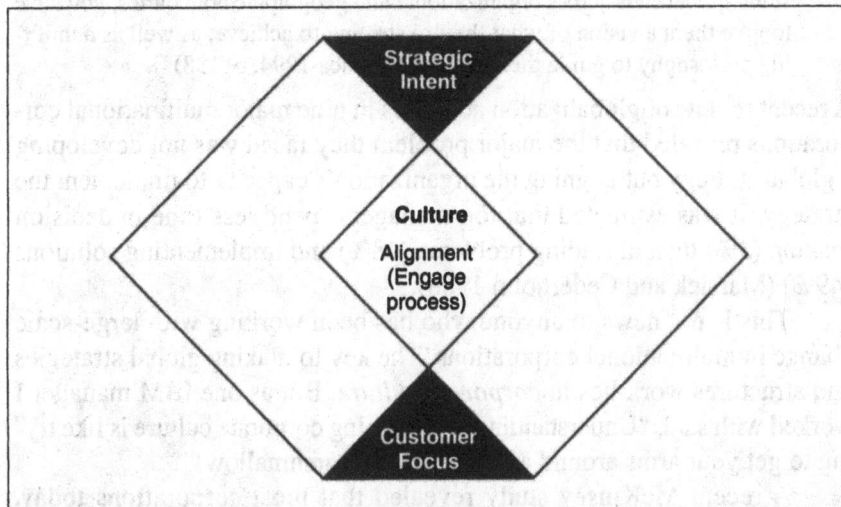

* Portions of this chapter have appeared in "Going Global from the Inside Out," *Training and Development Journal*, November 1991.

and product boundaries. Some people may be confused about the degree to which a company can be truly global unless it has a "pure" corporate culture. In a pure global corporate culture, there are no longer privileged areas for a home nationality—by product, people, or function. As *Fortune* magazine characterized it, "in a world without walls, a company without a country has an undeniable edge" (Stewart 1990). An often cited example is that a global organization must have members of its governing board from outside the home country. While this is useful, it is not a prerequisite for an organization to act and think like a global organization. What *is* necessary, however, is that the senior management and board have a *global mindset.* Without this, there is no hope that a company can become globally oriented and effective.

What are the elements of a global corporate culture? What are the competitive advantages? What companies have effective global cultures? What can be done to develop a global corporate culture in your company? These are the issues addressed in this chapter.

Once more, we take a cue from David Whitwam:

> You must create an organization whose people are adept at exchanging ideas, processes, and systems across borders, people who are absolutely free of the "not-invented-here" syndrome, people who are constantly working together to identify the best global opportunities and the biggest global problems facing the organization. If you're going to ask people to work together in pursuing global ends across organizational and geographic boundaries, you have to give them a vision of what they're striving to achieve, as well as a unifying philosophy to guide their efforts. (Maruca 1994, p. 138)

A recent review of globalization activities in nine major multinational corporations revealed that the major problem they faced was not developing a global strategy but aligning the organization's capacity to implement the strategy. It was estimated that top managers spend less time in decision making (3%) than in finding problems (48%) and implementing solutions (49%) (Marsick and Cederholm 1988).

This is not news to anyone who has been working with large-scale change in multinational corporations. The key to making global strategies and structures work lies in *corporate culture.* But as one IBM manager I worked with said, "Understanding and aligning corporate culture is like trying to get your arms around a 2,400-pound marshmallow!"

A recent McKinsey study revealed that most corporations today, domestic and international, believe that correct strategy formulation constitutes only 20 percent of organizational success. The remaining 80 percent lies in strategy implementation, which is becoming increasingly difficult in a world of constant change. There is growing evidence that the lack of an integrated global corporate culture has inhibited many American corporations in their attempts to implement global strategies. ITT, GE, and Corning Glass Works have all experienced difficulties competing with Japanese and European firms in recent years for reasons that have been identified as lack of speed in responsiveness, lack of flexibility in organizational structure, and lack of capacity to transfer technology to the right place in a timely fashion.

Each of these failures is a failure of implementation, not strategy. Failure of implementation invariably involves failures of organizational alignment. And failure of organizational alignment is directly related to corporate culture.

GLOBAL CORPORATE CULTURE

The development of a global corporate culture that is aligned with a new strategy and structure is for most corporations the last step in the integrated approach to globalization described in Chapter 3. It is not just a matter of doing business internationally or even having subsidiaries abroad. **Developing a global corporate culture that is aligned with and supportive of a new global strategy and structure involves forming integrating values, mechanisms, and processes that allow a company to move in new directions and manage constant change in a competitive marketplace**. The world leaders in aligning global corporate strategy and structure with culture and practices are old European firms such as Philips, Shell, and ICI, and new global Japanese firms such as Matsushita, NEC, and Toyota. In the United States, Motorola, General Electric, and 3M are leaders in globalizing their corporate cultures, but all admit to the need to monitor and improve their practices constantly.

One company that has recently undertaken some new and interesting approaches to developing a global corporate culture is the Paris-based AXA insurance group. One of the keys to AXA's globalization strategy is decentralization. But to achieve this, the leadership recognizes that a synergy and shared culture must be created throughout the company. To maintain a cohesive management culture worldwide, AXA has established several layers of management, including an executive committee, with five senior board members meeting once a week; a strategy committee, consisting of 15 members meeting every two months; a corporate committee consisting of 150 members meeting twice a year; and various "synergy" groups and task forces meeting regularly to deal with ongoing business. The company has about 200 people working in these groups. But AXA also promotes more unorthodox means of motivating management and providing a cohesive corporate culture. For example, 5,500 members of its management from all over the world spent a week together in the summer of 1995 at a chateau near Bordeaux, France, for a special training course to explain the AXA style of management. Other projects in the past involved an excursion to Niger to see the challenges of economic development and, in 1994, a trip to the Great Wall of China, where managers were required to sleep outdoors in sleeping bags to share experiences outside office life (Aldred 1995).

While AXA may represent an extreme example of developing a global corporate culture, many of the elements are absolutely correct. You must have multinational groups meeting at regular intervals to review the business globally, and you must bring together large groups of people to develop relationships across borders. These tactics encourage people to work well together even when structure, policies, and procedures break down in the face of a global challenge.

FIVE KEY FACTORS IN GLOBAL ALIGNMENT

Aligning global organizations to new global strategies and structures most often focuses on five key factors—organizational values, organizational communications, financial systems, information systems, and human resource systems. These elements woven together form the integrating values, mechanisms, and processes that allow a company to manage the implementation of globalization.

Organizational Values

Aligning values with strategy and structure is not just a matter of drawing up a list of positive ideas like integrity, teamwork, empowerment, and respect for the individual. To be sure, such an exercise may be a starting point, but until values are translated into performance systems, little will change in employee behavior. **The greatest single mistake that executives make in corporate culture change is to think that identifying and communicating values instills them into the corporate culture of an organization.** Changing the value structure of an organization is a relentless, time-consuming process that demands the time and attention of all departments in an organization. In many cases, it also unfortunately requires some high-profile dismissals of senior executives who continue to get business results through the wrong means; that is, in ways that are not in line with the new values of the organization.

This was true of Jack Welch's turnaround of GE. In fact, in a presentation to Ford senior managers to discuss his experience with corporate culture change, Welch told a stunned group of senior people that if 20 percent of them were not let go in the process of Ford 2000, it was unlikely that the program would be successful!

Organizational Communications

Many times the corporate communications department is left out of planning for organizational and corporate culture change. Yet corporate communications, both internal and external, should be a primary tool for shaping the corporate culture and a major resource in helping employees and the public understand the organization's vision, values, and culture. You should ensure that the communications department is involved not only in the communication of organizational changes but, when possible, in their development, so that its people understand the rationale behind organizational decisions. They can contribute both more effective communications to employees and a more transparent decision-making process. As we said in Chapter 4, creating a sense of due process is central to managing organizational complexity in a global organization. Good communication is an essential element of due process.

In Ford's corporate culture change to a global matrix organization, there has been an extensive communications program involving multiple meetings of hundreds of managers in different parts of the wold. Ford's communications department worked closely with senior management to draft ideas and develop the best means of communicating the changes to employees. FCN, the Ford Communications Network, which delivers four hours of daily television programming to Ford employees worldwide, produced continuous interviews with senior managers engaged in the development and implementation of Ford 2000. All 320,000 employees were exposed to constant information. These communication efforts were not one-shot but continued for months prior to the actual implementation and for months after the reorganization. Communication and information empower employees by making them part of the process, reassuring them that they can take initiatives to contribute to corporate culture change.

John Fulkerson, vice president of organization and management development for Pepsi International, speaks of the cultural differences that complicate building a company that can deliver consistently superior customer satisfaction through a global system. He believes that to make it work, you have to create HR systems that allow flexibility on a local basis but maintain consistency of vision and values at headquarters. In addition, Pepsi uses such communications tools as newsletters, video conferencing, and internal publications to convey consistent global and local messages. "Number one, you have to talk about what it is you're trying to communicate," says Fulkerson. "We're trying to convey how we provide value and the best product in the marketplace. So, we try to transfer knowledge through lots of discussions and personal conversations" (Solomon 1993).

Financial Systems

It is useless to change from a geographic to a global product organization without changing the financial systems that track and reward profits on a global product basis, in addition to a country basis. Yet many global product managers find themselves in a never-never land when an organization changes its structure abruptly. They may suddenly have profit-and-loss responsibility but no financial information with which to track their progress or evaluate their results.

Aligning financial systems with new structures and authority relationships is complex, particularly if you have chosen a global matrix organization. In a matrix organization, a number of people may be simultaneously responsible for profit and loss in a particular area. While most organizations try to designate a specific person to hold accountable, that person's ability to deliver is often dependent on one or two other people with whom they must cooperate to achieve the financial results they have targeted.

In Ford 2000, the financial executives were leaders in the change process, starting a change in their systems six months prior to the implementation of the new structure. There were still many areas that did not have adequate information when the global structure went into place on January 1, 1995, but the financial effort was moving in the right direction. Unfortunately, financial systems too often lag behind in organizational realignment. A common reason the financial area may not be up to speed in a large global restructuring is that information systems have not been redesigned and put into place. The accumulation and monitoring of financial information in line with the new structure is simply not possible.

Information Systems

Reorganizing the information systems is perhaps the most difficult of all aspects of organizational realignment, but not because information systems groups are resistant or slow. Two major complications are most often cited. The first is that the time and cost of changing system architecture, software, and, in many cases hardware are often staggering. It is not unusual for revision to take two to five years at a significant cost to the bottom line. The second complication is less obvious: the problem of new global managers not understanding their roles and responsibilities in a new global matrix organization. If you are a newly appointed global product manager but are unsure how you are to operate with the regional and local management and how you are to coordinate with the global functional management, it will be nearly impossible for you to specify the information you will need to have reported.

Information technology (IT) specialists cannot begin their work on new information systems until managers in the new organization understand their roles and responsibilities in decision making. Even when an initial set of reports is designed, needs will constantly shift as global market and competitive factors change.

More than 800 CEOs, CIOs, CFOs, MIS directors, and VPs of manufacturing and distribution in local organizations concluded that they were not receiving maximum benefits from information technology, according to a recent study conducted by Andersen Consulting (*Industrial Engineering,* December 1993). The global companies receiving the greatest benefits, however, reported that effective globalization of IT depended on other success factors—adoption of a global perspective, top-down agreement on critical challenges, development of a formal systems plan, and implementation of common systems. The survey also revealed that to meet the unique challenges of globalization, IT must be implemented across the entire company to develop a global information infrastructure.

So, in aligning your organization to new global strategies and structures, start as early as possible on reconfiguration of your financial information *and* develop an understanding of your decision processes so that your IT people can get their arms around the architecture needed to run the new organization.

Human Resource Systems

While it should not be the case, many times the human performance system takes the longest to put into place. Yet, time after time, it is clear that until a company aligns its performance appraisal, rewards, and management succession system with its new directions, people simply do not behave in new ways.

Charlene Marmer Solomon reports that after the Gulf War, Bechtel human resource employees worked day and night in a 14th-floor office in San Francisco's financial district, culling through 105,000 phone inquiries to supply the necessary manpower for their Middle East reconstruction operation. Gathering and transferring information from Bechtel's headquarters to the ground operations in Kuwait, they were able to mobilize 16,000 Americans, Britons, Filipinos, Australians, and others from 37 countries to rebuild Kuwait. She writes:

> Call it what you like—global, transnational, international—but when business looks to the entire world for capital and supplies, when there's an official company language, when human resource professionals become interested in work hours in Seoul and Stockholm, and when fluctuation in exchange rate for yen and Deutsche marks become meaningful, you've entered a global frame of mind. (Solomon 1993, p. 83)

In this case, Bechtel was able to mobilize human resource (HR) professionals quickly and with remarkable success.

Often, however, there is a delay in implementing human performance systems, which points to the lack of priority typically given to HR issues by senior executives. If the CEO does not understand the need for these systems and does not support an aggressive VP of HRD, there will be little progress in this area. In successful change efforts, like those of GE and Ford, the CEOs were intimately involved in management training, rewards, and management succession systems that placed the right people in leadership positions, sent a clear message about expected behavior, provided the skills to get there, then rewarded or punished behavior within a limited period of time. As Alex Trotman said, "The train is leaving the station. It's your decision whether you want to get on, but it's my decision when you get off if you're not riding with the same values as the rest of the passengers."

Unfortunately, a second reason for delay in the alignment of human performance systems with a new corporate culture often has to do with the senior HR management. Too often these people see themselves narrowly as compensation and benefit specialists and do not understand their new role as supporters of human resource development and, by extension, supporters of corporate culture alignment through organizational development. **Unless HR executives understand their unique position to influence and shape corporate culture, there is little chance that HR will be a valued partner in an organizational change process.**

One of the greatest levers that HR executives have in helping a company globalize is through training and development. The Pepsi-Cola International Management Institute, the Ford Executive Center, Andersen's Center for Professional Education, and Motorola University are all powerful training organizations that are strategically linked to company objectives and are perceived by top management as key levers in the implementation of any change in corporate culture. Many of these companies, like Motorola and Pepsi, deliver their programs through a series of regional training institutes throughout the world.

DEVELOPING A GLOBAL CORPORATE CULTURE

It is not easy to develop a global corporate culture. Again, we turn to Whirlpool CEO Whitwam:

> The hardest part of globalization is avoiding the temptation of trying to build Rome in a day. The purchase contract might state that you own the land. But you don't own the builders; they have to enter into the work contract of their own free will. . . . Most employees didn't sign up to be part of the globalization experience. Suddenly we give them new things to think about and new people to work with. We tell people at all levels that the old way of doing business is too cumbersome. . . . We spent a lot of time building trust and creating a common vision of our future. . . . We brought 150 of our senior managers to Montreux, Switzerland, and spent a week developing our global vision. We made those 150 people accountable for educating all of our 38,000 people around the world. (Maruca 1994, p. 143)

Whitwam used many different techniques to get his managers and employees aligned with the new global corporate culture and vision. But he did not try to homogenize them into a single entity. He had them build a common vision, but their ways of explaining the vision to their employees around the world varied according to local cultural traditions. This is a key lesson in building a global corporate culture and aligning organizations on a global basis. **To build a global corporate culture, you must** concentrate on the vision, values, and principles of the organization and allow regional and local managers to execute them with their people through their own cultural filters.

Recent studies have shown that it is impossible, as well as undesirable, to insist on uniform execution of a global organizational vision. Andre Laurent, a professor at INSEAD business school in France, conducted a study of several companies, after which he made the following observations:

1. **Multinational companies do not and cannot submerge the individuality of different cultures.** As strong as a corporate culture may be, people never give up their own national backgrounds and preferences. People can adapt, but in periods of crisis or uncertainty, they will retreat to their own sets of beliefs and cultural values. Since crisis and uncertainty are prime characteristics of global organizations, national culture often plays an important role in people's day-to-day behavior.

2. **Contact with other nationality groups can even promote determination to be different.** It is paradoxical that many people withdraw when confronted with cultural differences and reinforce their determination not to adjust and not to give up their own values. Unless intercultural contact is supported and guided to be a positive experience, it can often lead to the reinforcement of negative stereotypes. And others will resist integration or "homogenization," as they may see it, by emphasizing their own cultural heritage, history, and beliefs.

3. **It is useless to present new kinds of management theory and practice to individuals who are culturally unable or unwilling to accept it.** For example, performance reviews are difficult in most multinational corporations because of differences in personal style. Americans see themselves as open, direct, and blunt; Asians tend to be much more indirect, oblique, and subtle in giving feedback. Thus, something as apparently basic and common as a performance-appraisal system probably cannot be implemented uniformly on a global basis.

No corporate culture transplants with complete success overseas. Companies that try to graft their home culture onto local nationals will experience problems, the degree of which will depend on both the new regional or national culture within which they are operating and the national culture from which they come. I was a consultant to a major U.S. oil company trying to start up a joint venture in Siberia with a local Russian oil company. The project involved the enhancement of an existing oil field to improve its productive capacity. The American attitude was that they were delivering the capital and technology and that the Russians should listen to the way "things should be done." The Russian attitude was that they were delivering the opportunity (the oil field), as well as the workers and some 15 years of experience with the field, and that they should be considered equal partners. In this case, the Americans wanted *explicitly* to transfer their technical expertise *and* their corporate culture to the Russians to teach them how to think and act like Americans. The project reached a crisis after a year, during which the Russians ordered most of the Americans to leave. When asked why, they responded that they felt the Americans did not respect them and were not willing to work with them as partners.

Because a global corporate culture cannot be defined by the home culture of the corporation, you must change the mindset of managers and employees of the home country. American Express generates 85 percent of its revenues in the United States, yet much of its future growth is international. Ford 2000 is designed to integrate the U.S. operations with Ford of Europe and the rest of the world. Siemens has been dominated by its domestic German market but is now trying to reach out around the world to newly emerging markets. In each case, while a truly global corporate culture may not ultimately be required, the dominant home-country orientation must be realigned and many domestic managers must begin thinking about how they relate to global markets in an integrated global organization.

When a global corporate culture is created, it transforms a corporation and its management so thoroughly that it is difficult to discern a single-country bias—from the executive suite to the lowest (and arguably most critical) level of the organization.

MANAGING A GLOBAL CORPORATE CULTURE

We will divide the elements of corporate culture according to the basic management activities of any company. In this way, we can personalize the globalization process so that you, as a practicing manager, can identify with the kinds of changes you will need to make in your day-to-day management operations if you are to align your global corporate culture with your overall strategy and structure.

The three activities we will consider here are old in conception but new in interpretation—planning, organizing, and controlling. Staffing, the fourth key area for managing a global corporate culture, will be considered separately in Chapter 8, "Managing Learning," and leading, the fifth area, will be addressed in Chapter 6, "Managing Multicultural Teams."

Planning

Five planning activities directly affect your global corporate culture. These are

1. A globally inspiring mission.
2. A global corporate vision.
3. Global information sources and systems.
4. A globally fair and equitable system of resource allocation.
5. Decision-making criteria reflecting global and local values.

Let us briefly examine each.

Globally Inspiring Mission

It is easier said than done to create a mission that inspires people from many different cultural backgrounds and many different social, political, and economic circumstances around the world. One manager's inspiration, "to dominate the household cleaning products market worldwide," may be inspiring for people living in abundant post-industrial societies but may be a nightmare for other managers in the same corporation living in countries plagued by overpopulation and inadequate nutrition.

Global missions must be tested against many different social, political, and economic circumstances. One reason it is so difficult to achieve a culturally acceptable global corporate mission is that a mission statement is the connection of a corporation to the values of a society and its workforce. A global corporation by definition operates in many different societies with a multicultural workforce. Its mission must be attractive to the greatest number of people from the greatest number of cultural, social, economic, and political backgrounds.

One of the difficulties for global organizations—especially not-for-profit and public sector organizations based on volunteer support—is that if they decide to revise a mission that has been carefully developed over many years on a multinational basis, they may find themselves faced with resistance from a global volunteer population. There are, indeed, very few global values on which all people in the world can agree. Peace and children appear to be two of the more popular ones, which is why UNICEF and the American Field Service international student exchange program have gained such broad volunteer bases around the world.

Global Corporate Vision

The basic difference between mission and vision is that **a mission speaks to the purpose of the organization and a vision describes what the corporation will look like in achieving its mission.** It is somewhat easier to have an agreed-upon global corporate vision from a cultural perspective than a power perspective. Global corporate visions usually involve matters of structure, authority, and resources—all of which are complicated by issues of power, status, and personal ambition. Forming a global corporate vision, therefore, is a complicated process involving sophisticated visioning and equally sophisticated global negotiations with all the power figures who must participate in achieving the vision.

Ben Tregoe, the founder of Kepner-Tregoe, has said that "the last thing a company headed in the wrong direction needs is to get there more efficiently" (Peak 1991, p. 33). In recent years, global managers have found that global corporate visions, to be headed in the right direction, must embrace greater numbers of people. The shaping and realization of visions have also become increasingly dependent on suppliers and customers, as well as internal stakeholders. Managers in global organizations are discovering that all boundaries need to be broken, all stakeholders redefined, and all power-sharing processes and methods reviewed to arrive at a global vision.

Global Information Sources and Systems

As a manager in a global organization involved in planning, one of the first things you become aware of is the need for more and better information about global social, economic, and political conditions. For most global managers, global scanning becomes an obsession. Without scanning, you risk becoming paralyzed by the lack of information or being blind-sided by not having defined a broad enough range of variables.

You must review all your information sources and make sure you are scanning on a worldwide basis, as well as across many different functional, business, and technological areas. Only then will you be able to develop an adequate plan for your company.

A Globally Fair and Equitable System of Resource Allocation

A difficult and contentious aspect of a global corporate culture, and of global management in general, is the development of a fair and equitable system of resource allocation. It appears to be almost impossible to have everyone's agreement about the way in which financial, human, and other resources should be allocated. A common method of dealing with this problem in the financial area is through transfer pricing. This practice involves the development of a financial formula in which components of a production process result in various income credits being awarded to different geographic locations, depending on their contribution to the overall value of the finished goods or service. While the concept is worthy, agreeing upon the amount of value added by each component is often a time-consuming negotiation.

There are many other methods global companies have devised to ensure perceived fairness in the system. But there are also instances in which the consensus around resource allocation breaks down so severely that managers become fixated on negotiating their own internal power relationships to the detriment of their customers, their financial viability, and, indeed, their ultimate survival. In other words, on this issue it is possible to commit corporate suicide by paying more attention to internal power relations than to customers.

Decision-Making Criteria Reflecting Global and Local Values

Not only does the allocation of resources need to be seen as fair and equitable, but the decision process through which the allocation of resources is determined must be seen as taking into account local as well as global values. While all of this may seem to be just an exercise in democratic decision making, there is increasing evidence that sensitivity to local values is good business as well as good politics. The representation of diverse values, opinions, and perspectives is one of the richer assets of a global corporation, contributing to better strategy and a more thorough analysis of all options. The trick is to establish a means for polling these diverse views and negotiating a final decision that cannot, by definition, equally incorporate all concerns.

The fact is that many companies ignore diverse perspectives because they have not yet developed the global corporate cultural norms for managing diversity and the inevitable conflict that accompanies it. **During the years ahead, you will increasingly see that successful global companies have a means for managing global diversity of opinions, perspectives, and values in a way that enriches strategy and contributes to more creative and competitive operations.**

Organization

We have discussed the structure of a global corporation, but we have barely touched on its organization. They are two different issues. The structure is *where functions are placed;* the organization is *how they are coordinated.* Let's examine five specific aspects of organization that affect global corporate responsiveness:

1. Clear levels of authority and responsibility.
2. Empowerment.
3. Formal and informal networking and integration mechanisms.
4. Global-functional and cross-unit coordination councils.
5. Global corporate meetings and conferences.

Clear Levels of Authority and Responsibility

It is critical that authority be clearly designated within roles and responsibilities that are equally clear. One of the worst mistakes made by many global managers is to assume that people will somehow appropriately interpret their roles, responsibilities, and authority for themselves.

ABB Chairman Barnevik points out that clarity of roles, responsibilities, and authority in a complex matrixed global corporation is vital in allowing it to respond effectively to changes in the corporate environment. This is particularly true of the vertical delegation of authority and responsibility between global centers and local operating units. Clarity may seem impossible when geographic, functional, product, and business organizations are matrixed in different ways in different functions in different businesses in different products in different parts of the world! One of the greatest failings of newly globalized corporations, especially those with a matrix structure, is that they do not think through how their structure will *operate* on a global basis. As a result, they fail to develop the *policies, procedures,* and *mindset* necessary to run the organization globally.

To ensure an effective global organization, you must make the effort to clarify roles, responsibility, and authority for as many issues as possible. For those issues where no clear definition can be reached on a continuing basis, you must establish some form of decision making to allow for conflict.

Empowerment

Empowerment is a very difficult value to translate globally. The concept itself is largely culture-specific, emanating from the individually oriented American culture that assumes people want power and authority to act by themselves. There are also group forms of empowerment in which teams are given the authority and responsibility to manage themselves. This is done often in manufacturing and has been used successfully by Motorola, Ford, and many other companies.

When empowerment leaves the manufacturing setting, however, it becomes more difficult to embed in managerial ranks. The difficulty is compounded in a global matrix organization or a global product organization where there is some centralization of authority and responsibility aimed at achieving worldwide coordination of best practices, economies of scale, or global responsiveness to global customers. In such cases, there is a contradiction between the centralization aspects of globalization and the concept of empowerment and decentralization.

The fact is that globalization and empowerment are in some ways contradictory. They form a paradox. You are going to centralize to gain economies of scale, while simultaneously decentralizing and empowering for speed of responsiveness to local markets. Sorting out what gets centralized and what gets decentralized through empowerment is mind-boggling.

To further complicate matters, not all cultures respond well to the concept of empowerment itself. Mexicans, Thais, Indians, and many others who come from hierarchical countries, where obedience and respect for supervisors is an assumed behavior, are completely taken aback by the idea that they should take initiative and responsibility for their own actions. In many cases, such a foreign idea just cannot be implemented.

Because structural and cultural barriers to empowerment exist, you may need to explain the concept in terms of the ultimate objective of, perhaps, speed to market or efficiency of decision making. Local managers in each country will then determine how they can achieve the objective, perhaps using a management tool other than empowerment. By the way, companies often make the error of defining empowerment as a management philosophy, rather than a management tool. As a tool it can be appropriately applied, but as a philosophy it is assumed to be pervasive throughout the company. This is just not possible in a global organization.

Formal and Informal Networking and Integrating Mechanisms

One of the formal mechanisms used for networking and integrating global corporations is management rotation and training. Through global career pathing and frequent changes of responsibility and location, managers of global organizations develop a global perspective and at the same time become acquainted with people from throughout the world. This informal networking facilitates global decision making, especially at times when speed is essential and knowing the person at the other end of the line 10,000 kilometers away is imperative.

Global-Functional and Cross-Unit Coordination Councils

Another organizational mechanism to ensure global coordination of conflicting opinions, needs, and ideas is the continual use of global-functional and cross-unit coordination councils.

Grace Cocoa holds global operations and commercial meetings with representatives from all its plants to examine the total company's needs on an ongoing basis. It also has a seven-member global executive committee consisting of people from five countries who together represent all divisions. This group meets quarterly to review overall company strategy as well as to coordinate month-to-month operations.

Philips, in the face of intensifying Japanese competition, needed to improve its consumer electronics coordination among its independent national organizations. It created a World Policy Council that includes key managers from strategic markets around the world. Through this council, Philips co-opts country support for company decisions about product policy and manufacturing location. At IBM-Europe, country CEOs are autonomous in their country subsidiaries, but also sit on a pan-European board. This "glocal" structure achieves coordination across the company's European operations.

Coordination councils and other forms of international cooperation do mean more travel. Many managers who have worked in international or multinational organizations are used to taking a business trip to their territory or headquarters once a year. These people often fail to understand that when you form a global organization, the amount of travel necessary to keep its disparate parts together increases geometrically. Frequent global travel is not an option to be eliminated during budget crunches, but a necessity to keep the organization in coordinated, competitive condition.

Global Corporate Meetings and Conferences

Any successful global corporation, if it is to develop and sustain an integrated global corporate culture, must have a range of global meetings and conferences involving people from throughout the corporation. Ideally, on an annual basis, it should go one level lower than any normal decision-making groups or committees. In other words, if you have quarterly meetings of your vice presidents from various areas of the world, then you should have an annual meeting of vice presidents and directors.

The first reaction of many managers is that the travel cost cannot be justified. The second thought, if they are thinking, is that a global corporation cannot stay in business in a fast-changing environment without updating and coordinating not only the executive group, but also the senior operating people responsible for ironing out the day-to-day misunderstandings that inevitably occur in global operations.

In the end, we all must accept the fact that the decision whether there are or are not adequate resources for effective coordination of a global organization is not a matter of money, but of vision and priorities.

Control

The final building block of a global corporate culture is the means of recognizing and rewarding behavior and performance that contribute to the overall objectives and philosophy of the corporation. Every management textbook ever written about corporate culture notes that *corporate cultures are not established through visions and mottos, but through a reward-and-recognition process*. This process must acknowledge performance that is consonant with the corporation's values, philosophy, vision, mission, and direction. If these aspects of corporate life are out of line, the corporation will not perform to its potential.

There are four areas in which this reward process is applied in global corporations:

1. Incorporation of quantitative and qualitative data for performance review.
2. Globally consistent and culturally sensitive performance review standards and processes.
3. Measurement systems to encourage continuous improvement.

4. Globally consistent business-unit measurement and reward systems.

As we review each area of reward, reflect on how your company organizes these processes.

Incorporation of Quantitative and Qualitative Data for Performance Review

Given the complexities of global corporations with many rotating or matrixed boss/subordinate relations, it is becoming increasingly important to include qualitative as well as quantitative data in performance reviews. This time-consuming process has not been well-developed in many corporations, in large part because standards are so nebulous. Investment banks and other companies that have flat, de-layered organizations with shifting project teams use qualitative peer feedback because many times supervisors have not had enough contact with an employee to adequately evaluate performance at year's end. The same holds true for many managers in global organizations. They may report to someone who is on the other side of the globe or to several people in several parts of the globe. To accommodate this matrix organization, performance appraisal systems can be electronically operated through coded channels to allow people to have input from various points in the world without getting bogged down in paperwork.

Globally Consistent and Culturally Sensitive Performance Review Standards and Processes

Another difficult area in conducting individual performance reviews in global corporations is the cultural bias of the typical American performance review process. There are many cultures, the French for example, in which senior managers above a certain level are simply not subject to annual performance reviews. There are others, like the Indonesian, where performance reviews do not involve face-to-face discussion between a supervisor and employee but instead are done through a third party or some other impersonal mechanism to prevent loss of face.

A major challenge for global corporations is to devise performance appraisal systems that are simultaneously sensitive to these cultural differences, yet are perceived as valid and equitable in their measurement of employee contribution to total organizational achievements. Companies that have done this successfully have been very clear about their global corporate values and have allowed local variety in process, while requiring consistency in content.

Measurement Systems to Encourage Continuous Improvement

Total quality management and the Japanese concept of *kaizan* have etched the idea of continuous improvement into the corporate mindsets of many of the world's largest corporations. Whether TQM takes hold in operations as a long-term methodology depends on the corporate culture of an organization. In a global corporation that is process-driven, however, continuous improvement is a significant means of monitoring and refining processes, thereby enhancing corporate effectiveness. As such, it must be an integral part of a global corporate culture.

There is not enough space in this brief review to examine the elements of Demming's 14 principles that could be applied to global corporations. For a global manager, however, it would be a useful exercise to ascertain the relevance of implementing a continuous process improvement program for a global corporate culture.

In any case, successful global corporations, if they are to compete head-on with the Japanese, will need to take into account the fact that their competition will be operating on a philosophy of continuous improvement that will impose a hard competitive stance over the long haul. Any global manager who believes that it is possible to establish a product niche and sit on it without constant adjustment and improvement will be doomed to fall victim to the higher quality or lower cost of a global competitor. Your rewards system may need to incorporate special awards for process improvements, which should be publicized widely within the organization.

Globally Consistent Business-Unit Measurement and Reward Systems

Individual recognition and reward is one aspect of managing a successful global culture. Equally important, however, is the basis upon which business units are evaluated and rewarded and the degree to which the process and standards are considered consistent and equitable among units on a global basis. This rather complicated objective rests on perceived as well as actual contributions to the corporate bottom line. It goes without saying that without an appropriate definition of profit centers and the best financial policies for allocation, accounting, and control, there will be constant warfare between business units over their perceived and real contributions, both to corporate profit and corporate overhead.

Careful definition of financial units and accounting standards for a global organization can help you avoid painful misunderstandings and jealousies and time-wasting meetings, debates, and arguments. "Financial transparency," or something close to it, must be an objective of global corporate finance departments so that illusions of contributions and misunderstandings about the real cost structure of global operations can be prevented or filtered out. **A chief financial officer who appreciates her or his role as a developer of the global corporate culture, as well as the chief financial strategist and controller, is one of the most important assets that a global corporation can acquire.**

Developing a global corporate culture with appropriate management practices depends heavily on changing the individual attitudes and skills of executives, managers, and employees in the organization. Without a change in people's mindset, the best vision or global strategy will never get off the ground.

COMPETITIVE BENEFITS OF A GLOBAL CORPORATE CULTURE

One competitive advantage of a well-aligned global corporate culture lies in the flexibility to shift from local to global strategy when necessary to blunt a competitor's attack. It is relatively easy to adjust a global culture to local needs, but much more difficult to adjust a locally responsive culture to global needs.

Philips, the Dutch-based electronics giant, has been constantly frustrated in its attempt to overcome its multinational localized bias. Despite the fact that Philips has technological superiority over the Japanese in a number of areas, it has been unable to transfer and distribute the technology quickly enough to be competitive in the right markets. It has lacked the strategic coordination and the global corporate culture that facilitate rapid response. Explanations given for Philips's failure are all too familiar. They include suggestions that those who developed the product were too distant from the market. Others felt that there were barriers between research, development, manufacturing, and marketing that led to delays and cost overruns. Still others suggest that since worldwide subsidiaries were not involved in new product development, they have not been committed to distributing new products that were not tailored to local demands.

By contrast, Matsushita Electric Company, Philips's rival in worldwide electronics, has built global leadership through the development of a corporate culture that bridges such strategic gaps. Three characteristics of Matsushita's corporate culture contribute heavily to its success. First, it gains the input of subsidiaries into management processes. Second, it ensures that development efforts are linked to market needs. And third, it manages responsibility transfer from development to manufacturing to marketing (Bartlett and Ghoshal 1988, p. 3).

A globalized corporate culture can facilitate a longer-term corporate view. To use an analogy developed by McKinsey & Co., large globally integrated corporations are more "farmers" than "hunter-gatherers" (Bleeke and Johnson 1989, p. 67). Global hunter-gatherers identify the newest product resulting from the most advanced technology or latest fad and travel the globe trying to sell it in the best markets. The result is short product life cycles and a high-overhead marketing effort that is in constant change and adjustment. On products with high margins in introductory phases of their product cycle, this can be a profitable strategy. Global farmers, on the other hand, build long-term stable customer relationships and sell more mature, dependable products over a longer period of time. A global corporate culture, with a series of international checks and balances, tends to shift corporations toward developing and maintaining relationships rather than hunting/gathering products. This is because globalization encourages global efficiency and innovation, but not at the cost of being unresponsive to local long-term needs and relationships. To become global farmers, managers must have a highly refined understanding of the world, good global scanning skills, a sharp instinct for generic business strategy, and a deep sensitivity to cultural, social, economic, and political differences around the world.

Ericsson, the Swedish telecommunication company, appears to be everyone's choice as a model global corporate culture. It has done the best job of managing the need for global integration and local responsiveness, while developing excellent strategic coordination mechanisms. Three characteristics stand out: an interdependence of resources and responsibilities among organizational units through mandatory sharing of resources, ideas, and opportunities; a set of strong cross-unit integrating devices; and a strong corporate identification and well-developed worldwide management perspectives. By changing responsibilities, shifting assets, and modifying relationships among various geographic, product, and functional groups, Ericsson has built a diverse organization in which multiple perspectives exist not only within the decision-making process, but among the global managers themselves.

These diverse viewpoints, combined with a fluid structure, are complemented by a set of interunit integrating devices that form the core of the global corporate culture. The most critical aspects of Ericsson's corporate culture that enhance global competitiveness are a clearly defined and tightly controlled set of operating systems; a people-linking process that employs such devices as temporary assignments and joint teams; and interunit decision forums, particularly subsidiary boards, where views can be exchanged and differences resolved. These three elements provide the infrastructure necessary to manage diversity and ensure effective and timely decision making.

Ericsson's systems have been constructed to facilitate worldwide coordination, rather than central control. All of this requires good interpersonal relations on a worldwide basis. For this reason, temporary interunit transfers between headquarters and subsidiaries, as well as between subsidiaries, lie at the heart of the people equation. Ericsson's transfer process is much more intense than most, however. It often transfers a team of 50 to 100 engineers and managers from one unit to another for a year or two.

Ericsson's conflict-management forums tend to be in active board meetings (both headquarters and subsidiary), during which differences between headquarters and local subsidiaries are thrashed out with input from people with a wide range of perspectives and backgrounds.

PRACTICES AND TASKS FOR MANAGING ORGANIZATIONAL ALIGNMENT

The following is a list of the practices and tasks that you as a global manager can undertake to make sure that your global corporate culture is properly aligned with the organization's strategy and structure.

Skill 3: Managing Organizational Alignment

Key Question	How do you remain focused and coordinated?
Definition	Ability to develop and effectively communicate the vision, values, systems, and procedures necessary to execute a global strategy throughout a diverse population of employees and business units around the world.
Action and Mindset	Engage process
Personal Characteristic	Strategic

Key Practices and Tasks

1. Review your current corporate culture against the list outlined earlier. Determine *which corporate policies, procedures, systems, values, and practices facilitate or hinder the development of your global operations* within a three- to five-year strategy and structure.

1.1 Clearly restate your three- to five-year business strategy in terms of its implications for your global operations and your global corporate culture.

1.2 Compare your corporate culture today against your global business strategy to determine where you need to make adjustments to ensure adaptability to future competitive and market demands.

1.3 Ensure that your reward systems and criteria reinforce the global cultural values and behavior that you want to see in your unit.

2. Develop a *global strategy and structure that is fixed,* but a *global corporate culture that is process driven and flexible* to changing world conditions through the use of global task forces, temporary decision committees, regional coordination groups, and global integrators.

2.1 Determine where task forces can enhance decision making by bringing together key players who have conflicting interests, such as country or regional managers with global functional specialists or global product managers.

2.2 Consider creating an organizational effectiveness or organizational development group of internal consultants with international experience and cross-cultural skills who can troubleshoot conflict in any part of the world.

2.3 Look for extraordinary individuals who seem to have an ability to see many sides of an issue and use them for global troubleshooting and analysis, regardless of their full-time positions and responsibilities.

3. *Monitor your corporate culture* through periodic global employee surveys that reveal the degree to which your vision, values, systems, and procedures are understood and effectuated.

3.1 Get your customers involved in giving you feedback on your vision, values, systems, and procedures to determine whether you are effective in the marketplace in communicating your direction.

3.2 Look for opportunities to make your job and function as flexible as possible by establishing annual or semiannual cross-functional reviews and building in feedback loops on your performance from internal and external customers on a global basis.

4. *Benchmark* your business and operational policies, procedures, and practices against *international competitors*. Determine what changes need to be made to achieve world-class status.

    4.1 Examine the global business and operational practices of your global competitors and suppliers.

    4.2 Incorporate one new idea each year from a global competitor or supplier into your operations.

The management of global corporate culture could well be the most important task of a global manager. Herein lies the manager's and the organization's capacity to respond to rapid changes in the environment on a global basis, changes that affect the organization's survival and growth. To be a successful manager of a global corporate culture, you must be willing to occasionally break all rules, be addicted to change and "thrive on chaos," as Tom Peters (1988) would say.

SELECTED BIBLIOGRAPHY

Aldred, Carolyn. "Global Strategies Encompass Changing Corporate Culture." *Business Insurance,* April 17, 1995, pp. 41–43.

"Alignment of Business Objectives with IT Gives High Returns." *Industrial Engineering,* December 1993, pp. 9–10.

Allen, Robert F., and Charlotte Kraft. *The Organizational Unconscious: How to Create the Corporate Culture You Want and Need.* Englewood Cliffs, N.J.: Prentice-Hall, 1982.

Atkinson, Philip E. *Creating Culture Change: The Key to Successful Total Quality Management.* Bedford, UK: IFS Publications, 1991.

Bartlett, Christopher A., and Sumantra Ghoshal. "Organizing for Worldwide Effectiveness: The Transnational Solution." *California Management Review* 31, no. 1 (1988).

Bleeke, Joel A.; and Brian A. Johnson. "Signposts for a Global Strategy." *The McKinsey Quarterly,* Autumn 1989, pp. 60–71.

Champy, James. *Reengineering Management: The New Mandate for New Leadership.* New York: Harper Business, 1995.

Collins, James C., and Jerry I. Porras. *Built to Last: Successful Habits of Visionary Companies.* New York: Harper, 1994.

"Corporate Culture." *Business Week,* October 27, 1980, pp. 34–38.

Daniels, John L., and Dr. N. Caroline Daniels. *Global Vision: Building New Models of the Corporation of the Future.* New York: McGraw-Hill, 1993.

Deal, Terrence E., and Allan A. Kennedy. *Corporate Cultures: The Rites and Rituals of Corporate Life.* Reading, Mass.: Addison-Wesley, 1982.

Egan, Gerard. *Adding Value: A Systematic Guide to Business-Driven Management and Leadership.* San Francisco: Jossey-Bass, 1993.

Evans, Paul. "Management Development as Glue Technology." *Human Resource Planning* 15, no. 1: pp. 85–106.

Gouillart, Francis J., and James N. Kelly. *Transforming the Organization*. New York: McGraw- Hill, 1995.

Hampden-Turner, Charles. *Corporate Culture: How to Generate Organisational Strength and Lasting Commercial Advantage*. London: Piatkus, 1994.

Hickman, Craig R., and Michael A. Silva. *Creating Excellence: Managing Corporate Culture, Strategy and Change in the New Age*. New York: New American Library, 1985.

Kilmann, Ralph H. *Managing beyond the Quick Fix: A Completely Integrated Program for Creating and Maintaining Organizational Success*. San Francisco: Jossey-Bass, 1989.

Laurent, Andre. "The Cross-Cultural Puzzle of Human Resource Management." *Human Resource Management*, 25, no. 1 (Spring 1986): pp. 91–102.

Marquardt, Michael, and Angus Reynolds. *The Global Learning Organization: Gaining Competitive Advantage through Continuous Learning*. Burr Ridge, Ill.: Irwin Professional Publishing, 1994.

Marsick, Victoria J., and Lars Cederholm. "Developing Leadership in International Managers—An Urgent Challenge!" *The Columbia Journal of World Business* 22, no. 4 (Winter 1988): pp. 3–11.

Maruca, Regina Fazro. "The Right Way to Go Global: An Interview with Whirlpool CEO David Whitwam." *Harvard Business Review*, March-April 1994, pp. 135–45.

Miller, Lawrence. *American Spirit: Visions of a New Corporate Culture*. New York: William Morrow and Company, Inc., 1984.

Peak, Martha H. "Developing an International Management Style." *Management Review*, February 1991, pp. 32–35.

Peters, Thomas. *Thriving on Chaos: Handbook for a Management Revolution*. New York: Harper & Row, 1988.

Peters, Thomas; and Robert H. Waterman. *In Search of Excellence: Lessons from America's Best-Run Companies*. New York: Harper & Row, 1982.

Rhinesmith, Stephen H. "Going Global from the Inside Out." *Training and Development Journal*, November 1991, pp. 42–47.

Solomon, Charlene Marmer. "Transplanting Corporate Cultures Globally." *Personnel Journal*, October 1993, pp. 78–88.

Stewart, Thomas A. "How to Manage in the Global Era." *Fortune*, January 15, 1990, pp. 58–72.

Taylor, William. "The Logic of Global Business: An Interview with ABB's Percy Barnevik." *Harvard Business Review*, March-April 1991, pp. 91–105.

Winslow, Charles D., and William L. Bramer. *Future Work: Putting Knowledge to Work in the Knowledge Economy*. New York: The Free Press, 1994.

6

CHAPTER

Managing
Organizational Change

In 1983, Shell conducted a survey of how long business organizations survive. It revealed that corporations live about half as long as individual human beings. So the chances are that your organization will die before you do, and if it survives, it will have changed dramatically. The dominance

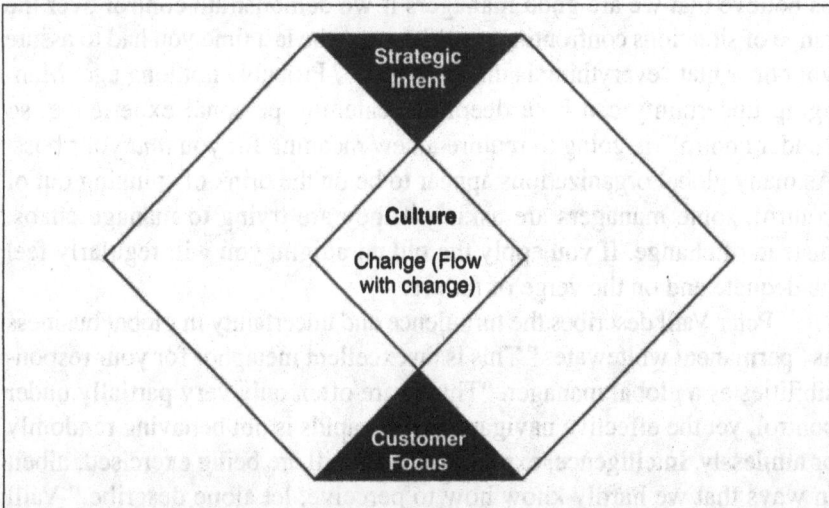

of continuous change in global business activities today demands not only new skills but also new comfort zones for you as a global manager. Your traditional role of making order out of chaos is shifting to one of continuously managing change and chaos to be responsive to customers and competitive conditions.

When Ford was developing the new Taurus, designers were pushed to the edge of their thinking by Alex Trotman, Ford chairman and CEO. When he dropped by one day to view the latest clay model, Trotman said, "That's not far enough. You're not scaring me yet." One of the designers later said, "I never thought I was going to get my hand slapped for not pushing too far." An industry observer says, "Trotman has almost purposefully created chaos and a feeling of global insecurity." Trotman, though, is not troubled by the prospect of failure nor awed by the complexities of his creation. "We're comfortable with discomfort," he maintains. He likes to test his ideas by arguing them with subordinates who are encouraged to "give me your off-the-wall ideas. That way, I can go to sleep at night knowing that what I think is valid. If I have a weak spot in my logic, we'll find it" (Taylor 1995, p. 139).

The idea that change, not stability, will be the regular and understood frame of reference for your life may constitute a shift for you. Taken further, it means that you will probably need to learn to "feel" differently and gain comfort with uncertainty. For some managers, it means they must change their self-concept and even their definition of self-worth. The modification of self-concept and self-worth emanates from the fact that most of us believe that we are good managers if we demonstrate control over the range of situations confronting us. When was the last time you had to assure your boss that "everything is under control"? Probably not long ago. Managing uncertainty can be a deeply threatening personal experience, so "under control" is going to require a new meaning for you *and* your boss. As many global organizations appear to be on the brink of spinning out of control, some managers are asking if they are trying to manage chaos, instead of change. If you apply the old paradigm, you will regularly feel inadequate and on the verge of failure.

Peter Vaill describes the turbulence and uncertainty in global business as "permanent whitewater." This is an excellent metaphor for your responsibilities as a global manager. "Things are often only very partially under control, yet the effective navigator of the rapids is not behaving randomly or aimlessly. Intelligence, experience, and skill are being exercised, albeit in ways that we hardly know how to perceive, let alone describe," Vaill says. Note that there is a critical difference here between a **lack of total control** and a **sense of helplessness**. Whitewater rafting places the right emphasis on the use of skill and ability to maintain equilibrium within a flow of forces beyond your control. Remember *wu wei*, nonaction that allows one to follow the "constant flow of transformation and change," as Chung Tzu calls it (Capra 1982).

Learning to "go with the flow" is a fundamental part of global management. But allowing yourself to let go without being swept uncontrollably into dangerous waters is among the most difficult global management skills to acquire. You must learn to exploit uncertainty for success.

UNCERTAINTY AND GLOBAL MANAGEMENT

Ralph Siu has fantasized about a game he calls Chinese baseball. "It's just like American baseball, except that when the ball is in the air, anyone is allowed to pick up any base and move it—anywhere!" This is a game, says Peter Vaill, that "no one knows how to play."

While global management may at times feel like Chinese baseball when you first approach it, there are obviously ways to play the game that can increase your chance of succeeding. Don Schon, in *The Reflective Practitioner* (1995), calls the lack of clarity international managers face in their work "the swamp." He suggests that people frequently depend on "technical rationality" to solve problems, while most problems in the swamp call for more right-brain, intuitive, action-learning approaches. Marsick and Cederholm note a similar pattern:

> International managers struggle with their judgment over problems that increasingly fall outside the realm of the right answer into this grey area of "the maybe," "the probably" and "the likely." To formulate the problem correctly and implement a solution when working internationally, managers must frequently depart from comfortable cultural norms. (1988, p. 6)

Of all the competencies we are examining, the management of uncertainty is one of the most difficult to understand and deal with. If you turn to a dictionary, you will see why managing uncertainty has its challenges. Consider the words and phrases associated with "uncertainty" in the *Random House Dictionary of the English Language*:

- Not clearly or precisely determined; indefinite; unknown.
- Vague; indistinct.
- Subject to change; capricious, variable, unstable.

- Ambiguous; unreliable; undependable.
- Dependent on chance or unpredictable factors.
- Unsteady or flickering; of changing intensity.

These words echo many global managers' characterizations of their world. Many new global managers I have worked with feel that events are not clearly or precisely determined, that everything seems ambiguous, unreliable, and undependable, and that their responsibilities, which were in the past knowable and manageable, have suddenly become unknown and unpredictable.

Ralph Stacey, in his excellent book, *Managing Chaos* (1992), talks about the need for managers to face the unknowable.

> This new approach is disturbing because it means accepting that you really have no idea what the long-term future holds for your organization. . . . The new approach is about sustaining contradictory positions and behavior in your organization. . . . The new approach is about positively using instability and crisis to generate new perspectives, provoking continual questioning and organizational learning through which unknowable futures can be created and discovered. . . .
>
> The new approach faces reality and accepts the consequent increase in levels of anxiety as necessary for creative activity. . . . This is perhaps the chief contradiction of all—the structures and behaviors necessary for stable normal management have to coexist with the informality and instability of extraordinary management which is necessary to cope with the unknowable. (pp. 17–18)

It may be some consolation that this is a common feeling. And it is a common feeling not only among global managers but among domestic-company managers trying to deal with increased complexity and uncertainty in the world. Michael McCaskey noted a wide range of sources of ambiguity for all managers in his study, *The Executive Challenge: Managing Change and Ambiguity (1986)*. You may feel a lack of confidence understanding what the problem really is, what is really happening, what you want, what your superiors want, who is supposed to do what, how you are to get what you want, and how to know if you have succeeded. Andy Grove extends the argument:

> As managers in such a workplace, you need to develop a higher tolerance for disorder. Now, you should still not accept disorder. In fact, you should do your best to drive what's around you to order. The fundamental idea is that you should run your managerial process like a well-oiled factory. But you as a manager need to be mentally and emotionally ready for the turbulence

generated by a megamerger in Asia or for the new shock waves engendered by a new technique pioneered by someone you never even heard of. (1995, p. 29)

Many observers believe that this sea change occurring at the end of the twentieth century is of a magnitude that occurs once every couple of hundred years. Without getting too far off course, let's take a minute to understand some of the bigger, broader picture within which our current discussion of managing change is embedded.

PHYSICS AND GLOBAL BUSINESS STRATEGY

Fritjof Capra, in his seminal work *The Turning Point* (1982), reminds us that at the beginning of the twentieth century physicists began extending their understanding of Newtonian physics to the atomic level. In the process, they discovered something quite shocking. The classical Newtonian laws that had explained so much observable physical activity for over 200 years became obsolete almost overnight. Two new principles challenging Newtonian physics that are relevant to our current investigation of global management are Heisenberg's uncertainty principle and the recent evolution of chaos theory.

Uncertainty Principle

Werner Heisenberg, a German physicist, discovered in 1927 what he called the "uncertainty principle." This states that the position and velocity of an object cannot be measured exactly at the same time, even in theory. For example, in wave theory, every particle has a wave associated with it. The particle is most likely to be found in that part of the wave where its undulations are most intense or uncertain. There is a continuous uncertain reaction between the particle and its wave, and as one is stabilized the other becomes more unstable. An accurate measurement of one, therefore, involves a relatively large uncertainty in the measurement of the other.

In global management, there are many instances that follow a similar pattern. Market forces and currency fluctuations in particular are at no time precisely measurable because they are constantly changing based upon a continuous exchange of currency and economies, 24 hours a day. We have the illusion of "knowing" exchange rates only because convention has established that at a certain time each day, each country's central bank "fixes" the rate of exchange as a result of the day's trading.

In investment banking, sophisticated mathematical formulations drive the equity derivatives business, as mathematicians, physicists, and computer scientists combine with traders in New York, London, and Tokyo to try to calculate in a split second the movement of hundreds of variables that affect the particular buying or selling of financial instruments now and in the future. Hedging, futures, listed options, SWAPs, and sophisticated alterations of complex global portfolios are done through extensive mathematical calculations to determine the best method and time to make a trade.

Chaos Theory

Ralph Abraham, an experimental mathematician at the University of California at Santa Cruz, and others in mathematics have founded a branch of mathematical vibration theory based on chaos. Their basic finding is that the Newtonian formula that allows one to establish laws that are at the same time explanatory and predictive is not applicable to complex systems. Chaos theory deals with complex phenomena whose course cannot be determined by timelessly valid laws; in other words, complexity that is beyond the rules of a predictable universe.

Chaos theory, however, maintains that there *are* patterns that flow from disorder, patterns that can be used in understanding the larger transformation of systems even if their changes cannot be predicted in detail. This search for patterns within uncertainty is akin to the drive for the bigger, broader picture, looking for the megatrends, that constitutes one of the critical attributes necessary for managing uncertainty.

The level of uncertainty is affected by our expectations, and a fundamental message of this book is that to be a competent global manager you have to recalibrate your assumptions about certainty, simplicity, and control. You must adjust your mindset to look at the broader picture, to look for trends and stress fractures on a global basis. If you refocus, with less expectation of finding rules and more expectation of finding the next significant movement in the evolving global environment, you will necessarily become less concerned about uncertainty because you will not *expect* certainty.

Stacey believes that there is too much emphasis in management today on stability, regularity, predictability, and cohesion. Instead, he believes that business should stress the management of "bounded instability," as he calls it. Bounded instability is a state in which behavior has a pattern, but it is irregular. He contrasts this with explosive instability, in which behavior and systems go completely out of control and sometimes self-destruct. These observations underscore the new management paradigm that includes chaos as a natural part of change. Just as the limits of Cartesian and Newtonian thinking have been reached in physics, the idea that everything relevant to successful management is knowable, hence controllable, must also be abandoned.

Many change formulae over the years have stressed change as a process to be controlled through the application of principles of management science. In such instances, people have viewed chaos as something beyond control. In this, as in the other complexities of global management, the answer to controllability is not either/or. You must simultaneously manage from both viewpoints, according to the circumstances, some of which are under control and some of which are out of control.

NEW MINDSETS FOR UNCERTAINTY

George Bernard Shaw once observed that all progress depends on unreasonable men. He argued that reasonable men adapt themselves to the world, whereas unreasonable men persist in trying to adapt the world to themselves.

The real human resource challenge in globalization is the development of right-brain, intuitive skills through which global managers can develop the personal mindset and behavioral capacities to operate in this uncertain global world. The basic thesis of this book has been that the world is becoming more complex and less predictable, requiring organizations that are more complex and less predictable and, logically, requiring managers that are able to deal with complexity and ambiguity. Managers who are successful in this world will have five basic capacities:

1. The ability to feel comfortable with ambiguity.
2. The capacity to see uncertainty as opportunity.
3. The desire to view things differently.
4. The ability to translate opportunity into concrete products, services, strategies, and structures.
5. The ability to see the potential obsolescence of all products, services, strategies, and structures.

Let's look into each of these a little further.

Comfort with Increased Ambiguity in Decision Making

Global management is more complex because one faces the challenge of managing increased ambiguity in decision making. This results from being exposed to many more variables and broader issues, which often have philosophical, moral, and cultural dimensions, as well as business considerations. This makes the decision process more ambiguous.

To attack this problem, global managers scan differently and track additional factors in their decision making. They are sensitive to various interests and needs. And in the end, they must be clearer than ever about their purpose, priorities, and vision in order to make decisions in the best interests of the corporation. The irony of all of this is that **the more ambiguous a situation becomes, the simpler and clearer the criteria for decision making need to be**.

Jimmy Carter is the best example of a recent global leader who made the mistake of dealing with complexity with complex criteria. Carter was undoubtedly one of the brightest presidents of the United States. He is extremely analytical and thorough in his decision making. In fact, he is so thorough that he found himself accused of inconsistency because for each problem he would conduct an exhaustive analysis in which he would become buried in detail, reaching conclusions that at times were contradictory to the last conclusion he reached on a similar issue.

Part of this dilemma is what I call the "decision-ascendancy" principle. According to this principle, the higher one goes in an organization, the more complex are the decisions and the less available is the necessary information to make the decision. Judgment and clarity of vision therefore become much more critical factors than at lower organizational levels.

This is not an odd phenomenon if you think about it. At lower levels of an organization, the information necessary to make a decision is generally available if you have the abilities to access and properly analyze it. When the weight of evidence for a decision after analysis is 70 percent to 30 percent, lower levels of management can make the final decision. But as one progresses up through an organization, the decision-ascendancy principle begins to function. The information available for analysis and action becomes more sparse, the judgment factor increases, and middle managers begin passing decisions up because they do not want to take the risk or they do not have the authority to make decisions in which the choice is not clearly supported by data and analysis.

By the time decisions reach the top of a corporation (or the Oval Office), the evidence is many times 51 percent in favor and 49 percent against a particular decision. It is then that the decision-making process moves from analysis to judgment. And judgment depends on clarity of vision, principle, and purpose, not on abundance of information and detailed analysis.

You should not assume, therefore, that the management of ambiguity requires "just a little more data or analysis" to come to a conclusion. Managers who take this path are waiting for the tough decisions to be made for them by the weight of available information.

Uncertainty as Opportunity

Traditional management philosophy has rewarded managers for closing off uncertainty. Companies have stressed probability analysis, moderate risk taking and risk analysis for loss prevention as key behaviors for which business recognizes and compensates managers.

But the ability to see uncertainty as opportunity is being tested today throughout Eastern and Central Europe as hundreds of Western lawyers and accountants pore over early market, technology, and political risk reports indicating a variety of uncertain horizons in the region. The future development of Eastern and Central Europe is not being fought out on their territory as much as it is in the offices of Western corporations worldwide, where the struggle continues between left brain and right brain for investment and trade opportunities full of uncertainty and risk. As a result, we find that there are two kinds of companies investing in these uncertain areas. The first are small entrepreneurial, wholly owned companies where an individual or family can decide to risk personal funds. The second are large corporations where the CEO is strong enough to offset the natural and responsible caution of the legal and finance departments.

Desire to View Things Differently

With all the talk about paradigm shifts, we often stress ability rather than desire. It is perfectly possible that many people do not shift their paradigms, not because they are unable to, but because they have absolutely no desire or motivation.

Motivating people to shift their world view, as Joel Barker writes in *Discovering the Future* (1989), is a fundamental aspect of leadership. The great leaders of the world, like Winston Churchill, Abraham Lincoln, Martin Luther King, and Mikhail Gorbachev, have been people who could motivate others to change their mindset. They have accomplished this either because of a vision of a better life or from an understanding of the pain associated with continuing their current view. Daryl Conner, president of ODR, Inc., and a specialist in change management, argues that "pain management" is one of the greatest reasons why people are willing to change their thinking and their lives. In fact, he and some other researchers believe that it is impossible for the vast majority of people to change significantly without a sufficient amount of pain being associated with their current state to drive them to seek an alternative.

One of the assumptions behind all management training and development, however, is that we can educate people to adopt new world views through "pull" rather than the "push" of pain. In fact, this is an implicit assumption behind much of HRD, not only in management training but also in coaching, counseling, and consulting. While there is no simple answer to the push/pull approaches to perceptual and behavioral change, it would seem that a balanced perspective is key. We should continue to search for pedagogical paradigms and methods that will attract people to new ways of viewing the world, while at the same time developing pain indicators that might assist in "pushing" change in the direction necessary.

Making Opportunity Actionable

There are thousands of opportunities that present themselves to people every day. Of these, there are hundreds seen by a majority of the population. Of those that are seen, however, relatively few are actually turned into products, services, strategies, and tactics to become new opportunities for service, profit, or change in the world.

To make opportunity actionable, global managers have to first view change as friendly, look beyond the chaos of the moment to the opportunities being opened by instability, and then move swiftly and decisively to act on intuition in a way that turns these opportunities into concrete products or services. This requires a combination of right-brain intuition, left-brain analysis, and right- and left-brain action that is seldom found in the general population, but that must be a quality of global managers.

Global opportunities often do not provide the luxury of detailed analyses to reduce risk and increase the chance of success. Instead, global managers must seize opportunities and move at a faster and harder pace than those managers who enjoy taking their time, examining all the angles and "feeling comfortable" that all their down-side risks are covered. This is not a game for the timid.

Drumming Obsolescence Out of Order

On the other side of the equation, a global manager must not only be able to seize opportunity from chaos but should also be prepared to drum obsolescence out of order. There are many organizations operating in the international arena who will eventually go out of business because of their obsession with past traditions, past ideas, and past success. Effective global managers understand that durability of global products and services is measured in months, not years. The number and speed of global competition, combined with global scanning information systems, means that any new product success is immediately spotted by the competition, and if there is a good market for it, the chances are that someone will be there with an alternative within a very short time. Realistically, effective global managers know that their most vulnerable products and ideas are those that have been most successful. These are prime candidates for obsolescence through erosion of market share to an aggressive competitor.

An effective global manager does not assume that the normal state of the world is a long-term cash cow. Instead, he or she is constantly analyzing what is winning today to determine its vulnerability tomorrow.

Anticipating future needs, seizing new opportunities, living with ambiguity, seeking new paradigms, and drumming obsolescence out of order are all aspects of the global-mindset, right-brain activity necessary for effective global management.

You have to know how to manage meaning to put together a globally inspiring mission statement, an organizationally motivating vision, or a personally engaging work plan. Meaning is the translation of a stimulus not into a response, but first to a concept—which in turn generates a response. The search for meaning, for ourselves, for others, for the world, is a profound lifelong activity that global managers are destined to undertake.

SEEING CHAOS AS A FRIENDLY ALLY FOR CHANGE

If you think "managing chaos" is an oxymoron, you must admit that "managing change" is as well. The difference between the two is that "managing change" gives a *false* sense of control, whereas "managing chaos" more accurately describes the need to stay with a process that is fundamentally beyond our control. According to Peter Vaill, "*comprehension* of what is going on in an organization" and "*control* of what is going on there are the unique things that the manager is supposed to bring to the system" (p. 77).

He believes, however, that the global manager's capacity to do this is history. An old-style manager who today tries compulsively to use linear, cause-and-effect thinking to understand dynamic, integrated holistic systems is, in Vaill's term, a "technoholic." This management style is irrelevant to the managerial skills necessary for successful global leadership today.

We need a new paradigm for understanding global management in an information society. The old illusion that change can be managed in a way that always includes a strong element of control must be smashed if global managers are to learn the art of change in an uncertain world. Andy Grove, the change guru at Intel, writes:

> You need to try to do the impossible, to anticipate the unexpected. And when the unexpected happens, you should double your efforts to make order from the disorder it creates in your life. The motto I'm advocating is, "Let chaos reign, then rein in chaos." (1995, p. 50)

Grove's observation leads to a method for managing change that I call the chaos-control theory of organizational change, which involves the ebb and flow of letting go and taking control. We will examine it in more detail below.

CHAOS-CONTROL THEORY OF ORGANIZATIONAL CHANGE

The chaos-control theory of change is built on four basic principles.

1. **The principle of unmanageable reaction:** People need to get used to new ideas, so all change has periods that are subject to chaotic, unpredictable, and unmanageable reactions.

2. **The principle of trustable process:** During these times, leaders need to trust process and allow the unmanageable aspects of change to play out, which may be far more helpful to the goals of change than anything that could be planned, managed, or controlled.

3. **The principle of constant reinforcement:** At the same time, change will not move forward unless there is consistent and continual pressure applied to break down barriers and reinforce and reward new behavior.

4. **The principle of consistent attention:** As a result, any leader who is serious about change must make time every day to

concentrate on the change process, either engaging in an active intervention or determining when no action is the best means to facilitate change.

Six phases of change transpire from these four principles.

1. Awareness of chaos
2. Interest in change
3. Acceptance of chaos
4. Experimentation with change
5. Adaptation to chaos
6. Installation of change

As you can see, I have formulated one phase that is out of control followed by a phase that is under control. The result is an alternation of letting go and taking charge. Note that the first step involves chaos, or letting go. **Any manager who is unwilling or unable to let things go out of control will more than likely fail to either initiate or sustain change**.

You must learn to manage both chaos and control as the two sides of change to successfully manage in a complex, geographically diverse organization. As you explore each phase of the chaos-control change theory, pay close attention to the organizational interventions available to you to encourage the organization in the direction of change.

Awareness of Chaos

Many organizations do not survive because they recognize too late that change is needed. There are many cases in the international arena, such as ITT's ill-fated attempt to operate in European competition with Ericsson and GE's inability to convert its consumer products group in the face of competition from Matsushita.

To develop an awareness of the need for change you must understand and accept the influence of chaos. Since chaos is always present as a destabilizing force to the current order, it can be viewed as a precursor of change and a friend to anyone interested in change. If its people do not accept this first basic principle of change, an organization will have little hope of proceeding through the next stages of change. Seeing chaos as friendly is not easy, but managerial intervention can facilitate the awareness of chaos.

Interest in Change

Once a potential for change has been identified, the organization needs to respond in a logical, left-brain manner. Many times, the first step is to generate interest by calling the need for change to people's attention. Oddly enough, many managers assume that when other managers and staff are aware that the organization is in trouble or faces an unusual opportunity, they will be interested in doing something about it. Experience has shown that this is not always the case. Frequently, people become aware of a trend that is negatively or positively affecting the organization but believe that outside forces beyond their control are the cause. As a result, they may struggle against these forces or adopt a posture of helplessness rather than orient their behavior in the direction of the change.

To develop real interest in organizational change, employees must feel that the change is meaningful to them. Farquahar, Evans, and Tawadey (1989) talk about the need to "sell the crisis" before it actually hits the bottom line. Marks and Spencer, an extremely successful British retailer, is a company that, although it aborted its move into the international market, found that the process helped its employees see the need for change in other areas to maintain their industry leadership.

One well-known method that can be used to plan and manage change is a **force-field analysis**. In this process, people are encouraged to analyze change by listing all forces inhibiting a desired change on one side of a line and all forces reinforcing the change on the other. These forces are weighted according to their estimated strength of influence, represented by the length of the line drawn to represent each force. For example, a major force pushing you to search for foreign markets might be competitive pressure in your home market. This would be represented by a long line. Another, less pressing reason you might consider foreign markets is that some of the newly emerging markets of Eastern and Central Europe need your products but have not yet developed the stability to make marketing to them as profitable as you would like. This would be represented by a smaller line. There might be another line representing a barrier to change, such as the cost of entry into Eastern European markets.

A basic premise of a force-field analysis is that more progress toward change will be made by overcoming the areas of least resistance than by concentrating on the forces for change. Experience has shown that reinforcement often leads to an equal and opposite force against the change process. Some Newtonian laws are still valid in organizational life.

Acceptance of Chaos

Once an awareness of chaos has been developed, strategic fracture lines have been identified, and force-field analyses have been conducted, you need to accept the fact that there may be some things best left unattended. I first learned this lesson during a short assignment with the U.S. government. I asked the State Department desk officer in charge of Soviet affairs for policy guidance concerning how much we wanted to tell the Soviets about managing change. The answer I received was a classic State Department response, but perhaps more insightful than it is usually given credit for. "We have studied the issues and determined it is best not to have a policy on this matter at the current time." This is *wu wei* in practice. Believe it or not, State Department personnel may be masters of managing change, at least accepting that at certain times no policy is better than some policy as one waits to see how factors beyond control play out.

It is difficult to get people to "let change go" after they have done their force-field analyses and begun to concentrate on how to manage various inhibiting factors. On the other hand, force-field analysis acknowledges that there are certain forces that may be too strong to tackle and that it is better to wait them out. Implicit is an acknowledgment that the process of change requires managing those things that can be changed, not managing those things that cannot be changed, and having the wisdom to know the difference, to paraphrase a well-known prayer.

In this case, the best organizational intervention to stimulate acceptance of chaos is to clarify which factors are subject to managed change and which are not. You must also during this phase in the change process identify things that will *not* be changed. Change creates enough resistance from people who have a reason to be threatened without creating resistance among people who think erroneously that they are next on the hit list. Better to identify areas where no change is anticipated and line these people up as allies for the changes that will occur.

Experimentation with Change

After becoming aware of the need for change, analyzing forces operating for and against change, and accepting what can and cannot be changed, the organization should experiment with a variety of ways to implement the change. Phase four moves the organization from anticipation to action, emphasizing new behaviors that are necessary to work on the forces that can be affected by action. Building commitment to change requires opportunities for people to feel secure about modifying their behavior and to become personally involved in the change process to make it meaningful to them and to give them a sense of satisfaction. As a result, you must plan, develop, and implement this phase of the change process in a logical fashion. You must ensure that the organization begins taking corrective action for any problems identified.

The most popular method to encourage experimentation is training. Whether the subject is globalization, quality, or customer service, training programs have evolved as a mainstay of organizational change. In addition to training, team development can assist your organization in managing change. Teams are mutually supportive but can also be highly entrepreneurial units when well managed. On a global scale, teams can be the key to organizational synergy, creativity, and innovation.

The corporate culture itself must, of course, be supportive of the change process. Rewarding behavior is often critical in allowing organizations and individuals to experiment with new forms of behavior. In other words, your organization must give permission to managers and staff to experiment in new directions, experimentation that may eventually advance the organization in unexpected ways.

Adaptation to Chaos

The best-planned and executed training programs do not result in behavior changes exactly according to the theories and practices advocated in the classroom. Instead, people must adapt what they have learned to their own circumstances to make it relevant and meaningful for them. The adaptation phase acknowledges that there are elements of chaos in every "back-home" situation, especially when you change geographic, functional, or product locations in a global organization. Allowances have to be made for local adaptation of global theories, practices, and mandates.

Ciba-Geigy's use of human resource management and Ericsson's use of strategic framing to create variety and breadth in decision making assist in adaptation to change. Many global organizations have spent much time on technology transfer (ITT, NEC, and Ericsson) and other methods of ensuring that centrally developed ideas are adapted to local needs. Many have realized in the process that technology must be adapted to the different cultures of the world.

In addition to technology transfer training, organizational intervention can involve international task forces and global/local teams working on adaptation procedures to improve global ideas for local application. When done within a "glocal" team, lessons learned at the local level can be fed back to the global level to modify future global initiatives.

Installation of Change

For any change to become installed or "embedded" in the corporate culture, it must be consciously and consistently reinforced over time. This so-called second wave of change is anchored in the organization's systems and procedures. It is most often directed toward middle management and will probably take a longer time to implement. Rewards are important throughout all phases of the change process, but especially in the installation phase. The only way that people will move from one phase to the next is if they have a positive, reinforcing experience that allows them to feel good about their new behavior.

Change does not take place in isolation, for all change is a complex renegotiation of the structure and processes that hold certain kinds of behavior in place. As a result, it is impossible to talk about installing change in an organization without talking about its corporate culture and the degree to which the corporate culture hinders or facilitates the change that is being implemented. At times it may even be necessary to destroy the old culture in order to embed new values, norms, and behavior. Olivetti has developed its own approach to the management of a major change, which has been summarized as "fire, hire, and build a new culture." In most instances, though, change of any magnitude affects an organization's corporate culture somewhat less dramatically, creating a need for a persistent long-term program of change directed at values, attitudes, and behavior. This is a very control-oriented, left-brain phase of the change process, and its operation needs to be highly analytical and rational.

You can intervene to assist in the installation of change not merely by encouraging people to behave differently but also by changing information systems to ensure that everyone understands the need for the new behavior. You can also change reward systems to ensure that people are recognized for their new behavior. Only in this way will change be installed and new behaviors become routine.

The catch, however, is that no behavior in a global organization can become truly "routine" again. Instead, there needs to be consistent scanning for new threats and opportunities to start the process all over again, to create new initiatives that will be processed through the six phases of organizational change.

ORGANIZATIONAL LEARNING

Ray Stata, chairman of Analog Devices, believes that the capacity and rate at which organizations and people learn may become the only sustainable competitive advantage of the future, especially in knowledge-intensive industries. He suggests that the management challenge is to accelerate organizational learning by building a change-oriented corporate culture that welcomes change, learns from it, and incorporates it into future plans on a total-systems basis.

Jack Welch, the change-oriented master of GE, has invented three new methods to enhance organizational learning during his second decade as chairman: work-outs, best practices, and process mapping. *Work-outs* are held in retreat settings. A group of 40 to 100 employees, selected by management from all ranks of an organizational unit, are taken to a hotel or conference site for a three-day session. The boss rolls out the agenda then leaves people for small-group brainstorming of as many ideas as they can think of for improving the quality and productivity of the organization. On the third day, the boss reenters the room and, with senior executives watching, must respond to employee suggestions with one of three answers: agree, disagree, or ask for more information. Many times the senior executives sit in the back of the room so there is no eye contact between the manager and his boss. A work-out saves money and brings the employee directly into the change process in a way that balances control and openness.

Best practices involves interviewing other companies to find out what is the secret of their success. Almost all companies interviewed emphasize processes, not function or structures. In other words, they do not focus on the operations of a single department, but on the processes that facilitate departments working together on a global basis.

Finally, GE, as a complex global organization, developed something called *process mapping* as a means of managing change on a global scale. Process mapping generates a flowchart showing every step, no matter how small, that goes into making or doing something. GE has discovered that when a process is mapped, the ability of managers to manage it is greatly enhanced.

To conclude, it might be useful to reflect on an observation made by two 3M officers in an article in *Executive Excellence.*

Every morning in Africa when a gazelle wakes up, it knows that it must run faster than the fastest lion or it will be killed. Every morning when a lion wakes up, it knows that it must run faster than the slowest gazelle or it will starve to death. So it doesn't matter whether you are a gazelle or a lion. When the sun comes up, you'd better be running. (Hershock and Braun, p. 20)

PRACTICES AND TASKS FOR MANAGING CHANGE

By incorporating these practices and tasks, you can develop a better feel for managing organizational change in the face of uncertainty.

Skill 5: Managing Organizational Change

Key Question	How do you remain flexible and open?
Definition	Ability to manage continuous change and uncertainty on a personal and organizational level, ensuring that an adequate blend of flexibility and control are achieved to enable the organization to be responsive to change in a timely fashion.
Action and Mindset Attribute	Flow with change
Personal Characteristic	Flexible

Key Practices and Tasks

1. Assume that *continuous global change*, rather than stability, is the norm and learn to navigate in "perpetual whitewater."

    1.1 Analyze which aspects of your job are subject to outside events and which should be reviewed for change from the inside.

    1.2 Determine the optimal shelf-life of your policies, practices, and procedures to ensure that they remain relevant to your industry and profession.

2. Create *new opportunities out of change and chaos* rather than try to reestablish the old order.

    2.1 Continuously examine the changing conditions around you for new products, policies, practices, or procedures that can increase your personal, professional, or organizational efficiency and effectiveness.

2.2 Search for and uproot outmoded practices and habits that hinder your ability to respond to change.

3. Manage *change as a cyclical process* of "taking charge" and "letting go."

3.1 Determine where you may need to increase your span of control to force you to manage in a more open way. Be hard on yourself in evaluating whether you are trying to micromanage the world! Force yourself to let go a little bit or you will never be able to manage your expanded responsibilities on a global basis. If you cannot trust the people you have in positions that report to you, change the people. But don't get caught in the trap of micro-management. It reduces everyone to an attention to detail that is stifling and ultimately destructive to your organization.

3.2 Evaluate your attitude toward change. Are you proactive in initiating changes needed in your job or department? Are you open to considering changes suggested by others? Do you encourage independent, innovative thinking from others concerning ways you can improve your work group's performance? Do you adequately communicate the reason for change to others in a forthright manner? Do you provide support for people experiencing difficulty in adjusting to change?

The management of uncertainty has one central message: As a global manager, you can no longer depend on rules or on traditional left-brain knowledge. Your ability to succeed will be based on judgment that is developed by broadening your perspective and by trusting people, organizations, and organizational process to go out of control from time to time. **Any global manager who is afraid to occasionally let go will be left behind, concentrating on control, while the world—and opportunities—flow away.**

SELECTED BIBLIOGRAPHY

Barker, Joel Arthur. *Discovering the Future: The Business of Paradigms.* St. Paul., Minn: ILI Press, 1989.

Bleeke, Joel A., and Brian A. Johnson. "Signposts for a Global Strategy." *The McKinsey Quarterly,* Autumn 1989, pp. 60–71.

Burke, W. Warner. *Organization Development: A Normative View.* Reading, Mass.: Addison-Wesley OD Series, 1987.

Calvert, Gene. *High Wire Management: Risk-Taking Tactics for Leaders, Innovators and Trailblazers*. San Francisco: Jossey-Bass, 1993.

Capra, Fritjof. *The Turning Point: Science, Society and the Rising Culture*. New York: Bantam Books, 1982.

Conner, Daryl R. *Managing at the Speed of Change: How Resilient Managers Succeed and Prosper Where Others Fail*. New York: Villard Books, 1993.

Drucker, Peter F. *Managing in Turbulent Times*. New York: Harper & Row, 1980.

Egan, Gerard. *Change Agent Skills A: Assessing and Designing Excellence*. San Diego: University Associates Press, 1988.

Farquhar, Alison; Paul Evans; and Kiran Tawadey. "Lessons from Practice in Managing Organizational Change." In *Human Resource Management in International Firms: Change, Globalization, Innovation*. Evans, Paul; Yves Doz; and Andre Laurent, eds. New York: St. Martin's Press, 1990.

The Forum Corporation. *Leadership: Training Workbook*. Boston: Ma: The Forum Corporation, 1990.

Geneen, Harold. *Management*. New York: Basic Books, 1982.

Gleick, James. *Chaos: Making a New Science*. New York: Penguin Books, 1989.

Grove, Andrew S. "A High-Tech CEO Updates His Views on Managing and Careers." *Fortune*, September 18, 1995, pp. 229–30.

Handy, Charles. *The Age of Unreason*. Boston: Harvard Business School Press, 1990.

Heifetz, Ronald A. *Leadership Without Easy Answers*. Cambridge, Mass.: Harvard University Press, 1994.

Hersey, Paul, and Kenneth Blanchard. *The Management of Organizational Behavior*. 3d ed. Englewood, Cliffs, N.J.: Prentice-Hall, 1976.

Hershock, Robert J., and David Braun. "Cross-Functional Teams Drive Change." *Executive Excellence*, July 1993, p. 20.

Imai, Masaaki. *Kaizen: The Key to Japan's Competitive Success*. New York: Random House, 1986.

Kanter, Rosabeth Moss. *When Giants Learn to Dance*. New York: Simon and Shuster, 1989.

Marsick, Victoria J., and Lars Cederholm. "Developing Leadership in International Managers—An Urgent Challenge!" *The Columbia Journal of World Business* 22, no. 4 (Winter 1988).

McCaskey, Michael. *The Executive Challenge: Managing Change and Ambiguity*. New York: Harper Collins, 1986.

Mintzberg, Henry. *The Rise and Fall of Strategic Planning*. New York: The Free Press, 1994.

Morgan, Gareth. *Riding the Waves of Change: Developing Managerial Competencies for a Turbulent World*. San Francisco: Jossey-Bass, 1988.

Naisbitt, John, and Patricia Aburdene. *Reinventing the Corporation*. New York: Warner Books, 1985.

Peters, Thomas. *Thriving on Chaos: Handbook for a Management Revolution*. New York: Harper & Row, 1988.

———. *Liberation Management: Necessary Disorganization for the Nanosecond Nineties*. New York: Ballantine Books, 1992.

Schon, Donald. *The Reflective Practitioner: How Professionals Think in Action*. New York: Basic, 1995.

Senge, Peter. *The Fifth Discipline: The Art and Practice of the Learning Organization*. New York: Doubleday, 1990.

Siu, R. G. H. "Management and the Art of Chinese Baseball." In Harold J. Leavitt and Louis Pondy, eds. *Readings in Managerial Psychology*. Chicago: University of Chicago Press, 1980.

Soros, George. *Underwriting Democracy*. New York: The Free Press, 1991.

Stacey, Ralph. *Managing Chaos: Dynamic Business Strategies in an Unpredictable World*. London: Kogan Page, 1992.

Stata, Ray. "Organizational Learning—The Key to Management Innovation." *Sloan Management Review*, Spring 1989, pp. 64–74.

Taylor, Alex III. "Ford's Really Big Leap at the Future: It's Risky, It's Worth It, and It May Not Work." *Fortune*, September 18, 1995, pp. 134–144.

Tichy, Noel. *Managing Strategic Change: Technical, Political and Cultural Dynamics*. New York: John Wiley & Sons, 1983.

Vaill, Peter B. *Managing as a Performing Art: New Ideas for a World of Chaotic Change*. San Francisco: Jossey-Bass, 1989.

Wheatley, Margaret J. *Leadership and the New Science: Learning about Organization from an Orderly Universe*. San Francisco: Berrett-Koehler, 1994.

PART FOUR

GLOBAL TEAMS AND PEOPLE

7

CHAPTER

Managing Multicultural Teams

Life can be tough on the frontier of globalization. Take the joint venture among three competing high-tech companies from three continents—Siemens AG of Germany, Toshiba Corporation of Japan, and IBM. They are trying to develop a new chip together in East Fishkill, New York. The Triad, as they call themselves, are working in an IBM facility in the Hudson River

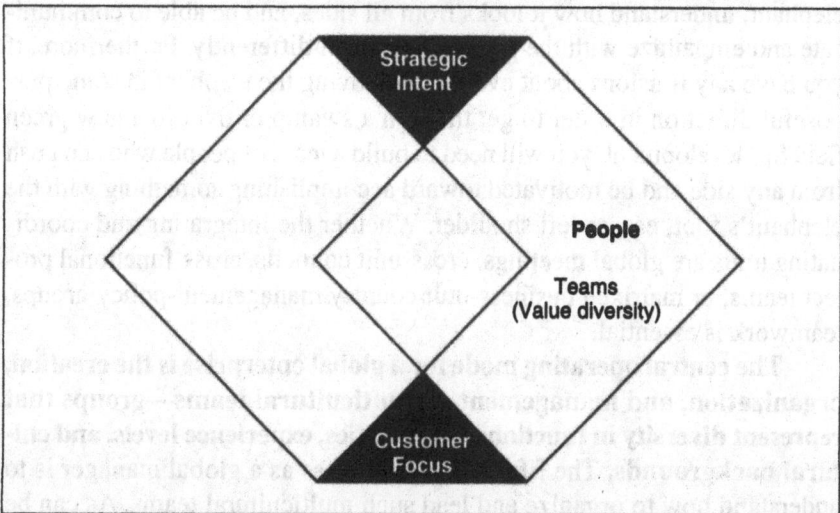

```
                    Strategic
                     Intent

                              People

                              Teams
                         (Value diversity)


                    Customer
                     Focus
```

valley with over 100 scientists from the three organizations. Not surprisingly, cultural factors are a major challenge in the operation. *The Wall Street Journal* reports:

> Siemens scientists were shocked to find Toshiba colleagues closing their eyes and seeming to sleep during meetings (a common practice for overworked Japanese managers when talk does not concern them). The Japanese, who normally work in big groups, found it painful to sit in small, individual offices and speak English; some now withdraw when they can into all-Japanese groups. The Americans complain that the Germans plan too much and that the Japanese—who like to review ideas constantly—won't make decisions. Suspicions circulate that some researchers are withholding information from the group. (May 3, 1994)

Global homogeneity was never a desirable vision culturally, creatively, or philosophically. But now it has become clear that living with and managing diversity will be a central theme of the coming century. The explosion of ethnic identities in Eastern Europe and the former Soviet Union, the reassertion of the value of diversity in the United States, and the restatement of the values of fundamentalist religious concerns in the Middle East and middle America all establish the management of diversity as a prime skill of the twenty-first century.

Too many people with one perspective spend a great deal of time denying the validity of another. So the first lesson in global and cross-cultural management is that your own perspective is just one side of the elephant. To be a truly global manager, you have to be willing to crawl around the elephant, understand how it looks from all sides, and be able to communicate and empathize with the people who see it differently. Furthermore, if you have any illusions about eventually moving the elephant in some purposeful direction in order to get through a swamp or over to a new green field for development, you will need to build a team of people who can push from any side and be motivated toward accomplishing something with the elephant's foot, ear, or left shoulder. Whether the integrating and coordinating units are global meetings, cross-unit councils, cross-functional project teams, or matrixed business-unit/country management-policy groups, teamwork is essential.

The central operating mode for a global enterprise is the creation, organization, and management of multicultural teams—groups that represent diversity in functional capabilities, experience levels, and cultural backgrounds. The fifth skill for success as a global manager is to understand how to organize and lead such multicultural teams. As can be

seen from the Siemens/ Toshiba/IBM venture, you must be able to effectively lead and direct a diverse group of people, many of whom have values, beliefs, behaviors, business standards, and traditions that are culturally
different from your own. In this sense, the requirements of global leadership extend well beyond traditional management practices, to reflect sensitivity to cultural diversity and understanding of different—and sometimes
conflicting—social forces. You will often be required to operate in an unfamiliar and uncomfortable organizational setting. This will demand enormous personal flexibility, as well as sensitivity.

   Diversity in the American workplace and multiculturalism in international enterprises both engender the need to compare, contrast, and
understand cultural differences in a new way, a way that does not melt and
homogenize but recognizes and employs difference for cultural synergy and
creativity. While the ideal may never be reached, you can take steps to
move toward it.

   Several cultural paradigms that affect our ability to rethink the new
global game are worth noting. The "we are all alike" syndrome is one that
many of us have experienced when we have visited a foreign land and come
back with the initial perception that all people are very much alike. We are
just one big human race. A second stage of understanding comes, however,
when we begin to uncover specific, subtle differences. We then realize that
although people have some significant similarities in their needs and feelings, they can also have strong differences in the way they *meet* these needs
and *express* these feelings. Finally, after continued contact, a third stage
is reached with the realization that people are both different and similar. An
organization, leadership, or management model must address both common
and uncommon threads. *Ultimately, we must acknowledge and address the
diverse behaviors and beliefs that other people hold.*

   The prevailing attitude of senior executives in American companies
seems to be, "If we can get our corporate culture and values right, then no matter where we operate around the globe, issues of strategy and local behavior
will be predictable and consistent." Some are saying that the template for values, beliefs, and behaviors of the enterprise must come from the values,
beliefs, behaviors, and attitudes of the parent corporation. It is becoming clear
that this is the wrong starting point. **Diversity—both domestic and international—will be the engine that drives the creativity of the corporation
of the twenty-first century.** Successful global managers will be those who
are able to manage this diversity for the innovative and competitive edge
of their corporations.

The difficult task for senior management today is to turn around the traditional thinking that suggests that values, beliefs, and behaviors need to be highly standardized from a central, corporate perspective. This shift in thinking will be particularly difficult for those American enterprises that have done little in the last 30 or 40 years to educate and train their managers to organize and manage the firm's resources from a multicultural or an international perspective.

IMPORTANCE OF TEAMS IN A GLOBAL ORGANIZATION

Effective, efficient multicultural teams are central to future global competitiveness and workforce motivation and management. Self-directed teams are critical for quality improvement, cross-functional teams for customer service and product development, and multicultural teams for the overall success of global enterprises. Behind much of this emphasis on teamwork is the realization that a better-educated workforce wants to take more responsibility for its work and accomplishments. With decentralization and de-layering, it is also clear that authority and responsibility will devolve onto people throughout the world who are both closest to the customer and able to operate in a multicultural environment.

The cosmopolitan management team is becoming a familiar sight in global organizations. Whirlpool International's management committee is made up of six people from six nations. IBM prides itself on having five nationalities represented among its highest ranking officers and three among its outside directors. Four nationalities are represented on Unilever's board and three on the board of Shell Oil.

In Figure 7–1, you can see nine types of teams important for effective global management (Gross, Turner, and Cederholm 1987). *Multicentered cosmopolitan headquarters teams* are developed from top management to oversee strategic directions for various parts of the business on a functional, product, or geographic basis. *Headquarters-subsidiary teams* ensure effective representation, coordination, and integration of "glocal" interests. *Strategic alliance teams* are part of new cooperative/competitive strategies to share development costs, technological advances, and proprietary approaches for global competitiveness. *Technology transfer teams* transfer organizational innovations from one geographic location to another. *Cross-functional teams* coordinate company programs such as quality improvement or customer service across functions. *Global functional teams*

FIGURE 7-1

Teamwork in Global Organizations

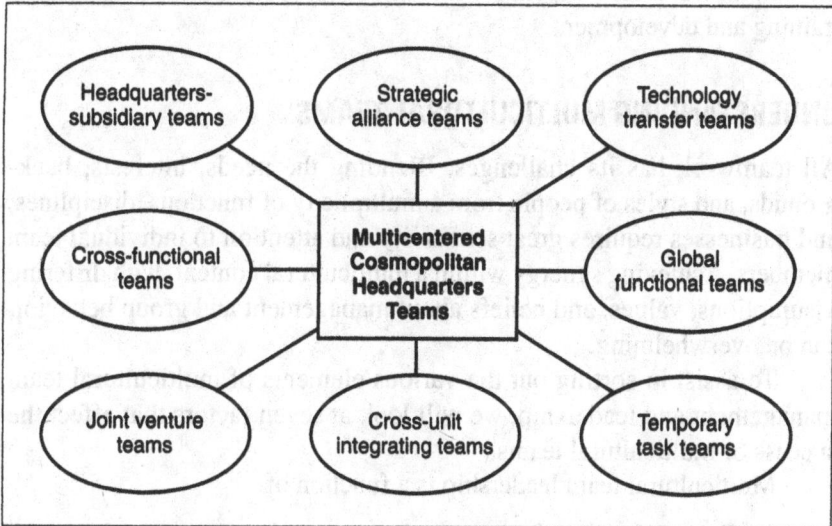

Source: Gross, Turner, and Cederholm, 1987.

coordinate strategies, policies, and procedures on a global basis for commercial, finance, administration, operations, or human resources. *Joint venture teams* manage the start-up and ongoing operation of new enterprises with a foreign partner. *Cross-unit integrating teams* coordinate strategies and plans between operating divisions or different businesses within the same global company. *Temporary project teams* are formed for temporary tasks, usually involving the study, research, and communication of special issues throughout the corporation.

These nine specialized teams are in addition to the normal workplace implementation teams that in most global corporations are multicultural. Many of these teams, as we have discovered already, are critical to the functioning of a global corporate culture that can integrate and coordinate the conflicting interests of complex global operations. 3M has had experience in multicultural team building through its European Management Action Teams (EMATS) program. While it was slow getting off the ground in 1988, EMATS has put a transnational training program, "Leadership for Growth," into place, bringing together 350 European 3Mers for two different rounds of training in 1989 and 1990.

It is imperative that you as a global manager feel comfortable leading a multicultural team if your organization is to be successful in the global marketplace. It is also imperative that these multicultural teams have some training and development.

UNDERSTANDING MULTICULTURAL TEAMS

All teamwork has its challenges. Blending the needs, interests, backgrounds, and styles of people from a multiplicity of functions, disciplines, and businesses requires great sensitivity and attention to individual team members. Achieving synergy within a multicultural context, with differing assumptions, values, and beliefs about management and group behavior, can be overwhelming.

To assist in sorting out the various elements of multicultural team management and leadership, we will look at seven factors that affect the success of multicultural teams.

Multicultural team leadership is a function of

1. *Personal styles* of team members.
2. *Functional cultures* of team members (e.g., finance, engineering, marketing).
3. *Corporate cultures* of the company, division, or unit represented by each team member.
4. *National culture* of each team member.
5. *Stages of team development.*
6. *Effectiveness of team functioning.*
7. *Stage of professional development* of each team member.

Obviously, no one person can keep track of all these variables at the same time, but they provide a good checklist of issues to be considered when teams are experiencing difficulty working together. As a global manager, you should at least be familiar with the various factors so that you can diagnose the cause of problems you may face in working with multicultural teams.

One of the best methods for understanding how teams function is an off-site team-building meeting. The team leader or outside facilitator helps the team assess the degree to which these factors may affect the team's operations by applying models, instruments, and exercises to each of the variables in the formula. Each variable has implications for managers, both domestic and global.

Personal Styles

There are a multitude of ways to assess personal styles but one that has been highly effective is the Myers-Briggs Type Inventory (MBTI). This brief test, based on the life-long insights of Carl Jung, can be self-administered and is an excellent way to open a team-building meeting. The purpose of the MBTI is to assess the way in which people access and process information—critical aspects of team functioning. Jung defined archetypal personal styles based on the interaction of four sets of preferred actions. These are:

Extrovert/Introvert

Sensing/Intuitive

Thinking/Feeling

Perceiving/Judging

While it would not be useful to try to make every multicultural team a group therapy session, team members and leaders should have some idea of how to distinguish cultural from personality factors in team functioning. The MBTI provides one method that is reasonably easy and nonthreatening.

People *access* information through sensing (S) or intuiting (N) information from their environment. Sensors tend to take in more detailed information by using their eyes, ears, nose, and touch to make contact with the environment. Intuitives (N) are big-picture people, looking for patterns, systems, the *gestalt* in the world around them. As a result, both S and N type personalities can read the same information or have the same experience but perceive different things. This can greatly affect a team's functioning. Ss may be looking for empirical data upon which to base decisions, while Ns may be looking at strategic directions.

Once people have accessed information, they *process* it in unique ways. Thinking people (Ts) tend to analyze the information they have accessed to determine what should be done in a particular situation. Feelers (Fs), on the other hand, will tend to classify information against a set of beliefs and categorize it as good or bad, right or wrong. These beliefs may be based on experience, upbringing, or religious and philosophical systems. You can see, however, that the criteria used in decision-making will thus be distinct for Ts and Fs. These characteristics have profound implications for interpersonal relations and team functioning. Within the dualities of sensing/intuitive and thinking/feeling, there are four basic archetypes: NT, NF, ST, SF. Each of these types perceives the world differently, not because of cultural differences but because of differences in personal style that are related to personality.

The application of the Jungian archetypes to team functioning holds that all four basic personal styles should be present in each team for a balanced effort. Teams with only Intuitives will excel in determining strategic direction but may not have any idea how to get there. Likewise, Sensors may have all the data but may not know or care where it leads. Thinkers will have everything analyzed but may miss the moral aspects of decision making. Feelers may be clear about what is right and wrong but may not understand how to communicate the results of a decision in a way that Ts will understand and follow.

The extrovert/introvert duality reflects whether people look to ideas (I) or other people (E) to verify their impressions of the world. Introverts march to their own drummer and enjoy time by themselves to reflect while extroverts develop synergy through people and prefer to work in teams. Extroverts are energized by people; introverts are sometimes exhausted by people.

The perceiving/judging category can have a great effect on team functioning as Ps prefer to think decisions through thoroughly, while Js are action oriented. Js without Ps rush to conclusions, sometimes in the wrong direction, and Ps without Js procrastinate in making decisions. Perceivers are open to all possibilities. They hesitate to come to closure on decisions because they want to take in more data to ensure that all angles have been covered. Judgers, on the other hand, want to make decisions and move on to the next topic on the agenda.

These few observations on the Myers-Briggs personal styles inventory do not do it justice. Our purpose here is not to be comprehensive, but merely to provide one overview of how personal differences affect multicultural team operations. For more information on Myers-Briggs profiles, see *Please Understand Me* by Keirsey and Bates (1984).

Functional Cultures

There has been some correlation between the MBTI and certain functional cultures because the requirements of various functional cultures tend to attract people with certain personal styles. CEOs, for example, tend to be ISTJ, ESTJ, INTJ, or ENTJ due to the need to analyze problems, make decisions, and be action oriented. Many highly creative entrepreneurs, on the other hand, are INFPs, who can allow things to remain open-ended and do not rely on others for advice and counsel. R&D specialists are often ISTPs, involved in detail and allowing for long, open-ended inquiry. Sales people are often ESTJs or ESFJs who are concerned about what others think and are looking to close sales to obtain revenues. Marketing people, on the other hand, are usually NPs who enjoy looking at the larger strategies of market targeting and the creative process of probing for the right message.

In addition to personal style, functional cultures also have their own norms of behavior, values, frameworks for analysis, and tests of significance. Marketing, finance, personnel, manufacturing, engineering, and design will emphasize varying aspects of policy decisions brought to a cross-functional team. This is one reason that cross-functional teams are now becoming such a rich source of information and creative decision making—and conflict.

The importance of cross-functional teams has been a cornerstone of TQM and customer-focused quality. As they attempt to ensure that customers are served in a seamless fashion that responds to their needs, many organizations have run into strong differences in functional cultures—their perspectives, values, and priorities. Global cross-functional management can build on the early experiences of TQM by examining how the movement has coordinated these myriad perspectives. You can gain a great deal of synergy from TQM and globalization if you consider them as complementary forces in your organization.

Corporate Culture

While national cultural differences have been documented for many years, the concept of corporate culture, first brought to the public's attention in a *Business Week* cover story in 1980, is quite recent. The *Business Week* story was followed quickly by four books that popularized the concept: Ouchi's *Theory Z* (1981), Pascale and Athos's *The Art of Japanese Management* (1981), Deal and Kennedy's *Corporate Cultures* (1982), and Peters and Waterman's *In Search of Excellence* (1982).

It is now generally accepted that each corporation has its own values and ways of operating. This is true of corporations within a national culture and, not surprisingly, of corporations in different countries. In the last two chapters, you have been reading about the characteristics of global corporate cultures. This is a new breed of corporate culture, our understanding of which is still evolving. For our purposes, however, the corporate cultural dimensions noted in Figure 7–2 provide a workable overview that you can apply to any organization, domestic or global. These three dimensions—organizational

FIGURE 7–2

Corporate Culture Survey Dimensions

Organizational Image	
Customer focus	The extent to which the company is concerned with providing quality service and searches out feedback to maintain quality. Employees feel a personal sense of responsibility for customers.
Environmental awareness	A concern for events outside the organization in terms of the competition and technology that affect the workplace. The company can adequately determine the effect of new services.
Excellence of performance	The extent to which a high standard is set internally and care is shown about the quality of work. Employees care about doing their best.
Organizational pride	The positive feelings of employees for their organization. People feel they are members of a superior company; their association brings them prestige.
Organizational mission	The clear communication of the organization's purpose and philosophy, which are are clear-cut and reasonable, worthwhile to society, and related to the work.
Shared values	
Innovation, change, and creativity	The extent to which value is attached to developing new ideas in spite of resistance or lack of resources. The company encourages risk taking; people are not punished for new ideas that don't work out. Rather, they are encouraged to reexamine such failures to learn from their mistakes.
Value of people	Being supportive and committed to employee development. A company strong in this area views its people as a major asset to be developed, cared for, listened to, and supported.
Egalitarianism	The degree to which all employees are treated the same, regardless of level or function. Employees feel highly valued and interact with one another on a first-name basis.
Bias for action	The commitment of an organization to the timely accomplishment of important tasks. Problems are attacked with energy and resolved; procedures are streamlined in the interest of ease; employees know how to find resources to get their jobs done.
Competitiveness	Reflected in the degree to which people are asked to work independently toward the achievement of common goals. In strongly competitive organizations, people do not share or exchange information, engage in win-loss competitions, and are not responsive.

Corporate Culture Survey Dimensions (continued)

Shared values (continued)	
Trust	The amount of confidence shared by management and employees that they will work in a fair and predictable manner. People have a favorable view of each other's actions and judgment.
Policies and procedures	The degree to which the formal organizational systems reinforce the activities and behaviors necessary. In a strong company, employees understand why policies exist and feel they facilitate getting their work done.
Rewards and incentives	The degree to which a company believes individuals should be recognized for performing in the company's interest. A strong company believes in providing monetary incentives as well as acknowledgement of those who do a good job.
Management behaviors	
Teamwork	Products and services result from team effort, and managers support extensive cooperation and interaction among employees.
Leadership	The ability of managers to articulate and motivate employees. Leaders help others succeed, follow up on delegated responsibility, and communicate effectively.
Communication patterns	Open and frequent communication is considered vital; information is transmitted; people have the facts necessary to do their jobs. The grapevine is not depended upon to get the work done.
Conflict management	The degree to which the company is committed to solving personal as well as professional problems in an open, honest, and caring fashion. In a strong company, people listen, discuss differences, and work out constructive solutions.
Camaraderie	The value placed on employee gatherings for the purpose of developing their sense of identity with one another. These include nonwork activities as well as recognition ceremonies and retirement parties.
Balanced decision making	The way in which organizations approach the process, acting in a deliberate, logical, and rational fashion as well as in a spontaneous and subjective manner, depending on needs.
Accountability	The organization's process of holding people responsible for accomplishing assigned tasks. Employees are clear about their responsibilities, have agreed upon performance objectives, and have received periodic and clear feedback on the accomplishment of these objectives.

Source: Moran, Stahl & Boyer, Inc., and Rhinesmith and Associates, Inc.

image, shared values, and management behaviors—conform to the way in which many national cultures view themselves, as you shall see in a moment. They become the basis for management of multicultural teams.

National Culture

The best recent attempt to examine the management implications of national cultural differences on management is Gert Hofstede's seminal empirical research project, *Culture's Consequences* (1980), which has been updated in *Cultures and Organizations* (1991). Hofstede presents an overview of four major cultural variables across 40 countries and examines their implications for managerial differences.

Other research is beginning to reveal considerable disparity in how nationalities approach basic management activities. For example, as you can see in Figure 7–3, Andre Laurent of INSEAD has discovered that there is wide variance in expectations of managers across 12 cultures. Nordic and Anglo-Saxon cultures prefer an open leadership style, in which managers can admit that they do not know all the answers but will be happy to find out an answer and get back to subordinates. Japanese, Indonesian, and French managers, on the other hand, expect their leaders to have at hand precise answers to questions their subordinates may ask.

FIGURE 7–3

National Differences in Expectations of Managers

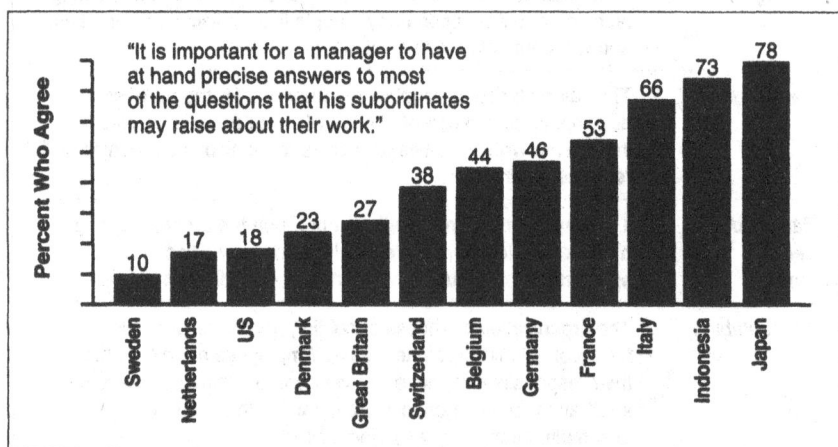

Source: M.E. Sharpe, Inc. Based on Andre Laurent, "The Cultural Diversity of Western Conceptions of Management," *International Studies of Management and Organization* Vol. XIII, no. 1–2, (Spring–Summer 1983): pp. 75–96.

Ten years before Hofstede's empirical study, I worked with Kluckhohn and Strodtbeck's cultural assumptions and values to develop a theoretical framework for integrating comparative management perspectives with differences in cultural values, beliefs, and patterns of thinking. I called it a model for Cultural-Managerial Analysis (C-M-A). It grew out of my doctoral dissertation, which was based on research I conducted in a rain forest hospital in Ghana. While it remains to be fully developed, the basic thesis is outlined in Figure 7–4. This framework provides an overview of the relationship between the major cultural factors—perception of self, perception of others, perception of the world, and patterns of thinking—and the three management activities that most affect multicultural team performance—planning, organizing, and leading.

The assumption is that most cultural differences are reflected in contradictory perceptions and incompatible patterns of thinking. One example of differences in the way in which cultures perceive the individual is illustrated in Figure 7–5, which shows the different levels of information needed for work relations. The concentric circles represent different levels of information needed by workers in high-context cultures and low-context cultures (Hall 1976). The higher the context, as in Japan, the more circles of information people need in order to work together. It is therefore necessary that you spend time with managers from the Far East, the Middle East, and even certain parts of Europe, such as France and the United Kingdom, providing information about yourself and your background before people will work with you. The lower the context, as in the United States, the less information people need. How many American managers have you heard say

FIGURE 7–4

A Framework for Cultural-Managerial Analysis

	Cultural Factor			
	Perception of Self	Perception of Others	Perception of the World	Patterns of Thinking
Planning Activity				
Planning	–	–	–	–
Organizing	–	–	–	–
Leading	–	–	–	–

Source: Rhinesmith and Associates, Inc., 1970.

FIGURE 7–5

FIGURE 7–5

Different Levels of Information Needed for Work Relations

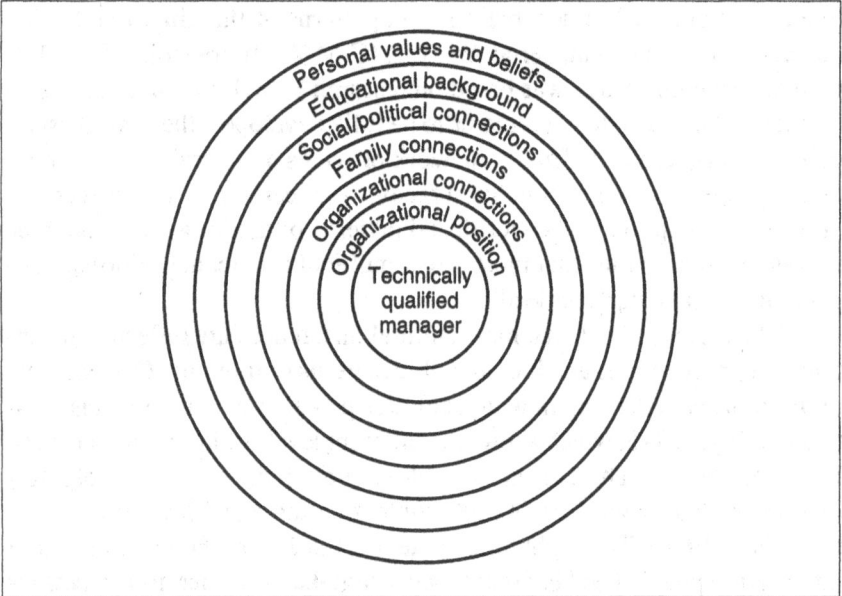

Source: Training Management Corporation and Rhinesmith and Associates, Inc., March 1992.

that all they need is someone who is technically qualified (center circle)? That they don't have to love people to work with them?

When you examine systematically, you can posit a pattern to the influences that cultural differences have on management. This is represented in Figure 7–6.

Planning activities, for example, are very much affected by people's perception of the world and by their thought patterns. Organizational structures, on the other hand, are affected by how people see themselves and their relationship to others. Leadership, as one might expect, is the most complex aspect and is affected by virtually all cultural variables. Figure 7–7 lists some of the management areas that can be affected by cultural differences in perception and thought patterns.

Finally, in Figures 7–8, 7–9, and 7–10, cultural variables are crossed with planning, organizing, and leading activities to suggest which cultural factors might affect each management activity.

As we have noted, most planning activities tend to be affected by beliefs about the world and patterns of thinking. Time horizons of plans, for

FIGURE 7-6

An Application of the Framework for Cultural-Managerial Analysis

	Cultural Factor			
	Perception of Self	Perception of Others	Perception of the World	Patterns of Thinking
Planning Activity				
Planning	–	–	xx	xx
Organizing	xx	–	–	–
Leading	xx	–	–	–

Source: Rhinesmith and Associates, Inc., 1970.

example, are greatly affected by the time perspectives held by people in different cultures. Americans tend to be oriented toward milestones and deadlines because they can substantially control their environment and affect their own success. In many African, Latin American, and Eastern European countries, however, people are less able to affect the world around them, due in part to lack of infrastructure or experience in managing environmental factors. The lack of adequate telecommunications, for example, severely reduces the productivity and extends the time it takes managers to operate in most of Eastern and Central Europe. The assumptions these managers have about the time it will take to accomplish something will therefore vary considerably from the assumptions of an action-oriented American.

Likewise, thought patterns can vary dramatically. Risk taking is one area in which there are very different ideas, again based on experience and assumptions about control. In general, Americans are moderate risk takers. In Russia, however, many people do not have any experience to judge the degree of risk involved in a deal. Without a context within which to understand the degree of risk or to gauge an American's response, they often propose very high-risk ventures.

Organization is also affected by culture. The cultural factors most affecting organizational preferences have to do with the way in which people perceive themselves and their relations with others. The best example in this area is the relationship between individualism and group identification. Americans and many other Anglo-Nordic cultures tend to be quite individualistic and egalitarian, putting great emphasis on individual freedom and a preference for informality.

FIGURE 7-7

Managerial Activities Affected by Cultural Differences

I. Planning	II. Organizing	III. Leading
• Nature of organizational objectives	• Centralization of authority	• Leadership role
• Time horizon of plans	• Work specifications	• Decision-making procedures
• Quantification of objectives	• Span of control	• Communication style
• Flexibility of plans	• Staff/line relationships	• Motivating techniques
• Planning methods	• Nature of job descriptions	• Delegation of authority
• Type of information collected	• Formal role relationships	• Coordination activities
• Amount of information needed for decision	• Committee use	• Subordinate development philosophy
• Application of scientific method	• Informal organization	• Problem-solving methods
• Risk taking/change attitude	• Flexibility to structural change	• Negotiating styles
		• Conflict management methods

More group-oriented societies, like the Japanese, and more formal cultures, such as the French, prefer more structured organizational relations, less informality, and in the case of Japan, much less emphasis on the individual. The group in Japan and rules and regulations of formal hierarchy in France define a person's place within a larger context. The individual is part of a larger system and is treated according to position rather than his or her personal needs and desires.

When people come together in global organizations and multicultural teams, chances of the occurence of some confusion and misunderstanding based on cultural differences can be quite high. As a manager of a multicultural team, you will have to adjust how you plan and organize your work, knowing that people will have different expectations of your leadership style and effectiveness. Some of the leadership activities subject to cultural interpretation are outlined in Figure 7–10. While this framework has not been tested empirically and needs further development, it points the way toward a more systematic understanding of the relationship between culture and management. With further development, this can become one of the many new tools global managers can use in their management of multicultural teams, as well as in their interaction with staff, joint ventures, customers, and suppliers worldwide.

FIGURE 7-8

Planning Cultural-Managerial Analysis

Planning Activity	Values — Perception of Self and Individual	Values — Perception of Relations with Others	Beliefs — Perceptions of the World	Beliefs — Patterns of Thinking	Language	Nonverbal Behavior
Nature of Organizational Objectives			• Availability of valued "good" • Role of providence • Happiness • Hard work • Man/nature relations • Role of religion	• Application of scientific methods • Systems thinking • Cause-and-effect assumptions		
Time Horizons of Plans			• Time orientation			
Quantification of Objectives			• Time measurement	• Level of abstraction		
Flexibility of Plans				• Cybernetic thinking		
Planning Methods			• Providence	• Problem-solving rationale • Cause/effect assumptions • Reasoning patterns		
Type of Information				• Problem-solving rationale • Level of abstraction • Reasoning patterns		
Amount of Information Needed for Decision				• Risk taking • Cybernetic thinking		
Application of Scientific Method				• Scientific methods • Cause/effect assumptions		
Risk taking/Change Attitude			• Change attitude	• Risk taking		

Source: Rhinesmith and Associates, Inc.

FIGURE 7-9

Organizing Cultural-Managerial Analysis

Cultural Factors / Planning Activity	Values		Beliefs		Patterns of Thinking	Language	Nonverbal Behavior
	Perception of Self and Individual	Perception of Relations with Others	Perceptions of the World				
Centralization of Authority	• Individualism	• Authority structure • Status					
Work Specialization	• Activity • Motivation						
Span of Control	• Self-esteem	• Authority base					
Staff/Line Relationships		• Authority base					
Nature of Job Descriptions	• Activity • Motivation	• Role flexibility					
Role of Formal Relationships	• Age/sex • Individualism	• Social relations • Relationship between sexes • Communication style • Activity					
Committee Use		• Authority structure • Opinion expression					
Informal Organization		• Communication patterns • Intermediaries					
Flexibility to Structural Change	• Cultural self-awareness	• Role flexibility					

Source: Rhinesmith and Associates, Inc.

Leading Cultural-Managerial Analysis

Cultural Factors / Planning Activity	Values		Beliefs		Language	Nonverbal Behavior
	Perception of Self and Individual	Perception of Relations with Others	Perceptions of the World	Patterns of Thinking		
Leadership style	• Cultural self-awareness • Activity • Motivation • Self-esteem	• Communication style • Role flexibility • Social relations				
Decision-Making Procedures	• Individualism • Age	• Opinion expression • Authority structure				←
Communication Styles	• Cultural self-awareness • Age	• Relationship between sexes • Social relations • Authority structure			• Verb structure (second person singular)	• Hand gestures • Facial expression • Posture and stance • Interdistance • Touching
Motivating Techniques	• Motivation	• Work/play		• Cybernetic thinking		• Eye contact • Smell • Voice tone • Time symbolism • Timing/pauses • Silence
Delegation of Authority	• Age/sex • Individualism	• Authority structure • Group member				→
Coordination Activities	• Activity	• Communication patterns		• Cybernetic thinking		→

(continued)

FIGURE 7-10 (concluded)

Leading Cultural-Managerial Analysis

Leading Activity \\ Cultural Factors	Values — Perception of Self and Individual	Values — Perception of Relations with Others	Beliefs — Perceptions of the World	Beliefs — Patterns of Thinking	Language	Nonverbal Behavior
Subordinate Development Philosophy	• Age/sex • Self-esteem	• Humanitarianism • Group membership	• Nature of man • Change attitude	• Cybernetic thinking		→
Problem-Solving Methods				• Problem-solving rationale • Cause/effect assumptions • Level of abstraction • Application of scientific methods • Reasoning patterns • Systems thinking • Cybernetic thinking		
Negotiating Style		• Status • Work/play • Intermediaries • Communication patterns	• Problem-solving rationale • Cause/effect assumptions • Level of abstraction • Application of scientific methods • Reasoning patterns • Systems thinking • Cybernetic thinking • Risk taking			
Conflict Management Methods		• Status • Work/play • Intermediaries • Communication patterns • Social relations • Communication style				

Source: Rhinesmith and Associates, Inc.

174

A word should be said here about stereotyping because it is a very mis-understood concept. Many people resist putting labels on themselves or others, whether it is an interpretation of personal styles as in MBTI or a description of national cultural behavior. These people either personally resist being "put in boxes" or feel that it is unfair and inappropriate to put others in boxes.

There are obvious pitfalls to generalizations. Any extreme use of a paradigm to characterize the behavior of others *all the time* will obviously lead to false assumptions. The idea of generalizations, on the other hand, is to describe the *most likely* response of people over time, based on a sampling of individuals and groups.

Anthropologists describe this as "value orientation," or the "preferred way" of thinking or acting by the majority of a particular population. Thus, we talk about the Japanese as group oriented and Americans as individually oriented. **This does not mean that there are no individually oriented Japanese or group-oriented Americans**, but simply that the majority of Americans and Japanese tend to fit into their respective identifiable category.

Figure 7–11 provides a graphic representation of the generalizations made in cultural analysis. This graph, which represents feelings in the United States concerning the relationship of man (in the generative) and

FIGURE 7–11

Stereotyping and Cultural Analysis

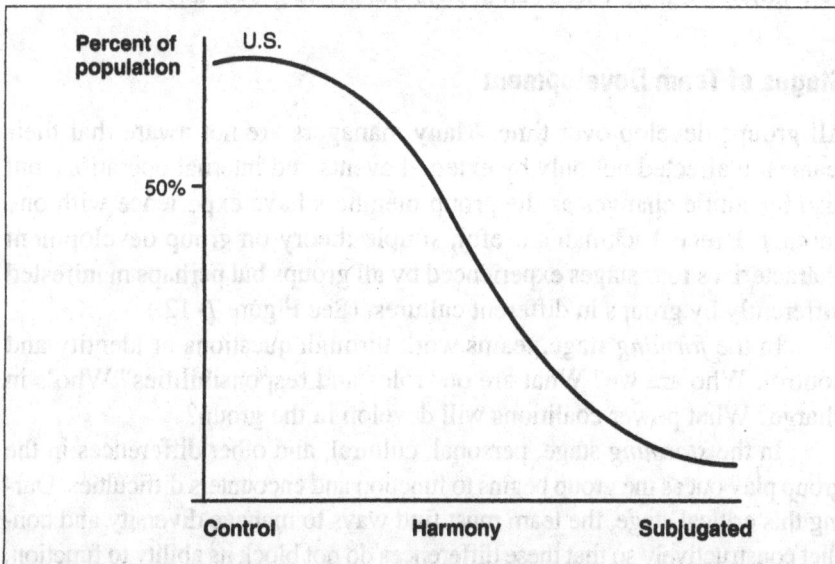

nature, reveals that while the majority of Americans may feel a large measure of control over their environment, there are obviously many who do not and others who believe that it is important to establish harmony with one's environment.

Obviously, many of the underclass of American cities feel very little control over their environment, as do many rural poor. These people, unsure whether they will be able to get through another day or another week, either due to the harshness of inner-city life or because of the unpredictability of floods and droughts, do not represent the dominant American profile of people who are involved in life planning and career development. Similarly, there is a growing number of people in the United States who are willing to give up some degree of dominance over their environment, feeling that, while America has the technology to cut through mountains, exploit timberland, and create products that destroy the ozone layer, "man" must at some point acknowledge the need to live in harmony with nature. The environmental movement in the United States is still not the dominant American profile, but it is gaining ground as a significant value orientation of the American people.

All in all, generalizations are necessary in dealing across cultures. People need to be able to contrast their own behavior with others so that they can explain and predict the likely reaction they will encounter if they behave in a particular way. To reject generalizations because of their misuse would be foolish. It is incumbent on all of us, however, *to acknowledge that individual differences can always transcend group norms.*

Stages of Team Development

All groups develop over time. Many managers are not aware that their teams are affected not only by external events and internal operations but also by subtle changes as the group members have experience with one another. Bruce Tuckman's useful, simple theory on group development characterizes four stages experienced by all groups but perhaps manifested differently by groups in different cultures. (See Figure 7–12.)

In the *forming* stage, teams work through questions of identity and control. Who are we? What are our roles and responsibilities? Who's in charge? What power coalitions will develop in the group?

In the *storming* stage, personal, cultural, and other differences in the group play out as the group begins to function and encounters difficulties. During this critical stage, the team must find ways to manage diversity and conflict constructively so that these differences do not block its ability to function.

FIGURE 7–12

Stages of Team Development

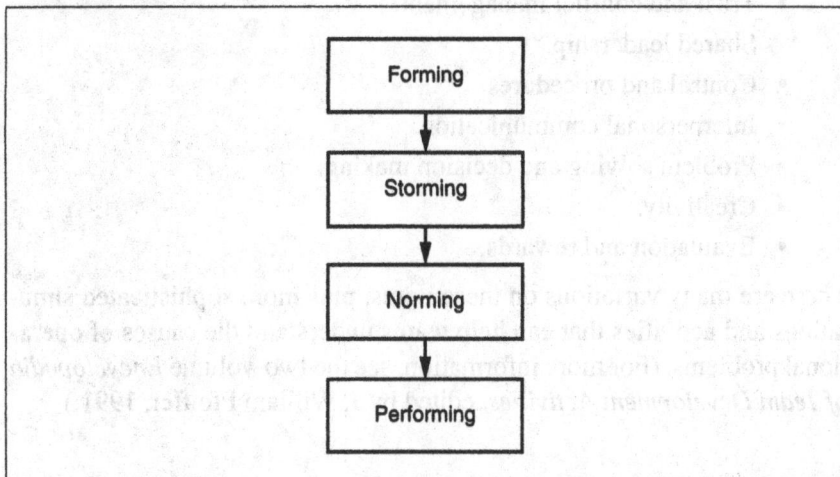

```
        ┌──────────────┐
        │   Forming    │
        └──────┬───────┘
               │
               ▼
        ┌──────────────┐
        │   Storming   │
        └──────┬───────┘
               │
               ▼
        ┌──────────────┐
        │   Norming    │
        └──────┬───────┘
               │
               ▼
        ┌──────────────┐
        │  Performing  │
        └──────────────┘
```

In the third phase, *norming,* the team develops its own norms of behavior, which are a composite of the differences represented by all team members. If the team works well, the new norms should facilitate the team in achieving its objectives.

In the final stage, *performing,* the team puts all its resources together toward accomplishing its mission. When operating well, it is not hampered by issues of internal functioning and is able to devote the majority of its energy toward the task at hand. When this happens, the team has become a fully functioning group.

If groups do not face up to the realities of the first three stages, they will not be able to reach stage four. Many teams become fixated on an early stage of development and continue to replay issues of forming (purpose, roles, and responsibilities), storming (power struggles, cultural misunderstandings) or norming (priorities or criteria and methods for decision making). In these cases, every problem the group faces seems to push it back to the same old issues.

Effectiveness of Team Functioning

There are a wide range of tests and questionnaires teams can take to assess their perceptions of team effectiveness. In general, these questionnaires are self-administered by team members. Their purpose is to gather information about how members see the team functioning on factors like these:

- Shared goals and objectives.
- Utilization of resources.
- Trust and conflict management.
- Shared leadership.
- Control and procedures.
- Interpersonal communication.
- Problem solving and decision making.
- Creativity.
- Evaluation and rewards.

There are many variations on these items, plus more sophisticated simulations and activities that can help teams understand the causes of operational problems. (For more information, see the two-volume *Encyclopedia of Team Development Activities*, edited by J. William Pfeiffer, 1991.)

Stages of Professional Development

You know from experience that team members are always at different stages in their professional development. The leadership style adopted by a multicultural team leader must take into account the particular needs of group members for support or delegation of responsibility.

A good framework for understanding leadership style under different staff and environmental conditions is Hersey and Blanchard's situational leadership theory. In their familiar model, a leader changes leadership style depending on the external situation as well as on the amount of professional experience and competence of the team. Leaders may be highly directive in times of crisis or when there is a great deal at stake. They may be more collaborative when there is time to consult with others to get their input to a decision that is still made by the leader. When more highly developed professionals are involved, the leader turns over authority to make decisions either to a group in which he participates or to an individual or team to whom he delegates. The less experienced the team and/or more urgent the need for a decision, the more directive the leader will be. The more experienced the team members and/or more time available for a decision or action, the more the leader can delegate responsibility to team members.

Such a view of leadership is, however, culturally dependent. In cultures where leaders are expected to have the answers to all questions, participative leadership may not be appreciated at any time. Many workers in highly stratified, hierarchical societies such as those in Asia and Latin America feel the boss loses face if he tries to be too much like the worker. In these cultures, everyone has a place and should accept the role society has assigned. If not, all those associated with the person, including subordinates, may lose face when a superior acts in a way that is not in accordance with his position.

GUIDELINES FOR DIAGNOSING THE EFFECTIVENESS OF MULTICULTURAL TEAMS

These seven variables constitute all the dimensions that you must consider in leading multicultural teams. You can use them in team-building meetings to check factors affecting teamwork. Various elements and instruments can also be used independently to diagnose specific interpersonal or group problems.

When forming a multicultural team or facilitating the development of such a group, however, it is best to begin as you would with a monocultural team until there is a problem that appears to have a cultural basis. While cultural differences can be important, many multicultural teams function very well due to similarities in professional and educational background, corporate socialization, and current interests and objectives.

One of the mistakes that many intercultural specialists have made over the years is to assume that cultural differences were the *primary* driving force in multicultural interaction. On close examination, many observers have found that most multicultural teams are driven *first* by personal factors and issues of team development, such as roles, responsibilities, power, and conflict. **Differences in national culture, while important, are usually secondary**. When they are present as a source of team difficulties, national cultural differences often revolve around thought patterns that directly affect problem-solving and decision-making styles, variety in leadership expectations, and differences in conflict-management styles. Many multicultural teams have also found that these differences are most pronounced during periods of stress. One way to test a multicultural team's effective integration is to place it under stress with stakes that affect their personal futures. Any differences that exist will probably surface. This is particularly true if the team is tired, jet-lagged, or suffering from any other physical adaptation to the local culture. Unfortunately, many managers do not know enough about cultural differences to determine whether or not they are a factor. For this reason, the work of Hofstede, Laurent, and Rhine-smith hold new hope for increasing the understanding and capacity of global managers to lead their multicultural teams more effectively.

There are a few guidelines you can apply to multicultural team analysis. When developing or diagnosing a multicultural team, a manager or facilitator should use the following order in examining potential team difficulties:

1. *Personal styles.* To what extent do personal differences create conflict or inefficiency?

2. *Stage of team development.* Are people clear about roles, responsibilities, power, and how to manage differences and conflict?

3. *Effective team functioning.* Where are there problems in team problem solving, communication, and decision making? Are the team norms of behavior well developed and understood? Are these norms functional or dysfunctional to team operations?

4. *Stage of professional development.* Are there problems created by team members overreaching their development stage or others assuming too much competence on the part of inexperienced members?

If you uncover problems in any one of these four areas and an answer does not appear to be found in any of the theories applied to these issues, you should look at the three sources of potential underlying cultural differences. It should be stressed, however, that this is usually a secondary rather than primary area of analysis, since the majority of problems that multicultural teams face are similar to those of any other team.

5. *National culture.* Are there differences in perceptions of self, others, and the world, patterns of thinking, language, or nonverbal behavior causing problems?

6. *Corporate culture.* Are there differences in corporate values and interests or norms and style of behavior creating difficulties?

7. *Functional culture.* Are there differences due to functions or professional disciplines?

With these seven areas for diagnosis, it is likely that a multicultural team leader, member, or facilitator will be able to determine the source or sources of ineffective team operation, which is the first step toward correcting it.

The objective of this exercise is not just to gain a better understanding of multicultural teams but to lead and develop teams that are flexible, mobile, adaptable, and able to solve complex problems anywhere in the world. They are horizontally coordinated, and because problems and solutions cannot be defined in advance, formal problem-solving meetings are less important than frequent communications and interaction that provide a fertile field for creative solutions to "creative problems."

NATIONAL CULTURE AND PERSONAL AND ORGANIZATIONAL LEARNING

As Andre Laurent has pointed out, the approach to organizational change cannot be the same in every culture. Therefore, the learning and development process itself will be more complex in a global than in a national organization. Laurent says:

> When a majority of German managers perceive their organization as a *coordinated network of individuals making rational decisions based on their professional knowledge and competence,* any process of planned organizational change in Germany will have to take this into consideration.
>
> When a majority of British managers view their organization primarily as a *network of interpersonal relationships* between individuals who get things done by influencing and negotiating with each other, a different approach to organizational change is needed in England.
>
> And when a majority of French managers look at their organizations as an *authority network* where the power to organize and control actors stems from their positioning in the hierarchy, another change model may be called for in France. (Evans, Doz, and Laurent 1990, p. 92. Emphasis added.)

As we can see in Laurent's description, German, British, and French managers have very different definitions of the nature of organizational life. In a multicultural team composed of German, British, and French managers, therefore, the stages of growth, while following Tuckman's thesis, will contain different concerns.

For example, in the forming stage of group development, a German will be concerned about developing clear roles and responsibilities and decision-making procedures. A Brit will want to get to know the other people in his or her group and understand how they can work together as a group of individuals. The Frenchman, though, will be concerned about power and authority, what the rights of the leader and the individual members of the group will be, and how much authority he will have over his own actions.

If you were an American manager of this group, how would you approach your team-building meeting to begin to "form" your group and create a common understanding of how you will work together? You first get everyone to acknowledge that there might be agendas, relate that to cultural differences in general, state some of your own biases as an American, and see if you can get people to deal with one another and the group's development within the context of cultural and personal expectations. That should give you enough to do in your first meeting!

LEADING MULTICULTURAL TEAMS

Leading multicultural teams requires both analytical (left-brain) and intuitive (right-brain) skills. From an analytical perspective, you need the capacity to understand the range of variables affecting multicultural team management, as outlined above. From the intuitive side, you need the qualities of leadership associated with any position of authority and responsibility. This includes the ability to shape, mobilize, and inspire a team in achieving its objectives.

Recent work on leadership by The Forum Corporation in Boston, Massachusetts, has revealed four basic skills, augmented by 20 management practices, of effective leaders. These have been transferred into a highly effective leadership training program that Forum conducts in many corporations. Below are outlined a series of basic leadership skills and practices Forum has identified as important for successful leadership in the United States. While these principles have been enormously successful in the United States, it is clear that multicultural teams contain people who may not respond as positively to these American practices. For each skill cluster, therefore, observations have been added on how various practices would relate to the leadership of multicultural teams.

Interpreting

The first skill cluster is the ability to interpret one's environment—from trends outside the organization to situations within the organization, to your team, and to yourself. There are five practices that constitute this **interpreting** skill cluster:

1. Seeking information from as many sources as possible.
2. Knowing how your own work supports the organization's overall strategy.

3. Analyzing how well members of your team are working together.
4. Knowing the capabilities and motivations of the individuals within your team.
5. Knowing your own capabilities and motivation.

As you have seen in earlier sections, these five areas are open to major differences in interpretation depending on cultural background. High-context cultures will seek more information from more sources and be concerned about placing issues and people in a broader context than low-context cultures. A Japanese or French manager, therefore, will want to gather more information about each team member and his or her background than will an American manager. On the other hand, a French manager may be less concerned about how well members of his team are working together than an American, since a French manager may believe that team members should work within the rules and procedures of the organization. An American manager, on the other hand, expecting more individualism from team members, will feel more responsibility to manage each member of the team. It is also more likely that an American would be interested in examining his or her own capabilities and motivations than, say, a French or German manager, both of whom may believe that once they have achieved a certain status or rank in the organization, their personal skills or motivations are not subject to scrutiny. Instead, they expect to be treated as positions, rather than people, and accorded the respect that is due the position.

Shaping

Shaping behavior entails creating the vision, values, and norms for your team in a way that reflects the values of your organization and enables your team to feel a sense of context and priority for what is important during turbulent and changing times. This skill has also been divided into five practices:

1. Involving the right people in developing the team's strategy.
2. Standing up for what is important.
3. Adjusting plans and actions as necessary in turbulent times.
4. Communicating the strategy to the organization as a whole.
5. Creating a positive picture of the future for the team.

Here again the impact of national cultural differences can be significant. Item 1, participation in team strategy, is a good example. The industrial democracy movement in Western Europe has resulted in laws and regulations that require much greater consultation with works councils and trade unions than in the United States. In Holland and Germany, management may not have a significant reorganization, even if there is to be no loss of jobs, without first explaining plans to the works council and getting its agreement. Such consultation is not normal practice in the United States, and many American managers are aghast to realize the constraints under which they have to operate in many countries where years of social democratic governance have resulted in a legally mandated, strong worker/management relationship.

The second leadership practice, standing up for what is important, is a logical, admirable act. It is probable, however, that the definition of *what* is important in any given situation will vary from culture to culture, as well as *how* one "stands up." Sometimes, the best way to stand up is by sitting down and working quietly behind the scenes. This is the much preferred style in French, Latin American, and many other cultures where leadership is perceived to be dominated by a strong authority figure who protects the rights of the group in highly personal or bureaucratic ways that many times may be executed informally.

A third area that may be interpreted differently is "communicating the strategy to the organization as a whole." Perspectives about information sharing vary widely. Japanese managers tend to believe that information should be shared very broadly because there is an understanding of strong company loyalty and confidentiality. American managers, on the other hand, will share some information but keep other information private if its leakage could endanger competitive positioning. Italian managers tend not to have grand strategies for their organizations but prefer to deal with situations as they arise and depend on creativity and ingenuity to get through barriers. Americans, though, are obsessed with planning, anticipating obstacles, developing contingency plans, and predetermining the methods, means, and priority of allocating resources in case of emergency. On this point, Italian and American managers can nearly come to blows!

The shaping and representation of group interests are therefore issues you must approach with some sensitivity and understanding of cultural differences.

Mobilizing

The third cluster of leadership activities identified in Forum's research is **mobilizing**—the motivation of people through communications, caring, and confidence. According to Forum's research, managers who are good at mobilizing are identified by the following activities:

1. Communicating clearly the results expected from others.
2. Appealing to people's hearts and minds to lead them in a new direction.
3. Demonstrating care for the members of the team.
4. Demonstrating confidence in the abilities of others.
5. Letting people know how they are progressing toward the group's goals.

Of all leadership behaviors, mobilizing is the one that is probably the most valid across cultures. Expressions of caring, attempts to communicate expectations and results, and displays of confidence in subordinate behavior are almost universally appreciated.

When in doubt, it is best to communicate positive feelings directly and personally. When the communication involves negative feelings, however, a third party should be considered, especially in countries where "face" is important. This is true not only for countries like Japan but also for many African, Central Asian, and Middle Eastern countries.

Inspiring

It goes without saying that people from different societies are inspired by different things. Some respond to images of nationalism, others to family or group loyalty, and still others to national ideology or religious beliefs. How you apply Forum's North American research becomes particularly challenging in inspiring multicultural teams.

The best practices for **inspiring** people that Forum has found are

1. Promoting the development of people's talents.
2. Recognizing the contributions of others.
3. Enabling others to feel and act like leaders.
4. Stimulating others' thinking.
5. Building enthusiasm about projects and assignments.

Even at this level, you will encounter variety in the way people are inspired in different societies. In Japan, for example, public praise as a mechanism of recognizing someone's contribution is embarrassing. In group-oriented cultures, public praise may single someone out for envy or retribution from others. There is a saying in Japan that the nail that stands up will be hammered down.

There can also be difficulty in enabling others to feel like leaders. In France, Latin America, and Russia, where there are strong expectations of control by an authority figure, giving up your authority—even temporarily—to be "one of the team" may not be seen as a strength but as a weakness. In such situations, the reasons and conditions under which you choose to turn over authority to others must be clearly spelled out if you are not to lose face or ultimate authority and respect.

INFLUENCING MULTICULTURAL TEAM PEER RELATIONSHIPS

While you may or may not be in a position to lead a multicultural team, it is likely that you will be a peer in a multicultural team that involves cross-unit coordination or global project management. In such situations, there may not be clear lines of authority, and your ability to make a contribution may depend on your ability to influence without formal authority.

Forum Corporation has also conducted extensive research on influencing skills. With the de-layering of organizations, managers are finding themselves in situations where they must convey their opinions through interpersonal influence rather than formal authority. Achieving this cross-culturally requires an understanding of cross-cultural *peer* relations, just as team leadership requires an understanding of *superior/subordinate* expectations across cultures.

Forum's research has identified three major behaviors with 21 practices that constitute effective influence. These are extremely important findings and very valuable for American managers. They can also be valuable in many other cultures but must again be subject to interpretation and sensitivity in a multicultural setting. Forum has had great success in running its influence and leadership training seminars in Europe where these factors have been discussed and adjusted for European cultural attitudes.

The three behaviors identified as most crucial for influence in situations with little or no formal authority are **building influence** through relations, processes, and expected results; **sustaining influence** by promoting joint accountability for high-quality decisions, and **sustaining influence** by demonstrating commitment to improvement.

Building Influence: Defining Relationships, Processes, and Expected Results

Forum's research has identified six practices associated with building influence.

1. Bringing together people with different perspectives.
2. Supporting and helping associates.
3. Setting group goals as well as individual goals.
4. Communicating needs clearly to people in your organization who provide you with goods and services.
5. Encouraging others to express their ideas.
6. Clarifying each person's role in carrying out the work.

This is an extremely helpful list that you can easily use in multicultural team leadership. There are obvious areas of congruence. The first practice, bringing together people with different perspectives, is one of the major strengths of multicultural teamwork, assuming it can be sensitively managed and that the ensuing differences can be worked into some decision pattern, be it consensus, consultative, or participative. The third practice, setting group as well as individual goals, is one of the fundamental ways global managers can work in interunit task forces to establish what sociologists call "superordinate goals"; that is, goals that extend beyond the narrow interests of any one faction to the group as a whole. The fourth practice, communicating needs clearly to people who provide you with goods and services, is even more important in a global organization where you may be separated from your support system, suppliers, and even team members by thousands of kilometers.

The last practice, clarifying roles and responsibilities, can be a double-edged sword. I had an experience in East Africa once where job descriptions were so strictly laid out and adhered to, much in the British tradition, that there was little ability to increase productivity in a small office because people refused to be cross-trained, claiming the new responsibilities were not in their job descriptions.

Sustaining Influence: Promoting Joint Accountability for High-Quality Decisions

Once influence has been built, it must be sustained over time. The eight practices associated with sustaining influence are all oriented toward promoting joint accountability for high-quality decisions. This works well in more egalitarian societies or in societies with a consensus or participative decision-making orientation. However, in societies like France and Russia, where leaders are expected to take charge and make decisions, encouraging joint responsibility for decisions may be seen as a managerial weakness.

These suggested practices are

1. Demonstrating competence by bringing relevant knowledge and skill to the group.
2. Sharing responsibility for solving problems.
3. Evaluating the views of others according to logic rather than according to personal preference.
4. Cooperating rather than competing with others.
5. Understanding which decisions need to involve others and which can be made alone.
6. Seeking creative ways to resolve conflict.
7. Looking for causes of problems in work processes rather than blaming people.
8. Seeking to understand the problems of other work groups.

From a multicultural perspective, this list is loaded with potential pitfalls. While most cultures respect competence and expertise and some, like Germany, absolutely require it for influence, there are other cultures, such as those of Italy, Latin America, and the Middle East, in which relationships and family are more important than competence and expertise.

Perhaps the most difficult practice cross-culturally is item 3, in which you are supposed to depend on "logic." As you know, if there is one area of cross-cultural relations in which there are massive differences, it is in patterns of thinking. There is even little congruence in logic between NTs, STs, NFs, and SFs within the same culture! When you add the ambiguities inherent in holistic versus linear thinking patterns, inductive versus deductive reasoning preferences, and value-based versus situation-based ethical criteria, the term *logic* is nearly drained of its meaning.

Sustaining Influence: Demonstrating Commitment to Improvement

You can probably see for yourself that the list below contains some areas to watch out for from a cross-cultural perspective.

1. Creating enthusiasm about work.
2. Making decisions that are consistent with agreed-upon goals.

3. Promoting innovation.
4. Admitting one's own mistakes and uncertainties.
5. Following through on commitments.
6. Considering requests to change plans and goals with an open mind.
7. Contributing suggestions aimed at improving work processes and products.

As mentioned earlier, admitting your mistakes is useful only under certain circumstances and within certain groups where that has already been established as a positive norm. It is not viewed as positive by your average multicultural group unless the group members have been socialized into it through corporate culture.

The rest of the list is fairly safe cross-culturally in terms of content, but you must always pay attention to the process. Remember that while there are many similarities in the needs that people have around the world, there is wide variety in how these needs are expressed. The same holds true for feelings and the satisfying of needs. We may all have the same feelings of happiness and sorrow, but when, where, and how we express them vary in sometimes surprising ways.

Likewise, we may all need recognition, security, and achievement, but when, where, and how we have these needs met differs by culture. The challenge and the fun are in understanding where, when, and how you can reach out to people from other cultural backgrounds to enable them to work with you most effectively in achieving your company's objectives.

PRACTICES AND TASKS FOR MANAGING MULTICULTURAL TEAMS

Multicultural team leadership has its challenges, but also its rewards. You may have become intrigued by the prospect of working effectively with people from many cultures, one of the most exciting aspects of becoming a global manager. You can implement these practices and tasks to make yourself a more competitive multicultural team leader.

Skill 5: Managing Multicultural Teams

Key Question	How do you work with others from different backgrounds?
Definition	Ability to manage teams that represent diversity in functional skills, experience levels, and cultural backgrounds with

cultural sensitivity and self-awareness,
using differences for creative innovations,
while managing conflicts constructively.

Action and Mindset Attribute   Value Diversity
Personal Characteristic   Sensitive

Key Practices and Tasks

1. Learn and use an understanding of the basic *dimensions of cross-cultural behavior* and their impact on managerial style and organizational functioning.

   1.1 Read some of the books contained in the bibliography for this chapter. There are many good ones covering all major regions of the world. Do you want to know how Arabs think, or Brazilians behave, or Americans manage? There are books listed that will help you in each of these areas, and many more. One book that you will find especially helpful is *Doing Business Internationally* by Brake, Walker, and Walker. It examines 10 cultural variables, such as time, space, structure, communications and power, and how people in different parts of the world deal with each of these issues in a way that affects multicultural team management.

   1.2 Apply management ideas from other societies to your own business unit to improve its productivity and/or effectiveness. Try to find ideas from foreign companies that can enhance your operations not only within that region but across the organization.

2. Examine the cultural assumptions and values behind your *products, services,* and *management practices* to determine whether you are being "culturally blind" to issues that could derail your competitiveness or your personal effectiveness. To begin, ask your foreign customers or colleagues to give you a list of cultural facts they believe could adversely affect your organization's effectiveness.

3. Develop *cultural self-awareness* that allows you to contrast your own culture with other cultures to allow flexible movement from one culture to another.

   3.1 Read books that describe the cultural perceptions, values, and behavior of people from your culture and become aware

of the biases you bring to your job as a result of your
national background.

    3.2 Ask a colleague from another culture to give you semiannual
feedback on how your management actions are seen from his
or her cultural perspective.

4. When on a multicultural team, reflect on the personal, cultural,
and developmental aspects discussed in this chapter to improve
the effectiveness of your work.

    4.1 Become acquainted with your Myers-Briggs profile. Ask
your human resources department to give you a copy of the
standards used and the results for your multicultural team
and customer management groups.

    4.2 Read *The Wisdom of Teams* by Katzenbach and Smith to
understand the difference between a "group" and a "team"
and what you can do to make your group a team.

Along with flexibility, cross-cultural sensitivity is the second-most-
often-mentioned desired characteristic of a global manager by chief executive officers and senior managers from global organizations around the
world. Developing cultural self-awareness is a valuable exercise for any
manager. It is critical for the management of multicultural teams, though
curiously, most international organizations are reluctant to provide adequate
cross-cultural training to any but a few managers who are being transferred
overseas as expatriates.

The truth is that a successful global organization must provide cross-
cultural exposure and develop cross-cultural sensitivity in *all* its managers,
whether domestic or international, so that they are able to work with other
parts of the organization around the globe with whom they are interdependent, not to mention global customers, suppliers, and competitors.

As you cultivate greater sensitivity to multicultural team members,
remember the "Lessons from Geese," an anonymous analysis from which
managers throughout the world can learn.

*As each goose flaps its wings, it creates an 'uplift' for the bird
following. By flying in a V formation, the whole flock adds 71
percent more flying range than if each bird flew alone.*

Lesson: People who share a common direction and sense of
community can go further and get where they are going more
quickly and easily because they are traveling on the thrust of
one another.

Whenever a goose falls out of formation, it suddenly feels the drag and resistance of trying to fly alone and quickly gets back into formation to take advantage of the "lifting power" of the bird immediately in front.

Lesson: If we have as much sense as a goose, we will stay in formation with those who are headed where we want to go.

When the lead goose gets tired, it rotates back into formation and another goose flies at the point position.

Lesson: It pays to take turns doing the hard tasks and sharing leadership with people, as with geese, who are interdependent on each other.

The geese in formation honk from behind to encourage those up front to keep up their speed.

Lesson: We need to make sure our honking from behind is encouraging—not something less than helpful.

When a goose gets sick or wounded or shot down, two geese drop out of formation and follow it down to help and protect him. They stay with the goose until it is either able to fly again or dies. Then they launch out on their own with another formation or catch up with the flock.

Lesson: If we have as much sense as geese, we will stand by each other like that.

SELECTED BIBLIOGRAPHY

Brake, Terrence; Danielle Walker; and Thomas (Tim) Walker. *Doing Business Internationally: The Guide to Cross-Cultural Success.* Burr Ridge, Ill: Richard D. Irwin, 1995.

Christopher, Robert C. *The Japanese Mind.* New York: Fawcett Columbine, 1983.

Davis, Stanley M. *Comparative Management: Organizational and Cultural Perspectives.* Englewood-Cliffs, N.J.: Prentice-Hall, 1971.

De Menthe, Boye. *Korean Etiquette and Ethics in Business.* Lincolnwood, Ill.: NTC Business Books, 1987.

_____. *Japanese Etiquette and Ethics in Business.* 5th ed. Lincolnwood, Ill.: NTC Business Books, 1988.

Elashmawi, Farid, and Philip R. Harris. *Multicultural Management: New Skills for Global Success.* Houston: Gulf Publishing Co., 1993.

Evans, Paul; Yves Doz; and Andre Laurent, eds. *Human Resource Management in International Firms: Change, Globalization, Innovation.* New York: St. Martin's Press, 1990.

Gannon, Martin J., and Associates. *Understanding Other Cultures: Metaphorical Journeys through 17 Countries*. Thousand Oaks, Calif.: Sage Publications, 1993.

Gibney, Frank. *Miracle by Design: The Real Reasons behind Japan's Economic Success*. New York: Times Books, 1982.

Gross, Thomas; Ernie Turner; and Lars Cederholm. "Building Teams for Global Operations." *Management Review*, June 1987, pp. 32–36.

Hall, Edward T. *The Silent Language*. New York: Doubleday & Company, 1959.

_____. *The Hidden Dimension*. New York: Anchor Press, 1966.

_____. *Beyond Culture*. Garden City: Anchor/Doubleday, 1976.

Hall, Edward T., and Mildred Reed Hall. *Hidden Differences: Doing Business with the Japanese*. Garden City, N.Y.: Anchor Press/Doubleday, 1987.

Harris, Philip, and Robert Moran. *Managing Cultural Differences*. 2d ed. Houston: Gulf Publishing Company, 1987.

Harrison, Phyllis A. *Behaving Brazilian*. Cambridge: Newbury House Publishers, 1983.

Hersey, Paul, and Kenneth Blanchard. *The Management of Organizational Behavior*. 3d ed. Englewood Cliffs, N.J.: Prentice-Hall, 1976.

Hofstede, Gert. *Culture's Consequences: International Differences in Work-Related Values*. Beverly Hills: Sage Publishing Co., 1980.

_____. "Motivation, Leadership and Organization: Do American Management Theories Apply Abroad?" *Organizational Dynamics*, Summer 1980, pp. 42–63.

_____. *Cultures and Organizations: Software of the Mind*. London: McGraw-Hill, 1991.

Katzenbach, Jon R., and Douglas K. Smith. *The Wisdom of Teams*. Boston: Harvard Business School Press, 1993.

Keirsey, David, and Marilyn Bates. *Please Understand Me: Character and Temperament Types*. Del Mar, Ca: Prometheus Nemesis Book Company, 1984.

Kiezun, Witold. *Management in Socialist Countries: USSR and Central Europe*. New York: Walter de Gruyter, 1991.

Laurent, Andre. "The Cross-Cultural Puzzle of Human Resource Management." *Human Resource Management* 25, no. 1 (Spring 1986): pp. 91–102.

Laurent, Andre. "The Cultural Diversity of Western Conceptions of Management." *International Studies of Management and Organization*. Vol. XIII, no. 1–2 (Spring, Summer 1983): M.E. Sharpe, Inc. pp. 75–96.

Lawrence, Paul R., and Charalambos A. Vlachoutsicos, eds. *Behind the Factory Walls: Decision Making in Soviet and US Enterprises*. Boston: Harvard Business School Press, 1990.

Little, Reg, and Warren Reed. *The Confucian Renaissance*. Sydney: The Federation Press, 1989.

Macharzina, K., and W. H. Staehle, eds. *European Approaches to International Management*. Berlin: Walter de Gruyter, 1986.

"Managing a Three-Country Team Project." *Electronic Business Buyer*, May 1994, pp. 68–69.

Mole, John. *Mind Your Manners: Culture Clash in the Single European Market*. London: The Industrial Society, 1990.

Moran, Robert, and Philip Harris. *Managing Cultural Synergy*. Houston: Gulf Publishing, 1982.

Muna, Farid A. *The Arab Executive*. London: Macmillan Press, 1980.

Myers, Isabella B. *Gifts Differing*. Palo Alto, Ca: Consulting Psychologists Press, 1980.

Nakamura, Hajime. *Ways of Thinking of Eastern Peoples.* Honolulu: East-West Center Press, 1964.

Nydell, Margaret K. *Understanding Arabs: A Guide for Westerners.* Yarmouth, Me.: Intercultural Press, 1987.

Pedersen, Paul. *A Handbook for Developing Multicultural Awareness.* Alexandria, Va.: American Association for Counseling and Development, 1988.

Pfeiffer, J. William, ed. *Encyclopedia of Team Development Activities.* San Diego: Pfeiffer & Co., 1991.

Phillips, Nicola. *Managing International Teams.* Burr Ridge, Ill: Richard D. Irwin, 1994.

Rhinesmith, Stephen H. *Bring Home the World: A Management Guide for Community Leaders of International Exchange Programs.* New York: Walker and Company, 1985.

————. *Cultural-Organizational Analysis: The Interrelationship between Value Orientations and Managerial Behavior.* Cambridge: McBer and Company, 1971.

Ricks, David A. *Big Business Blunders: Mistakes in Multinational Marketing.* Homewood, Ill.: Dow-Jones-Irwin, 1983.

Ronen, Simcha. *Comparative and Multinational Management.* New York: John Wiley, 1986.

Terpstra, Vern, and Kenneth David. *The Cultural Framework of International Business.* 2d ed. Pelham Manor, N.Y: South Western Publishing, 1985.

Tourevski, Mark, and Eileen Morgan. *Cutting the Red Tape: How Western Companies Can Profit in the New Russia.* New York: The Free Press, 1993.

Trompenaars, Fons. *Riding the Waves of Culture: Understanding Cultural Diversity in Business.* London: The Economist Books, 1993.

Tuckman, Bruce W., and M. A. C. Jensen. "Stages of Small Group Development Revisited." *Group and Organization Studies* 2, no. 4 (December 1977): pp. 419–27.

8

CHAPTER

Managing Learning

Personal adaptation to changing conditions, culture, and operating requirements of a global enterprise represents a significant and largely unfunded training deficit. Development of global managers in most American businesses has been *ad hoc,* rather than systematic, and there is a great need

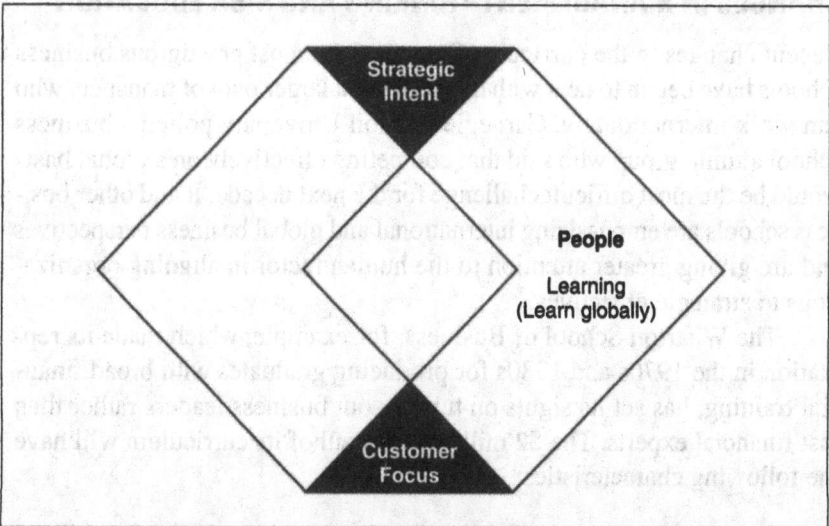

to develop a more orderly movement toward the mindset, skills, and practices of effective global management.

Whatever the challenges, it is clear that you as a global manager will have to manage accelerated change in your life and in the life of your organization. Regrettably, the management of global learning has been developed only in a few forward-thinking companies.

HRD IMPLICATIONS OF GLOBALIZATION

All this talk of a new global world lifts the human resource function of most organizations into a higher orbit. HRD can no longer focus only on *compliance* (compensation, benefits, and labor relations) but must now include *facilitation* (of global attitudes, knowledge, skills, and corporate culture).

Tom Peters, in his book *Thriving on Chaos: Handbook for a Management Revolution* (1988), notes that "every firm over two million dollars in revenues should take steps to examine their international market opportunities in the next 12 months. And every firm over $25 million should be alarmed if it is not doing 25 percent of its business globally, including some with Japan" (p.150). While this may be a bit of an overstatement, it places the emphasis on the right "syl-*la*-ble," as they say. Survival and competitiveness in the future will depend on an organization's global capacities; this, in turn, will depend foremost on the talents and the training of its people.

CHANGES IN MANAGEMENT THINKING AND MBA EDUCATION

Recent changes in the curricula of some of the most prestigious business schools have begun to deal with the need for a larger pool of managers who can work internationally. Carnegie-Mellon University polled a business school alumni group who said that competing effectively on a global basis would be the most difficult challenge for the next decade. It and other business schools are emphasizing international and global business perspectives and are giving greater attention to the human factor in aligning organizations to strategic objectives.

The Wharton School of Business, for example, which made its reputation in the 1970s and 1980s for producing graduates with broad financial training, has set its sights on turning out business leaders rather than just financial experts. The $2 million overhaul of its curriculum will have the following characteristics:

1. Place greater emphasis on "people skills."
2. Add more global perspective.
3. Foster creativity and innovation.
4. Promote real-world problem solving.
5. Examine business issues from the viewpoint of several disciplines.

This "MBA for the 21st Century," as *Business Week* calls it, is one manifestation of innovative thinking that will be necessary for global organizations in the next decade ("Wharton . . . " 1991). U.S. business increasingly recognizes the need for a global perspective in everything from sourcing finances, technology, markets, and people to scanning the globe for competitors. Most American companies, however, are short on people with adequate training and experience to play the global game at the same skill level as the Japanese, Dutch, Germans, or Swedes. These countries have been forced by the nature of their geography, home market, and competitive advantage to compete internationally—and even globally—over the last 40 years.

The United States, on the other hand, has remained more insular from an economic, if not political and military, perspective. Its greatest strength of the past—a domestic market unsurpassed anywhere in the world—has now oddly enough put American business at a disadvantage in the new business game, which demands global thinking, global marketing and global adaptability. To change these thinking patterns in a fundamental way may take years, if not a generation. During that time, American corporations, not its school systems, will need to take the lead in identifying the new skills and thinking patterns necessary to prepare managers to become more globally effective.

We have been discussing the mindset and skills managers need to operate effectively on a global basis. It is one thing to identify and describe these areas and quite another to develop them. Let's consider what an integrated plan would look like for developing managers to operate successfully in a global organization.

A GLOBAL MINDSET FOR GLOBAL PLAYERS

It seems apparent that different skills are necessary at different stages of organizational global evolution. You will recall the domestic and global mindsets we described in the second chapter. Figure 8–1 recapitulates the

FIGURE 8-1

Comparison of Traditional and Global Mindsets

	Traditional Mindset	Global Mindset
Strategy/Structure	Specialize	Drive for broader picture
	Prioritize	Balance contradictions
Corporate Culture	Manage job	Engage process
	Control results	Flow with change
People	Manage self	Value diversity
	Learn domestically	Learn globally

attributes of each. Let's review these again, now that we have been through an examination of each, to outline the kind of transition you and other global managers are undertaking to operate effectively in a global organization.

Strategy/Structure

First, remember that none of these paradigm shifts is mutually exclusive. In the case of strategy and structure, for example, we are *not* arguing that functional expertise is no longer necessary. We are only pointing out that functional expertise is insufficient to enable you to be a successful global manager.

Functional Specialization + The Broader Picture

I have seen many excellent engineers who are also good domestic managers fail in the global arena. The major reason is that they are used to a highly defined engineering perspective. The more intuitive, freewheeling scanning necessary for global management presents them with the need for a radical adjustment in their thinking that many fail to make.

As mentioned in the last chapter, Fritjof Capra has stressed the shift from a mechanistic to a holistic world. John Naisbitt has stressed the transition from physics to biology as a metaphor for change. Peter Drucker has emphasized the need for understanding the "new realities," which are global, generational, and epic. These are not small thoughts, insignificant thinkers, nor small perspectives. To understand them requires a broad view of the world and your role in it. I hope this book has helped you understand where you need some additional knowledge, information, or skills and given you motivation to "go for it." It is clear that we will all need to continue learning for a long time if we are to deal successfully with the many challenges and opportunities the world offers us.

Prioritization as Key to Action + Life as a Balance of Contradiction

We have seen the American penchant for *action*. We have also seen how the complexity of global organizations requires the management of simultaneously contradictory forces and interests. We have discussed the implications of this for your thinking and for your personal ability to manage complexity. The acceptance of some aspects of global management as unresolvable through prioritization is an important fact of life to confront. It is sometimes better, as we saw in the case of the State Department, to have no policy than to have a clearly defined policy about an issue on which there are irreconcilable differences.

This is a hard reality for many of us who have spent most of our working lives being rewarded and praised for prioritizing projects, making decisions, and taking action. It is important to understand, however, that living with contradiction does not mean being paralyzed by it. The contradictions of centralization versus decentralization and regional versus global product priorities will need to be *managed* but cannot be *solved*. As soon as you understand what must be managed on a continuing basis, you will feel less compelled to "fix things." You might want to read an excellent book on this subject by Barry Johnson entitled *Polarity Management: Identifying and Managing Unsolvable Problems*.

Corporate Culture

With a greater emphasis on the compatibility of corporate cultures in mergers and acquisitions, joint ventures, and strategic realignments, your ability to understand and manage these aspects of corporate culture are more important than ever, even if you are dealing with domestic enterprises. In the global arena, the need to align corporate culture by engaging process is acute.

Manage Job + Engage Process

We have seen in our two chapters on corporate culture that managing alignment and change simultaneously is another paradox that must be dealt with. From a mindset perspective, it means refocusing your attention from just the tactical aspects of doing your job to the strategic needs of the business and how it makes money.

The real question is *How do you relate to your company's value chain?* How does the company make money as its products and services move from R&D through engineering, manufacturing, marketing, sales, distribution, and follow-up service? How does your job or function relate to that sequence, and where are you adding value—even if it is outside your function, your business unit, or your country?

Control Results + Flow with Change

Again, balance will be necessary. We are not advocating that you ignore the need to be on top of your job, only that an effective global manager will establish a corporate culture in which room is left for surprises. This will enable you to take advantage of unforeseen opportunities for competitive benefit.

"No surprise" corporate cultures and corporate managers close down innovation, creativity, and the kind of behavior necessary to thrive in a fast-changing global marketplace. That's all there is to it.

People

The 1990s marked the resurgence of people as the most important factor in competitiveness. In the 50 years since World War II, there has been great emphasis on technological advances and the role of technology in global competitiveness. It is now clear, however, that unless people can effectively use the technology and operate anywhere in the world with anyone, there will be little capacity for global organizations to take advantage of the advances.

Manage Self + Value Diversity

Managers today are encountering new demands in self-management as well as team management. On the personal side, you are being asked to see yourself as a product or a business. Companies are saying that they no longer take responsibility for your career, just your skills, and that you will have to manage your own career. And in the process, you will also have to work with diversity.

It will be impossible to be a competent global manager, or any other kind of manager for that matter, if you cannot value and manage diversity. In many organizations, whether or not they are global, a shift from individual competitive behavior to cooperative group behavior is undeniably underway. While this has often been associated with Japanese management and the Total Quality movement, it appears to have deeper roots in a generational shift.

People under 40 are measurably more group- and cooperatively oriented than those over 40. Self-managing groups are used from the shop-floor through high levels of management. As we have seen, global teams are self-managing their way to a newly interdependent world in which people from different cultures, different functions, and different backgrounds come together to *work together* for their own benefit and the benefit of their organizations.

This does not mean that you will not be judged *individually* and that you do not have to perform individually. It does mean that there is a shift away from individual achievement at the expense of the team or your colleagues. This new thinking is evident on a global basis in its most vivid form—strategic alliances between former or current competitors.

Learning Domestically + Learning Globally

Americans have traditionally sought to become experts in their fields and masters of their professions by comparing themselves with others in their organizations or perhaps their industry. Seldom have U.S. businesses benchmarked themselves against the rest of the world or thought about learning from practices in other countries. And Americans are not alone in this. Most managers and organizations measure themselves against their domestic peers.

The move to global learning was made early by a few people who were fortunate enough to be exposed to other cultures when they were young. Exchange students may not realize it, but one of the greatest gifts they are given is a chance to learn the power and possibilities of another culture. While appreciation of cultural difference is essential in today's global world, there are an amazing number of people who have never had a truly other-cultural experience. So it is not part of their mindset. Sadly, these people are losing many opportunities for their own enlightenment and for discovering new perspectives that could benefit their organizations.

The movement from domestic to global leadership involves a transition not only in geographic focus but also in attention to process over structure, seeking out change rather than defending against it, exploiting chaos rather than avoiding it, and moving to a more free-flowing, open, integrated-systems mindset that stresses adaptability. We cannot say too often that shifting from a domestic organization to a global corporation is not just a matter of strategy and structure but of culture and people. It entails a fundamental change in style as well as substance. In fact, style—global style—has *become* substance in producing a competitive edge for the company.

From these observations, it should be evident that the HRD function is critical to the success of a firm's globalization effort. The development of a sophisticated global strategy and structure, as we have often said in this guide, is a good starting point. But until the right people have developed the appropriate mindset and skills, a globalization effort will never get beyond the executive suite. Let's see what an integrated global HRD program would look like.

TWELVE WAYS TO DEVELOP GLOBAL MANAGERS

According to Gillette Chairman and CEO Alfred M. Zeien, it takes at least 25 years to build an international management corps that possesses the skills, experience, and abilities to take a global organization from one level of success to the next! All aspects of a human resource management system must be used in this education process. But few companies today can afford 25 years to build an adequate corps of people to operate globally. How, then, do successful companies develop global managers?

Almost every study of global corporations has concluded that without an integrated and forceful human resource function, the talent and mindset necessary to manage these new complex organizational forms will not be developed and the organizations will eventually fail. Unfortunately, my experience in consulting with many globalizing companies has revealed that in more cases than anyone would like to admit, the human resource professionals have not been adequately prepared for their new global responsibilities. Even where there are far-thinking people, many CEOs still have not realized the primacy of culture and people in global success.

The thoughts below, therefore, are not just for HRD professionals but for *all* global managers. We will examine 12 components of an effective global HRD strategy, which is integral to the corporate culture glue that holds a global organization together. These are:

1. Global sourcing.
2. Assessment and selection.
3. Global orientation centers.
4. Global mindset education.
5. Global business training.
6. Cross-cultural management training.
7. Culture and language training.
8. Multicultural team building.

9. Staff exchanges and network development.
10. Relocation transfer, mentoring and reentry.
11. Career pathing.
12. Performance management.

Too often the assumption is that the major contribution HRD can make to developing global managers is a series of training programs to expand awareness, add knowledge, or promote new skills. This assumption has been encouraged by the ready availability of experts who claim to have some relevant knowledge or skill that can be transferred to increase executive effectiveness.

In Figure 8–2, you begin to see how an integrated strategy might be used to develop a global mindset and various skills for global managers. It is immediately evident that a multipronged approach must be taken because some of the preferred characteristics should be present in selection, while others can be transferred through education, and still others must evolve over time through experience. We will examine each strategy to see how it plays out in real-life policies and practices.

1. Global Sourcing

Acceptance of global sourcing as part of a global HRD function is one of the first changes that managers have to make in the transition to a global corporation. Multinational corporations have for many years seen themselves as the ultimate achievement in international human resource policies, because most of them have had a philosophy of staffing all overseas operations with nationals from that country. This philosophy has been seen as a far-reaching advance from the international corporation, which staffed most of its senior executive posts overseas with expatriates from the home country. Procter & Gamble, after decades of routinely appointing managers from its domestic operations to key positions in overseas subsidiaries, came to understand that this practice not only was insensitive to local cultural needs but greatly underutilized its pool of non-American international managers who were often more appropriate for international assignments than American managers.

Much of this philosophy, however, was developed in the 1960s and 1970s under pressure from the developing world, and later from the industrial world, for the development of local executive talent and skills. It eventually also became good financial policy for many corporations as the costs for expatriate relocation and maintenance skyrocketed.

FIGURE 8-2

Mindset, Skills, and HR Practices

S = *Skill*

HRD Practice	Competition / Big Picture	Complexity / Contradictions	Alignment / Process	Change / Diversity	Teams / Opportunity	Learning / Global
Global sourcing	M					
Assessment/selection	M	M	M	M	M	M
Orientation centers					M	M
Global mindset education	S M	S M	S M			S M
Global business training	S M	S M	M			M
Cross-cultural management training	M	M	S M	M	S M	M
Culture and language training						
Multicultural team building		M	S	M	S M	M
Staff exchanges and network development	M		S M		M	M
Performance management		S M	S	S		S
Relocation transfer, mentoring, and reentry	S M	S M	S M	S M	S M	S M
Global career pathing	S M	S M	S	S M	S M	S M

M = *Mindset*

Unfortunately, the move from international or multinational to global must jar this cozy congruence of philosophy and finances. **Global corporations cannot afford to be geographically bounded in their human resource policies**. Global corporations must be able to recruit, train, and place their best experts and most effective managers in the geographic locations where the demands of the market, technology, and the environment require the best skills, regardless of nationality.

2. Assessment and Selection

A good global human resource strategy cannot begin too early and *must be strategically linked,* especially for globalization. Far too many companies have decided to globalize, then looked around for global managers. Developing global managers, like developing global corporate cultures, is a three- to five-year endeavor. If you or your company anticipates going global in any sense of the term in the next five years, you cannot lose a minute in putting a global HRD plan into place.

A great deal needs to be done to define assessment and selection methods for the skills and characteristics (knowledgeable, analytical, strategic, flexible, sensitive, and open) we have outlined. At Matsushita, for example, managers are selected for international assignment on the basis of a set of personal characteristics known by the acronym SMILE:

- Specialty (the needed skill, capability, or knowledge).
- Management ability (particularly motivation).
- International flexibility (willingness to learn and adapt).
- Language facility.
- Endeavor (perseverance in the face of adversity).

Skills, however, are not always easy to assess. At this point, the best and easiest to assess are in the management of the competitive process (specialty), language, and perhaps endeavor. A new tool available from Moran, Stahl & Boyer's international division is an assessment instrument, the Overseas Assignment Inventory, which attempts to determine the cross-cultural sensitivity and adaptability of managers for assignment overseas. It is a research-based instrument, developed over 20 years of experience with a wide variety of clients.

Such an assessment instrument, however, must be combined with on-the-job coaching and a career path that provide opportunity for managers to correct areas of weakness and develop new skills and attitudes for effective global management. If it is seen only as a deselection instrument, it will never pass the tests of organizational reality. Line management does not want to hear that the only bauxite engineer available for an important assignment in Peru cannot go because he failed a test for cross-cultural sensitivity.

3. Global Orientation Centers

Assessment and selection are only the first steps in preparing qualified global managers. When working in a diverse global organization, there is a constant need for orientation of people with many different backgrounds to the corporate culture and its values and vision. In global corporate training, a company selects a major value or competence and periodically trains the top layers of management in internationally integrated groups of 20 to 40 people. The training serves to compare and contrast perspectives on the issue at hand and to develop wide-ranging global relationships that are important in managing the conflicting interests that inevitably arise in global operations.

Management training is insufficient if done on a country-by-country basis or outside the context of the corporation's global vision and values. Corporate global training programs must be utilized—just as corporate advertising campaigns are used with customers—to establish corporate identity and image with employees.

Arthur Andersen Consulting is one of the world's largest consulting firms. With 2,200 partners spread throughout the world, it needs to constantly share changes in its corporate strategy, tactics, values, and culture with all its people worldwide to ensure continuity of practice and operations with its global clients. To achieve this, Arthur Andersen has established its Center for Professional Education in St. Charles, outside of Chicago. Each partner must spend at least one week there each year of his or her career. Multinational groups of managers are given the latest information about the corporation and have an opportunity to network with one another about global trends and future needs.

To build a common commitment to the company at Matsushita, white-collar employees spend a great part of their first six months in what the company calls "cultural and spiritual training." They study the credo of the company and the "Seven Spirits of Matsushita." Philips has a similar entry-level training program ("organizational cohesion training"), as does Unilever.

Global orientation centers can be excellent places for corporations to conduct research about their global markets and operations, as the managers who come through these centers can be polled on any number of current or future issues. Too few corporations use these centers for research as well as education and are missing valuable input into the global planning process.

4. Global Mindset Education

Global mindset education is a new concept I have developed in conjunction with the preparation of this book. It has been tested most extensively at ARCO International and AT&T and involves a two- to three-day course that introduces managers to the basic themes of this book—the forces driving globalization, evolution of global organizations, and the six global management skills involved in managing competitiveness, complexity, alignment, change, multicultural teams, and learning. This is an orientation, rather than a skill-building process, to help managers understand what they will be going through as individuals. After this introductory course, they are prepared and motivated to take a more formal global business curriculum in which they will learn the technical and business knowledge to which they will apply their new global mindset and skills.

Another effort that takes mindset training a step further is a 4½-day program entitled "Leading and Managing in a Global Organization." This course, designed for the top 500 managers of WR Grace to facilitate its globalization effort, focuses on 41 behaviors that managers need in order to operate in a global organization. The 41 behaviors are divided into six clusters that reflect the basic ideas in this book: thinking systemically, managing complexity, managing organizational alignment, managing change, managing multicultural teams, and managing learning. Managers receive 360-degree feedback on the behaviors and devise a plan for importing their effectiveness to a global organization. The course, developed by Warner Burke of Columbia University and I, has gained widespread interest as a means of orienting managers to the challenges of managing in a company that is going global.

5. Global Business Training

Executive education and development have become big business in the United States. In 1990, more than 16,000 executives attended university or other educational institutions of general management, while another 50,000 participated in internal programs, and more than 3,000 were enrolled in one of the 100 executive MBA programs offered in the United States. It is estimated that by the year 2000, executive education will be an even bigger business:

- University general management and functional programs: 22,000 at an estimated cost of $12,600 per attendee.
- Internal corporate programs: 60,000 at a cost of $5,800 per executive.
- Executive MBA programs: 4,000 at an average cost of $36,000 for two years.
- Hundreds of thousands of managers in two- and three-day programs at an estimated cost of $200–$300 per day (Moulton 1991).

Yet at this point the share of money and space allocated to training *global* managers is infinitesimal. By 2000, the percentage will undoubtedly be much larger than it is today. The training challenge is considerable, with the traditional need for knowledge in global strategies, structures, markets, products, and finances, as well as global and regional knowledge.

Before its decision to break up into three companies, AT&T announced an objective of earning a much greater portion of profit outside the United States. For a company that was almost exclusively American until the 1980s, this presented a major human resource challenge. Figure 8–3 is a sample of the AT&T Global Business Curriculum. It includes business training, as well as global and area studies. At the most basic level, there are international systems and national area studies with which global managers must be conversant. This means some basic acquaintance with global economic, political, and social trends and some of the institutions affecting those trends, such as international trade and banking institutions, the Exim Bank (U.S. Export-Import Bank), and GATT (General Agreements on Trade and Tariffs).

AT&T managers must also have some basic understanding of foreign exchange, central banking, international transportation, telecommunications, tax, and legal considerations that may affect their industry. How AT&T's late-1995 decision to splinter the corporation will affect its excellent global training program is not known as this goes to press.

On a regional level, every global manager should know the major political and economic regional organizations like the EEC, European Investment Bank, LAFTA (Latin American Free Trade Association), Asian Development Bank, and other regional organizations that affect international trade and commerce.

It goes without saying that the successful global manager *has* to be competent in professional/technical skills. This requires not just marginal competence but more likely *superior* competence, as the world-class suppliers,

FIGURE 8–3

AT&T's Global Business Programs

Global Symposia	Global Business, Management, and Leadership
• Rising to the European challenge • Asia, Japan, and the Pacific Rim • Running a business anywhere in the world • Latin America and Mexico	• Elements of a global business • Managing a global business; money and results • Strategies for competing globally • Tactics for competing globally • Finance in the global marketplace • Global management: advanced business simulation • Product management in global markets • Strategic global marketing • Cross-cultural business negotiations and communications • Doing business in . . . (country specific) • Language programs—survival communications • Introductory communications—business/social communications • Business cases: global and international investments

customers, and competitors with whom you interact daily become better educated and more experienced. In addition to the competition, the increasing need for technology transfer means that international managers and representatives must not only know their product but be able to adapt, adjust, and customize it to local needs. The ability to tailor products and teach local professionals how to work with the concepts and ideas behind the product, as well as the product itself, requires a much higher skill level than that required to sell a product or service domestically.

The days are gone when corporations can put people out to pasture by sending them on an international assignment. **Today, global companies send their best and brightest abroad for seasoning and testing in preparation for executive leadership positions.**

6. Cross-Cultural Management Training

As you have seen in Chapter 6, managing multicultural teams requires balancing disparate expectations about leadership, communications, coaching, appraising, and decision making, not to mention different patterns of thinking that affect problem-solving preferences and many other subtle aspects of organizational life.

Perhaps the single greatest effort to acquaint managers with cross-cultural management methods has been conducted by Ford in connection with its 1995 global reorganization. As part of the implementation of its new organizational structure, in which 25,000 employees found themselves working with new colleagues, many of whom are in other countries, Ford conducted a leadership preparation program for its top 3,000 managers. The senior executive team, including the president and the group vice presidents for marketing and sales, manufacturing, and product development, also spent time examining the cross-cultural implications of their work.

Such high-profile attention from a major American corporation is unusual. In general, there have been few systematic attempts to acquaint global managers with ways of comparing cultural approaches to management. But perhaps Ford will point the way for other companies to begin to understand the importance and challenges of the multicultural dimension of globalization.

7. Cultural and Language Training

Can anyone question that some form of cultural and language training is necessary for employees who are relocating abroad? Remarkably, recent surveys of multinational corporations indicate that almost 50 percent of them do not have any predeparture language or cultural training, although most provide in-country training.

While predeparture language and cultural training for an expatriate and accompanying family should be routine practice in a global corporation, other groups also need cross-cultural sensitizing. These include managers who travel internationally but hold positions in their home country, as well as managers in the home country who have to interact with foreign counterparts, customers, or suppliers. Few companies do an adequate job for these populations. The recent wave of cross-border mergers and acquisitions has given rise to a need for greater cross-cultural training and awareness for many corporations. In Western Europe in particular, many companies are being rocked by acquisitions of companies with completely unfamiliar corporate and national cultures. Those who believe that Europeans are cross-culturally and globally more sophisticated than Americans because of their proximity to people of other nations are learning that exposure and understanding are two different things.

Country Knowledge

On a national level, you cannot appreciate the context within which you are operating without some understanding of social and economic development policies, the relationships among trade, export, industrial, and agricultural policies, and currency, taxation, and banking. Most countries have far more centralized economic and industrial policies than the United States, so Americans may be surprised by governmental attitudes and regulations on foreign trade and investment.

Cross-Cultural Knowledge and Skills

Becoming a truly competent global manager is ultimately a personal challenge, a challenge not only to learn about the world and the application of business principles, technology, and competitiveness to the international arena but ultimately one of accepting and adjusting to unfamiliar values, experiences, and lifestyles. A successful global manager understands cultural differences and approaches multicultural teams and foreign business opportunities with an open attitude and willingness to explore the synergy of these differences. You must also cultivate the analytical and behavioral skills to operate globally with people of different values, beliefs, and expectations concerning business and international management.

While it is helpful to have some knowledge of local customs and cultural conditions, a truly global manager must have a broader framework within which to analyze many cultures on a functional basis. You must examine:

* The way people of any society *perceive themselves* as individuals or as part of a collective group.
* The way people in a society *perceive their relations with others* in terms of formality, obligations, and depth.
* The way people in a society *perceive the world* around them, both animate and inanimate, from their relationship with nature and the environment to attitudes toward time and space.
* The *patterns of thinking*, including problem solving, linear versus holistic analytical patterns, high and low contextual needs, and inductive versus deductive reasoning patterns.

To these four dimensions, we can add the importance of language and nonverbal behavior. These two areas are greatly affected by cultural differences, and while the first has been well studied, country-by-country analysis of the second still lags far behind. You should consider:

- The *influence of language on culture,* from its ability to handle abstract thinking to its capacity to convey sense of time, urgency, and deadlines.
- The way in which *nonverbal behavior* affects interpersonal and business relations, including the use of silence, hand gestures, postures, colors, smells, and sounds.

Most people agree that the best way to obtain cross-cultural skills is to live in another culture, but many companies are reluctant to have many expatriates abroad because of the high cost. Samsung, however, has decided to go global and put its money where its mouth is. In September 1991, Samsung's HR department started sending 400 selected employees for one-year visits to 45 countries. Each is given $50,000 to spend as he or she pleases in the assigned country. Most study the local language and travel around the country, learning the culture and making friends. Samsung has currently budgeted $100 million for the program until 1996. Along with the newly established Samsung Global Management Institute, this initiative is central for enabling Samsung to achieve its goal of becoming a $200 billion company by the early twenty-first century.

Samsung is doing the unthinkable by most Western standards. Many of the major Western Fortune 1000 companies have fewer than 400 expatriates with full-time operating responsibilities. But Samsung has decided that a major investment in the development of global managers will build the foundation for its future strategic positioning. It will not take Samsung 25 years to build a corps of managers to operate globally.

The investment that most Western corporations actually make in training opportunities for international managers, especially at the levels of global and regional studies and cross-cultural and attitudinal comparisons, remains amazingly sparse. Nevertheless, the HRD field can prepare people in these areas if corporations will take the time and spend the money to allow their employees to attend available courses.

8. Multicultural Team Building

The most advanced area of global management and organizational development is multicultural team building. Grace Cocoa has been using multicultural team building in its plants and its global functional groups, as well as with its multinational global senior management team, for the last several years. Hoffman-La Roche, the Swiss-based pharmaceutical company, also uses strong team management methods and stresses the multicultural components of managing its international research and development teams.

In spite of the fact that multicultural team building is growing in popularity in global organizations as both an integrating mechanism and a method of increasing work productivity and effectiveness, there has been remarkably little systematic work in defining the specific characteristics of a well-functioning multicultural team. The analysis presented in Chapter 6 offers one approach.

9. Staff Exchanges and Network Development

Staff exchanges are an underutilized tool for building a global corporate culture. Most companies have not designed guidelines for conducting beneficial staff exchanges, which are little known in global corporations. The biggest problem in arranging staff exchanges is to be clear about the purpose, length, and structure of the proposed exchange. If you are clear about the purpose, the rest will follow. Personal biases such as "You can't learning anything in two weeks" should be ignored. The fact is, if you are interested in establishing acquaintances and testing chemistry between people at opposite ends of the globe in order to facilitate daily telephone contact, two-week staff exchanges work. If, however, you need to exchange staff to gain professional knowledge, skills, market information, or specialized orientation, then a period of at least four weeks is more appropriate. Staff exchanges of three months to a year fall into another category and are generally used for more in-depth technical or professional training and development for individuals who will be taking over responsibilities in another location.

Ericsson is built on networks and actively develops them. It has developed a policy of sending large numbers of people back and forth between headquarters and subsidiaries for a year or two. Where NEC may transfer a new technology through a few key managers, Ericsson will send a team of 50 or 100 engineers and managers from one unit to another. This flow is often two-way, as a means of strengthening the global corporate culture in addition to transferring technology.

One of the most sophisticated international trainee programs has been devised by Gillette, the Boston-based global consumer products company. Gillette has 57 manufacturing facilities in 28 countries with 31,200 employees. Since 1983, Gillette has developed almost 150 high-potential managers who are now on their way to important jobs worldwide. The Gillette program is oriented toward young people from countries outside the United States who could be on a fast track for future leadership in the company. The trainees are university graduates with a business background and good social skills, adaptable, younger than 30, mobile, single, and fluent in English. They work in their own countries for 6 months, then spend 18 months at one of Gillette's three international headquarters in Boston, London, and Singapore. While on these assignments, they perform real jobs and have responsibilities against which they are assessed to determine the next move after the traineeship is completed. Gillette emphasizes foreign experience not just for its youngest trainees. Expatriate experience is common throughout the organization. Of the top 40 Gillette executives, approximately 80 percent have had at least one foreign assignment, and more than half have worked in three or more countries.

10. International Mentoring and Reentry Planning

Reentry is a major obstacle for many managers who accept an assignment abroad. **A global organization that does not adjust its corporate culture, policies, and procedures to deal with reentry problems will never have a talented and adequate cadre of global managers.** Too many managers have become disillusioned upon their return from an overseas assignment. Several factors contribute to the difficulty:

- There is a definite drop in organizational status when one returns from an expert position in an outpost to a normal line job at home.
- There usually are financial and status benefits associated with expatriate living that do not follow the manager and family home.
- There is a period of cultural adjustment, many times to the different pace of life in one's home country.
- These problems are exacerbated if an expatriate has not been kept up to date with headquarters' thinking while abroad and does not have a real job on returning.
- Finally, this process may be further complicated when there are no opportunities to apply the knowledge and perspectives gained abroad and no appreciation of the way in which foreign experience could benefit operations in the new location.

To avoid these pitfalls, a carefully developed plan of information sharing, job planning, and cultural appreciation must be put into place. Mentors should be assigned to share information with managers when they are abroad. These same mentors should represent the career interests and job possibilities for managers as they return. And the corporation should work to develop a set of global corporate values that includes an appreciation for and incorporation of foreign experience into local management practices, whether "local" is in the field or at headquarters.

11. Global Career Pathing for the Global Management Cadre

Thirty years ago, when Charles Handy started to work for a famous multinational company, he was given an outline of his future career. The outline ended with his being chief executive of a particular company in a particular far-off country. He left before his career had advanced very much but notes that today "not only did the job they had picked out no longer exist, neither did the company I would have directed nor even the country in which I was to have operated."

Let this be a word to the wise who may think that global career pathing means establishing a predictable course for the future. A recent review conducted by *The Economist* of 15 global corporations from the United States, Europe, and Asia cites the following factors in planning for international careers:

- Top managers should have worked outside their own country.
- Local managers should have worked outside their own country and a corporate center.
- Corporate center staff should have worked abroad.
- International experience should be provided early in a career.
- International jobs are both jobs to be done and development opportunities.
- Organizations must "stretch" to meet their global human resource obligations and needs.
- The manager, spouse, and family must be treated as one unit.

AMP, a $4 billion manufacturer of electrical and electronic connectors with headquarters in Harrisburg, Pennsylvania, has 31 wholly owned companies outside the United States and derives more than 60 percent of its sales from abroad. AMP developed the concept of a "globe-able person" to describe the kind of people they need to run the company. According to William Hudson, president and CEO, a globe-able person is someone who has a minimum of five years of living in another country and culture and has been sufficiently immersed in the culture "to know what it's like to think like somebody else" (John S. McClenahen, "Global Grasp," *Industry Week*, June 7, 1993, 51–53).

Unilever, with one of the best and oldest of the global human resource programs, believes that management development should be centrally controlled because only in that way can it develop the managers needed by an international concern. Unilever has a system of personnel planning and development lists. Ericsson works with a worldwide management planning system. Rhone-Poulenc has an international human resource committee. Fiat internationalizes all management projects.

It is not necessary for everyone, but some well-identified management cadre must be on a global career path. This cadre should include anyone who has the talent or aspirations to eventually be in the executive suite. In many of the world's most sophisticated global corporations, the identification, monitoring, and transfer of the top cadre of senior executives is the responsibility of none other than the corporation's board of directors or management committee. This practice is standard at ICI, British Petroleum, and Philips, for example.

There are obvious complications in a global sourcing philosophy at a time when dual-career marriages create a greater desire on the part of many managers to "stay put." There is no easy answer to this issue, but you must develop HRD policies that are sufficiently attractive to the family as a whole so that they are seen as conducive to family life as well as corporate life. With the influx of a new generation of managers who are increasingly demonstrating new and different values, the incentive packages for global service will need to be modified accordingly. Companies have experimented with a variety of approaches. One answer is to view the development of a global career path as a combination of achievement, financial, and cultural needs. Achievement and upward mobility must be blended with financial incentives but modified by cultural backgrounds and values that may alter what is perceived to be the most attractive package for success in global management. Perhaps we need social scientists in addition to financial compensation and benefits specialists to help delineate a global career path in a global corporation.

12. Performance Management

As a manager, you know that the best way to encourage new behavior is to set goals around new directions and reward them, either financially or with other kinds of recognition. An integrated approach to global management development, therefore, cannot be effective without building the desired behavior into the performance management system of your organization. Very simply, this means that global managers not only must be offered orientation, training, and educational opportunities but must be coached and counseled into taking advantage of these opportunities and, in the end, must have their performance and rewards managed against the successful development of these competencies. You can accomplish this by installing within your organization a global career path that rewards and nurtures people through the predeparture, overseas assignment, and reentry process, a progression that has been such a dismal failure at so many international and multinational corporations, leaving employees with the sense that an overseas assignment is punishment.

A recent study in Europe has revealed some interesting differences in the way managers from different countries see the criteria for career promotion (Laurent 1986). The responses to an international questionnaire distributed to managers of a major American multinational corporation with an excellent reputation for human resource management indicated that American managers felt the single most important criterion for a successful career was ambition, or drive. French managers believed that being labeled as having high potential was the critical factor for success, while British managers felt it was important to create the right image and be noticed for what they do. German managers believed that technical expertise and creativity were critical for a successful career.

The subject of successful criteria for international assignments is not new by any means. Nasmiji Itabashi, one of the founders of international education in Japan, identified as early as 1934 that to be an "international person," as he described it, one had to cultivate the following qualities:

• Sincerity and dependability.
• An understanding of one's own culture and institutions.
• A global perspective and insight.
• Proficiency in at least one foreign language.

This is still not a bad list. In fact, it is insightful in many ways, not the least of which is an emphasis on cultural *self-awareness* over the learning of other specific cultures. And there are many people from the third world who would tell you that if American managers learned more about sincerity and dependability, they would gain many more contracts and have many more successful joint ventures abroad than has been the case over the last 50 years.

Successful global companies today are clear about their promotion criteria for global managers. Philips uses four criteria that are known throughout the company as the basis for assessing executive potential. These are:

1. Conceptual effectiveness (vision, synthesis, professional knowledge, and business directedness).

2. Operational effectiveness (individual effectiveness, decisiveness, and control).

3. Interpersonal effectiveness (network directedness, negotiating power, personal influence, and verbal behavior).

4. Achievement motivation (ambition, professional interest, and emotional control).

Developing a truly global career path system requires not only policies but clear corporate values that are communicated throughout the organization.

One of the best ways to create the matrix minds by which a global corporation rises or falls is through mobility. In the 1970s, over 90 percent of top management of American multinational corporations did not have passports. Today, many companies are using temporary assignments of up to one or two years to broaden executive thinking and facilitate corporate decision making.

But you must not become caught in the trap of the international corporate service corps of roving managers who never come home again. IBM has a policy that 99 percent of its people on overseas assignment are temporary, with positions waiting for them back home; only 1 percent of its expatriate managers are careerists in the international arena. The international perspectives gained through service abroad thus become integrated back into the home organization.

GLOBAL MINDSET CHALLENGES FOR THE TWENTY-FIRST CENTURY

Reflecting on the point we have come to in our journey, it might be useful to take a moment to address the implications of our observations for the global mindset as we stand at the edge of the millennium. Five basic themes emerge, which will keep us all stretched and challenged for the foreseeable future. These are:

1. Rethinking all boundaries.
2. Multinational, multicultural, and intercultural interaction and cooperation.
3. Decentralization, intrapreneurship, and entrepreneurship.
4. Retraining.
5. Personal flexibility and adaptability to change.

Rethinking All Boundaries

Boundaries are not what they used to be, physically, organizationally, or psychologically, and boundary redefinition will occur on all levels. *Geographic boundaries* are being reorganized daily. With these changes comes a reconceptualization of who we are, who our neighbors are, and in some cases, who our enemies are. This is certainly the case today in Western, Eastern, and Central Europe. Between EC 1992 and the reconfiguration of Eastern Europe and the Soviet Union, the world has been turned upside down for a large portion of its inhabitants.

Structural, functional boundaries, as a result of decentralization, delayering and cross-functional coordination, are being redrawn as part of the large themes of customer-driven organizations and Total Quality Management (TQM). While these changes have been driven by global competition and more educated customers, they have been facilitated by advances in microchip technology and vast computerization of global manufacturing, transportation, and marketing operations.

Strategic alliances are daily transforming life-long competitors to tentative allies, requiring new kinds of risks and new forms of cooperative/ competitive behavior. As a result, the boundaries among *teams, competitors, and allies* have broken down. Teams are increasingly diverse and multicultural, and your ability to work with constantly changing teams relies on a stronger corporate culture and common shared vision, values, and methods of operation.

Multinational, Multicultural, and Intercultural Interaction and Cooperation

Culture, in all its glory, has taken center stage. Increased diversity in the American workforce; ethnic strife in Eastern and Central Europe; cultural differences in cross-border joint ventures, mergers, and acquisitions are all trends that have demonstrated how little many of us know about cultural differences and how to manage them. This will be a growth area for the twenty-first century. The new emphasis on culture will take three forms.

An area that has been only tentatively developed is *cultural self-awareness training*. In this field, people are taught what biases and beliefs they have based on their own background as a means of better understanding and relating to people from other cultural backgrounds. Cultural self-awareness, which has great HRD potential, would enable people to operate in many different countries, without specific-country training for each world area.

We must not only learn to be culturally self-aware in order to work with people from other cultures, we must also become facile in our ability to adapt to a range of foreign environments that themselves may have a great variety. *Cultural adaptability* may be less amenable to training, but programs are being created to help.

Cross-cultural management requires that we adapt our personal management styles for multicultural teams and have a much better understanding of comparative management practices as they exist in different countries around the world. Cultural-managerial analysis and similar frameworks are being developed to provide analytical perspectives from which various management practices can be related to cultural values, then merged together for global cultural synergy.

Decentralization, Intrapreneurship, and Entrepreneurship

Creativity, innovation, and spontaneity are watchwords for success in a fast-moving world. Corporations around the world are shedding bureaucracy and finding ways to encourage experimentation among their employees. Continuous improvement, driving out waste, and skunk works are among the methods used to encourage more innovation in global organizations. Three factors push in this direction. Entrepreneurship and innovation require mindset changes, as well as structural adjustments, to free people to move toward systems thinking. *Think globally, act locally* is one of the context-building phrases of the twenty-first century. Global efficiency and local responsiveness find their answer in mass customization, the method by which *mass products* like Cabbage Patch Kids dolls are customized for individuals by special order. John Naisbitt and Patricia Aburdene's *Megatrends 2000* (1990) was published simultaneously in 19 countries, and in each case the local publisher included local examples of the trends the authors identified in the

United States and around the world. Just-in-time inventories; long-term, limited supplier relations on the supply side; and promises like that of Domino's pizza on the distribution side represent the move to relationship-building *quick, creative responsiveness*. Suppliers win contracts by delivering materials just in time and producers win customers by producing products just in time (in the case of Domino's, 30 minutes). Speed, responsiveness, flexibility, innovation—these will be the competitive advantages of the future.

Retraining

Global corporations have not yet begun to deal with the challenge of retraining. Several factors are converging to make retraining a major human resource requirement during the next century. The dramatic *global workforce dislocation* in Eastern and Central Europe will be the scene of human trauma for many years to come. Millions of people will lose their jobs through privatization, including government and Communist Party workers and former security and military personnel, because newly privatized companies cannot be profitable without drastic reductions in the workforce. Estimates of redundancy in most of the formerly socialist countries run between 10 percent and 25 percent of the workforce. We have never dealt with a dislocation of this scale in modern history.

In the United States and Western Europe, *management dislocations due to downsizing, acquisitions, and mergers* have become commonplace. Workers, technicians, professionals, and executives are faced with the need for retraining as acquisitions and mergers produce redundant positions and excess headcount. Downsizing to retain competitive advantage as the low-cost producer also places pressure on middle management as well as blue-collar workers.

Basic structural readjustments are occurring throughout the Western world as major portions of the world's economies experience *shifts in the transition from the industrial to the information age, and from the industrial to the service economy*. The result is displaced workers, outdated skills, and new skills, such as computer literacy, that will place great new demands on the human resource function.

Personal Flexibility and Adaptability to Change

A basic theme of this book has been the need to develop new managers who are more flexible and adaptable than those of the past. People are familiar with a base rate of unemployment and base rates of inflation. I suggest that we may be experiencing an escalation in the *base rate of change*. All societies exist within a certain rate of change that has become comfortable and manageable. In the former Communist countries change was imperceptible, and in Western Europe and the United States it has been perhaps 5 percent. Eastern and Central Europe are now experiencing a complete breakdown of their societies and a change rate probably exceeding 50 percent, while the United States and other parts of the world have roughly doubled their rate to 10 percent. All this places great pressure on people to adjust to new circumstances in ways that are totally new.

We have hardly begun to develop the *new change professions* that will be necessary to assist people through these transitions. Indeed, in general we have not recognized the transition itself, let alone conceptualized it, analyzed it, and trained people to deal with it. I am involved in training students at Moscow State University to become organization development specialists. It is an almost impossible task. The macro socioeconomic-political context is so unstable that most Western theories about micro-change on an individual, a team, or an organizational unit are irrelevant.

NEW DIRECTIONS

These trends constitute major challenges and opportunities for human resource professionals for many years to come. We need everything from research to conceptualization to theory building. We also need to develop new intervention methods, from selection and assessment to training and performance management, to enable people and corporations to meet the demands of the twenty-first century. It is an exciting time—and a complex time—but one with great potential for human resource people who have the skills and motivation to rise to the occasion.

Organizations that follow the integrated agenda recommended here can make significant progress on the human side of globalization work. Given the accelerating needs of customers from Europe and Japan, it is particularly urgent for U.S. organizations to develop new ways to align their people and cultures with their global strategies and structures. In the end, what America may need is a Baldrige Award for Global Competitiveness. U.S. corporations may have to be challenged to adopt best practices in global strategy, structure, culture, and skills in the same way they are being challenged to tackle quality. If it can develop corporations that are consumer driven, quality focused, and globally effective, American business will have gone a long way toward restoring America's competitiveness and ensuring its continued prosperity into the twenty-first century.

PRACTICES AND TASKS FOR MANAGING LEARNING

You may want to examine the list of practices and tasks associated with managing personal and organizational learning to determine where you should begin to work in this area.

Skill 6: Managing Learning

Key Question	How do you learn new skills and perspectives?
Definition	Ability to manage personal and organizational learning and improvement on a continuous basis through the exploration of new fields of knowledge and new cultural perspectives and through seeking feedback on a global basis.
Action and Mindset Attribute	Learn globally
Personal Characteristic	Open

Key Practices and Tasks

1. Examine what *global trends could affect your work* over the next three years and begin now to develop methods for using these changes as new opportunities for personal and organizational growth.

   1.1 Search for best practices in your job on a global basis, both within your organization and within your industry or profession.

   1.2 Develop one new idea each year to increase your productivity or your organization's competitiveness, the seeds of which you have obtained from outside your home country.

2. Develop a *working knowledge of international relations, international economics, and cross-cultural differences* that will promote effective interaction with foreign suppliers, customers, and partners.

2.1 Attend an internationally oriented seminar, workshop, or conference at least every other year to broaden your exposure to international thinking and perspectives.

2.2 Read magazines and newspapers that reflect the national or regional perspective of your target audience.

3. Consider personal and organizational *learning as a lifelong process.*

3.1 See yourself as one of the new "knowledge workers" and constantly gather, analyze, and reflect on information on a global basis, utilizing global resources for new concepts, perceptions, and opportunities for personal, professional, and organizational effectiveness.

3.2 Get at least 40 hours a year of training, either inside or outside your company. This should be done regardless of your level of responsibility, even if you are the president of your company!

4. Develop a *sense of meaning and purpose* in personal and organizational life that transcends the immediate job or annual objective and can be related to a higher or broader contribution to the human condition. Write your own vision statement about your work and include your personal reasons for staying in your job, profession, or organization—the motivation that gets you up in the morning. Make sure you are coming to work for a *purpose.*

The commitment to lifelong learning is not a casual one to make. It requires the willingness to live with unfinished business, the faith that people can constantly grow and develop for the better, and the sense that there is some larger reason for existence than making a buck. People and organizations who are committed to learning as a central aspect of life not only survive better but are often more attractive to others, more vibrant in their ideas, and more fulfilled in their pursuits.

You must determine where you and your organization stand in the identification of needs for the global mindset, behaviors, and skills that will make your people effective throughout the world. You may want to convene a task force or find some other way to examine the critical success factors for your business, what populations should be targeted for development, and what combination of human resource strategies and tactics (selection, training, etc.) should be used against each population, mindset attribute, behavior, and skill.

Being a competent global manager or a socially responsible global organization requires an integrated approach to developing the skills needed to flourish, while knowing that competency alone will never be enough to replace a sense of mission.

SELECTED BIBLIOGRAPHY

Abdoolcarim, Zoher. "Building up Human Resources." *Asian Business,* December 1993, pp. 42–44.

Anatal, Ariane Berthoin. "Odysseus' Legacy to Management Development: Mentoring." *European Management Journal* 11, no. 4 (December 1993): pp. 448–54.

Anfuso, Dawn. "HR Unites the World of Coca-Cola." *Personnel Journal,* November, 1994, pp. 112–116.

Austin, Clyde, ed. *Cross-Cultural Reentry.* Abilene, Tx: Abilene Christian University Press, 1986.

Bolman, Lee, and Terrence Deal. *Reframing Organizations.* San Francisco: Jossey-Bass, 1991.

Boyatzis, Richard E.; Scott S. Cowen; David A. Kolb; and Associates. *Innovation in Professional Education: Steps on a Journey from Learning to Teaching: The Story of Change and Invention at the Weatherhead School of Management.* San Francisco: Jossey-Bass, 1995.

Capra, Fritjof. *The Turning Point: Science, Society and the Rising Culture.* New York: Bantam Books, 1982.

Derr, C. Brooklyn, and Gary Oddou. "Internationalizing Managers: Speeding Up the Process." *European Management Journal* 11, no. 4 (December 1993): pp. 435–41.

Desatnick, Robert L., and Margo L. Bennett. *Human Resource Management in the Multinational Company.* Westmead, England: Gower Press, 1977.

Drucker, Peter F. *The New Realities.* New York: Harper & Row, 1989.

Ettorre, Barbara. "A Brave New World: Managing International Careers." *Management Review,* April 1993, pp. 10–15.

"The Fast Track Now Leads Overseas: Global Companies Now Want Top Managers Who've Been Around." *U.S. News & World Report,* October 31, 1994, pp. 94–95.

Fombrun, Charles, Noel M. Tichy, and Mary Anne Devanna. *Strategic Human Resource Management.* New York: John Wiley & Sons, 1984.

Handy, Charles. *The Age of Unreason.* Boston: Harvard Business School Press, 1990.

Hayes, Michael. "Internationalising the Executive Education Curriculum at General Electric: A Case Study of Trends in the 1980s." *Journal of Management Development,* February 1991.

Ibe, Masanobu, and Noriko Sato. "Educating Japanese Leaders for a Global Age: The Role of the International Education Center." *Journal of Management Development,* February 1991.

Johnson, Barry. *Popularity Management: Identifying and Managing Unsolvable Problems.* Amherst, Ma: HRD Press, 1992.

Korn/Ferry International and Columbia School of Business. *21st Century Report: Reinventing the CEO.* New York: Korn/Ferry International, 1989.

Labbs, Jennifer J. "How Gillette Grooms Global Talent." *Personnel Journal,* August 1993, pp. 69–76.

Laurent, Andre. "The Cross-Cultural Puzzle of Human Resource Management." *Human Resource Management* 25, no. 1 (Spring 1986): pp. 91–102.

Macoby, Michael. *The Gamesman: The New Corporate Leaders.* New York: Simon and Schuster, 1976.

Marquardt, Michael, and Dean Engel. *Global Human Resource Development.* Englewood Cliffs, N.J.: Prentice-Hall, 1993.

Marsick, Victoria J., and Lars Cederholm. "Developing Leadership in International Managers—An Urgent Challenge!" *The Columbia Journal of World Business* 22, no. 4 (Winter 1988): pp. 3–11.

McCall, Morgan W., Jr.; Michael Lombardo; and Ann M. Morrison. *The Lessons of Experience: How Successful Executives Develop on the Job.* New York: Lexington Books, 1988.

Moran, Robert T.; Philip R. Harris; and William G. Stripp. *Developing the Global Organization: Strategies for Human Resource Professionals.* Houston: Gulf Publishing, 1993.

Moulton, Harper. "Executive Development and Education: An Evaluation." *Journal of Management Development* 9, no. 4 (1991): p. 8.

Moynihan, Michael. *Global Manager: Recruiting, Developing and Keeping World Class Executives.* London: The Economist Intelligence Unit, 1993.

Naisbitt, John. *Global Paradox: The Bigger the World Economy, the More Powerful the Smallest Players.* New York: William Morrow & Company, 1994.

Naisbitt, John, and Patricia Aburdene. *Megatrends 2000: Ten New Directions for the 1900s.* New York: William Morrow & Company, 1990.

Odenwald, Sylvia. *Global Training: How to Design a Program for the Multinational Corporation.* Burr Ridge: Business One Irwin, 1993.

Peters, Thomas. *Thriving on Chaos: Handbook for a Management Revolution.* New York: Harper & Row, 1988.

Rhinesmith, Stephen H. "Open the Door to a Global Mindset." *Training and Development Journal,* May 1995, pp. 34–43.

Solomon, Charlene Marmer. "How Does Your Global Talent Measure Up?" *Personnel Journal,* October 1994, pp. 96–108.

———. "Repatriation: Up, Down or Out?" *Personnel Journal,* January 1995, pp. 28–37.

"Wharton Rewrites the Book on B-Schools." *Business Week,* May 13, 1991, p. 43.

PART FIVE

THE CONTINUATION

Chapter 9
Preparing for Your Global Future

9

CHAPTER

Preparing for Your Global Future

We are nearing the end of our exploration, but just the beginning of your adventure as you implement many of the ideas and concepts we have discussed in your future work. You should be feeling a little more "world-wise" than when you began and increasingly comfortable with your new, more global mindset.

There is still much uncharted water, personal, organizational, and international. The transformation of Eastern Europe and the former Soviet Union from centrally planned and structurally driven political and economic systems is giving way to free markets and process-driven democracies. The roles and relationships of the United States, Japan, and Germany in a post–cold war world have just begun to evolve. The speed and pace of technological change continue to challenge all organizational strategies and affect each of our lives.

It is apparent that globalization is something larger than a change in the strategy or structure of an organization. It is also probably greater than the global corporate cultures we have been discussing or the people like you and me who are coping with these transformations. Andy Grove, our guide to living with chaos, notes:

> Globalization . . . simply means that business knows no national boundaries.
> Capital and work—your work!—can go anywhere on earth. The consequence

of all this is painfully simple: If the world operates as one big market, every employee will compete with every person in the world who is capable of doing the same job. There are a lot of them, and many of them are very hungry. (p. 230)

So there are threats as well as opportunities in this brave new world. And it will be prudent for all of us to attend to both.

REFLECTING ON OUR JOURNEY

This book has introduced new ways of looking at your job, your organization, the world, and your life. I have tried to prepare you for the world that Andy Grove has described and some of the ideas he has advocated. A global mindset and six new global management skills, these are the resources that you will take with you into global management and the global twenty-first century.

All of the new perspectives and management skills in the world, however, need to ultimately be weighed against the meaning and purpose of your actions. One of the most astute observers of these issues has been James Carse, a philosopher from New York University. His powerful little book *Finite and Infinite Games* (1986) has challenged us all to look at our lives as "infinite, open-ended cooperative games" played for the purpose of continuing the play, rather than winning. In other words, make sure that in the process of winning your battles, there is also some cumulative positive result in your life.

Using some of Carse's ideas about games, let us review where we have been and where we may be going as we finish our discussion of globalization and launch out to test these ideas in the competitive world of global business.

I. Context

Going Global *"No one can play the game alone"* (Carse 1986, p. 45). No one can play a global game alone. We all need colleagues to cope with the complex, broad-based world that is the new business arena. You will find that there are many people who are willing and able to play the game with you as you try to develop as many infinite, rather than finite, games as possible.

It is impossible to gain a balanced picture of the world if you only look at your side of the elephant! Working as a successful manager in a global organization therefore requires you to constantly **drive for the broader picture**.

Americans are at a cultural disadvantage in looking for larger contexts. We mentioned earlier that the anthropologists who have studied the subject characterize Americans as low context. In a low-context culture, people are happy to accept the situation as they see it if it meets their needs. In fact, they are inclined to believe that the world as they see it *is* reality. They need only reinforce those things they like and overcome those things that stand in the way for life to be very good. This is what sociologists call an "instrumentalist" view of the world—you do whatever gets you there.

Many people who teach cross-cultural relations have noted that one source of difficulty between the French and Americans is that while Americans are constantly asking How? the French are asking Why? *How* leads to pragmatic descriptions of ways to get things done; *why* leads to philosophical considerations of the broader, historical framework for the current situation. This is the difference between high and low context.

The Japanese culture, as we have seen, also drives toward high context, not from a philosophical viewpoint like the French, but from a group perspective. The Japanese need to know what groups you belong to, where you fit into social, economic, and educational hierarchies, and what your family background and history have been before they can place you in the current situation and determine how to deal with you. One might say that if the American question is How? and the French is Why? the Japanese equivalent might be Where?

In any case, you can see how both the French and the Japanese are more driven to the bigger, broader picture than Americans. We have already discussed the impact of different thinking patterns on French, Japanese, and American approaches to exploring systems versus rational, linear perspectives. If you are an American working in a global organization, you will need to practice systems thinking and systems analysis, forcing yourself into the broader picture to understand the forces affecting global organizational life. In the process, you will come to appreciate contradiction as part of the more complex arena of world operations, rather than as an impediment to your current project.

Global Mindset and Skills

"Finite games can be played within an infinite game; but infinite games cannot be played within finite games" (Carse p. 8). Finite games are, very simply, win-lose. While we play many finite games in the world of global business in our competition for customers, suppliers, technology, and profits, to be successful we must play a strategic game that is larger than any of the local tactical contests we may win.

Michael Macoby, in his best-selling book of 1976, *The Gamesman*, describes the devastating end faced by managers who spent their entire lives winning battles but losing the war. Such people win innumerable games but lose any sense of cumulative purpose or accomplishment. Remember in global gamesmanship that the purpose of the exercise is to keep the larger game (better life for people of the planet) going and to ensure that you have a broad enough mindset to encompass the needs of others in your global play.

II. Strategy/Structure

Managing Competitiveness
"The rules of a finite game are the contractual terms by which the players can agree who has won" (Carse p. 9). Make no mistake about it: Global management is filled with win-lose, competitive games. In areas like managing the competitive process, you must understand the rules by which others play. Cross-cultural negotiating styles, international marketing techniques, global entry, and development strategies are all aspects of the global win-lose, finite game that you play as a global manager every day. If you do not play these finite games well, your life as a global manager may be remarkably short.

At the same time, Carse has a message for you as an individual—and perhaps for your corporation. He stresses that you always have the option to focus on the larger picture, the infinite game, and walk away from finite games that threaten to destroy your larger purpose, mission, or values. These are the elements of the infinite game that prevent you from becoming one of Macoby's victims of finite play.

Managing Complexity
"Finite players play within boundaries; infinite players play with boundaries" (Carse p. 12). The complexity of global organizations can suffocate you, but it doesn't have to. Carse has a way out: Play *with* boundaries rather than *within* them! To do this you need to focus on your conceptual skills and concentrate on "reframing" your current view of the world, emphasizing balance as you deal with all the contradiction and complexity of a global business. Developing a balanced perspective about the global world in which you work requires not getting bogged down in details. If you are "driving for the bigger, broader picture," this should help, but in addition you must apply your intuitive and analytical skills to continuously reframing the world you deal with. Reframing has been a subject of great

inquiry in recent years. A number of good books have been written about how to think creatively and intuitively to get out of boxes in your life, such as those by Lee Bolman and Terrence Deal (1991) and by Joel Barker (1989). Barker calls it "paradigm shifting," Carse calls it "playing with boundaries." You can *call* it whatever you want, but the actions you should take are to look at problems from different angles, brainstorm new visions, and try to ensure that you do not get caught in old ways of thinking that bog you down.

We have discussed the need to live with contradiction and the paradoxes inherent in global organizational life. We have noted the need to incorporate contradiction into more comprehensive systems thinking and to understand that the most important ingredient in simultaneously holding contradictory ideas is balance. What we have perhaps not emphasized enough, however, is that you will probably not be motivated to do any of these things unless you appreciate contradiction for the energizing role that it can play in a global organization. **Contradiction is the essence of diversity**. Contradictory ideas, opinions, and perspectives arise from any multicultural setting. Brainstorming, a technique in which people are allowed to put up contradictory ideas without discussion, many times leads to new creative ideas that derive from contradictory viewpoints on a flip chart. In addition, **contradiction is the engine of opportunity**. Every situation is skewed toward a particular strength on one side of the picture. Usually the entrepreneurial initiative will flow from the opposite, or underutilized, side—the side that no one else sees because everyone is preoccupied with managing the current state. Looking for contradiction in the current state of things will often point the way to the next generation of product, structure, or process that will be the competitive edge of the future. The full exploration of contradiction, when it goes against your current strength, is key to ensuring the success and relevance of your organization in the future. Above all, **contradiction is the natural state of the world**. Remember the Tao and yin and yang, symbolized by the flowing opposite halves of a circle. This symbol has reminded people for generations that the world is *rich* in its contradictions, and that there is great opportunity and pleasure to be gained from understanding and appreciating the flow.

III. Corporate Culture

Managing Alignment   *"Culture . . . is an infinite game. Culture has no boundaries. . . . For this reason it can be said that where society is defined* *by its boundaries, a culture is defined by its horizons"* (Carse, pp. 52 and 59). If culture is an infinite game, then corporate culture is unquestionably central to global management. If a culture is defined by its horizons, a corporate culture must be outward looking, rather than inward focused, to be healthy and successful.

In the last 25 years, I have seen many organizations fail because they became too focused on defining their structure, their boundaries, their authority relationships, and their allocation of internal resources, not realizing that "the old order changeth" around them. On the other hand, corporate cultures that focus on the horizons of new opportunity, the possibilities of a new world order, and the visions of emerging ideas and people are flourishing in today's global business environment.

The twenty-first century will likely be dominated by headlines of new technological breakthroughs, but the most taxing breakthroughs must come in our ability to manage our corporate cultures and people in response to these new technologies and the changes they rain down on our lives.

It doesn't matter what position you have because your stature in a particular organization can neither protect you from global change nor make you capable of dealing with it. What will make you a successful global manager is your willingness to **trust and engage process**—a theme you have encountered often in this book.

Managing Change *"The rules of the infinite game must change in the course of play"* (Carse p. 11). To stay relevant to the present and the future and to enable play to continue, "the rules of an infinite game must change in the course of play." Indeed, change must become the norm, not the exception. The secrets to living with uncertainty are, first, you must look for new order in disorder, which comes from putting on different lenses and new paradigms. Second, you must become comfortable with white-water rafting and structured process, in which you are neither in control nor wholly out of control. You must recognize that managing change will mean managing periods of alternating chaos and control.

You will also have to become comfortable with conflict, focusing on the opportunities that conflict provides for innovation and learning for yourself and your organization. Concentrate less on defending your position and more on understanding the possibilities and opportunities inherent in the other person's view. Like a black-belt judo expert, you must learn to use your opponent's momentum to move you both in new directions.

This will entail some potentially threatening work on your own psyche. Psychologists have long believed that we fear most in others those things we have not resolved in ourselves. Personal growth and development will be important for keeping pace with continuous change, as well as for dealing with the diversity of a global organization.

IV. People

Managing Teams *"No one can play the game alone. One cannot be human by oneself. There is no selfhood where there is no community. We do not relate to others as the person we are; we are who we are in relating to others"* (Carse p. 45). The Teamwork Era has arrived. While John Naisbitt and Patricia Aburdene have proclaimed the "triumph of the individual," this is not an isolationist but a global, team-oriented, adventuresome person who is a willing partner in personal and organizational development. It is also an era of team play. Real white-water rafting, outward bound, and other learning-play experiences will support integrated, interdependent, self-managed teams. Teams will construct constant learning loops, becoming self-managing in process as well as content, interpersonally as well as in the office— self-correcting while continuously upgrading their standards of excellence.

In the end, however, the real advantage of teamwork in a global organization has best been described by Carse. Through cultural diversity and the rich variety of perceptions, values, and beliefs available in global organizations, we can become much more than we ever could in a monocultural situation. We are truly enriched if "we are who we are in relating to others."

Managing Learning *"Because infinite players prepare themselves to be prepared for the future, they play in complete openness. To be prepared against surprise is to be trained . . . to be prepared for surprise is to be educated"* (Carse p. 23). Personal and organizational learning are paramount to global success. As we have seen in the last chapter, global managers must be trained in basic knowledge about the world, but more important, they must be educated to be open to surprise and uncertainty. Remember that to be educated is a state of being; to be trained is a state of preparedness. We have offered many thoughts on how you can prepare yourself for surprise—new theories, suggested actions and arenas for personal and organizational development. Expanding these and building them into an integrated whole that works for you is your life's work as a global manager.

You will never stop learning, for you will never know enough. **Being open to surprise is not a rational act; it is an act of faith**—faith in your own ability to flow with the future, faith in others' willingness to support you, and faith in some fundamentally larger forces in the world that use you for higher and better purposes than you can rationally construct.

V. The Continuation

Future   *"A finite game is played for the purpose of winning, an infinite game is played for the purpose of continuing the play"* (Carse p. 3). In the end, perhaps the most important skill for a global manager is the ability to "manage meaning." Meaning comes from continuous play—from the ability to work toward something larger than the next win. Managing meaning involves understanding not only the functional utility of an event, technique, or operation but also its context within the broader aspects of life, within the needs of the current situation, and within the needs, hopes, and fears of the people with whom you are working.

The key to all we have described in this journey is learning—personal learning, team learning, and organizational learning. Learning, in turn, is dependent not only on training and education but on an open attitude and curiosity about the world around you. I cannot imagine an effective global leader who is not curious about the world. To be an effective global manager, you must do more than exist; you have to thrive. Rather than cope, you must take the initiative. And instead of reacting, you must create.

Global management at its best is a testimonial to many of humanity's better attributes—openness, creativity, resilience, adaptiveness, understanding, sensitivity, empathy, analysis, anticipation, challenge, and, yes, control.

Andy Grove's prescription is to focus on adding value. He writes:

> The point is, the cliches of globalization and the information revolution have real meaning . . . to your career. . . . I can offer you no sure-fire formula for success. But here are three key questions:
>
> 1. Continually ask, "Am I adding value or merely passing information along? How do I add more value?" By continually looking for ways to make things truly better in your organization. In principle, every hour of your day should be spent increasing output or the value of the output of the people for whom you're responsible.

2. Continually ask, "Am I plugged into what's happening around me? Inside the company? The industry?" Are you a node connected to a network of plugged-in people, or are you floating by yourself?

3. Are you trying new ideas, new techniques, and new technologies?— and I mean personally. Don't just read about them.

People do not always face up to the changes they have to deal with, yet you can't be ready for the future until you've survived the crucible of change. And the key to survival is to learn to add more value today, and every day. (p. 230)

In this journey, I have shared some of my own beliefs, doubts, and convictions about the world and the world of global management. My challenge to you now is to develop your own philosophy of your life as a global manager. You are at the center of a rapidly evolving world. It has great potential, and if you grab onto it and go for the ride, you will have a wonderful and challenging life.

Sister Corita, a Catholic nun who incorporated abstract color with poetry and prose in paintings, created one of my favorites. She quoted Italian writer Ugo Betti: "To believe in God is to know that the rules are fair and that the world is full of wonderful surprises."

Be open to these surprises and move in the world with a spirit that inspires you and others to live life to its fullest. Good luck.

SELECTED BIBLIOGRAPHY

Barker, Joel Arthur. *Discovering the Future: The Business of Paradigms*. St. Paul, Minn: ILI Press, 1989.

Bolman, Lee, and Terrence Deal. *Reframing Organizations*. San Francisco: Jossey-Bass, 1991.

Bridges, William. *Transitions: Strategies for Coping with the Difficult, Painful and Confusing Times in Your Life*. Reading, Mass.: Addison-Wesley, 1980.

Carse, James. *Finite and Infinite Games*. New York: Ballantine Books, 1986.

Grove, Andrew S. "A High-Tech CEO Updates His Views on Managing and Careers." *Fortune*, September 18, 1995, pp. 229–30.

Kennedy, Paul. *Preparing for the 21st Century*. New York: Random House, 1993.

Koestenbaum, Peter. *Leadership: The Inner Side of Greatness*. San Francisco: Jossey-Bass, 1991.

_____. *The Heart of Business: Ethics, Power and Philosophy*. Dallas: Saybrook Publishing, 1987.

Macoby, Michael. *The Gamesman: The New Corporate Leaders*. New York: Simon and Schuster, 1976.

BIBLIOGRAPHY

Abdoolcarim, Zoher. "Building Up Human Resources." *Asian Business,* December 1993, pp. 42–44.

Adler, Nancy. *International Dimensions of Organizational Behavior.* Boston: Kent Publishing, 1986.

Adler, Nancy, and Dafina N. Izraeli, eds. *Women in Management Worldwide.* Armonk, N.Y.: M.E. Sharpe, 1988.

Aldred, Carolyn. "Global Strategies Encompass Changing Corporate Culture." *Business Insurance,* April 17, 1995, pp. 41–43.

"Alignment of Business Objectives with IT Gives High Returns." *Industrial Engineering,* December 1993, pp. 9–10.

Allen, Robert F., and Charlotte Kraft. *The Organizational Unconscious: How to Create the Corporate Culture You Want and Need.* Englewood Cliffs, N.J.:Prentice-Hall, 1982.

Anatal, Ariane Berthoin. "Odysseus' Legacy to Management Development: Mentoring." *European Management Journal,* 11, no. 4 (December 1993): pp. 448–54.

Anfuso, Dawn. "HR Unites the World of Coca-Cola." *Personnel Journal,* November 1994, pp.112–16.

"AT&T Global Service." *New York Times,* March 11, 1992, p. D4.

Atkinson, Philip E. *Creating Culture Change: The Key to Successful Total Quality Management.* Bedford, UK: IFS Publications, 1991.

Austin, Clyde, ed. *Cross-Cultural Reentry.* Abilene, Tx: Abilene Christian University Press, 1986.

Auteri, Enrico, and Vittorio Tesio. "The Internationalization of Management at Fiat." *Journal of Management Development,* February 1991, pp. 26–27.

Baatz, E. B. "Fourth Annual CEO Survey." *Electronics Business,* April 1993, pp. 38–44.

Barker, Joel Arthur. *Discovering the Future: The Business of Paradigms*. St. Paul, Minn: ILI Press, 1989.

Bartlett, Christopher A., and Sumantra Ghoshal. "Organizing for Worldwide Effectiveness: The Transnational Solution." *California Management Review* 31, no. 1 (1988).

———. *Managing Across Borders: The Transnational Solution*. Cambridge: Harvard Business School Press, 1989.

———. "Matrix Management: Not a Structure, a Frame of Mind." *Harvard Business Review*, July–August 1990, pp. 138–45.

———. "What Is a Global Manager?" *Harvard Business Review*, September–October 1992, pp. 124–32.

Birkinshaw, Julian. "Encouraging Entrepreneurial Activity in Multinational Corporations." *Business Horizons*, May–June 1995, pp. 32–38.

Bleeke, Joel A., and Brian A. Johnson. "Signposts for a Global Strategy." *The McKinsey Quarterly*, Autumn 1989, pp. 60–71.

Bolman, Lee, and Terrence Deal. *Reframing Organizations*. San Francisco: Jossey-Bass, 1991.

Boyatzis, Richard E. *The Competent Manager: A Model for Effective Performance*. New York: John Wiley, 1982.

Boyatzis, Richard E.; Scott S. Cowen; David A. Kolb; and Associates. *Innovation in Professional Education: Steps on a Journey from Learning to Teaching, The Story of Change and Invention at the Weatherhead School of Management*. San Francisco: Jossey-Bass, 1995.

Brake, Terrence; Danielle Walker; and Thomas (Tim) Walker. *Doing Business Internationally: The Guide to Cross-Cultural Success*. Burr Ridge, Ill: Richard D. Irwin, 1995.

Bridges, William. *Transitions: Strategies for Coping with the Difficult, Painful and Confusing Times in Your Life*. Reading, Mass.: Addison-Wesley, 1980.

Burke, W. Warner. *Organization Development: A Normative View*. Reading, Mass.: Addison-Wesley OD Series, 1987.

Calvert, Gene. *High Wire Management: Risk-Taking Tactics for Leaders, Innovators and Trailblazers*. San Francisco: Jossey-Bass, 1993.

Campbell, Alexandra J., and Alan Verbeke. "The Globalization of Service Multinationals." *Long Range Planning* 27, no. 2 (1994): pp. 95–102.

Capra, Fritjof. *The Turning Point: Science, Society and the Rising Culture*. New York: Bantam Books, 1982.

Carnevale, Anthony Patrick. *America and the New Economy: How New Competitive Standards Are Radically Changing the American Workplace*. San Francisco: Jossey-Bass, 1991.

Carse, James. *Finite and Infinite Games*. New York: Ballantine Books, 1986.

Champy, James. *Reengineering Management: The New Mandate for New Leadership*. New York: Harper Business, 1995.

Chesanow, Neil. *The World-Class Executive*. New York: Rawson Associates, 1985.

Christopher, Robert C. *The Japanese Mind*. New York: Fawcett Columbine, 1983.

Cleveland, Harlan. *The Future Executive*. New York: Harper & Row, 1972.

Cohen, Roger. "For Coke, World Its Oyster." *New York Times*, November 21, 1991, p. D1.

Collins, James C., and Jerry I. Porras. *Built to Last: Successful Habits of Visionary Companies*. New York: Harper, 1994.

Conner, Daryl R. *Managing at the Speed of Change: How Resilient Managers Succeed and Prosper Where Others Fail*. New York: Villard Books, 1993.

Copeland, Lennie, and Lewis Griggs. *Going International: How to Make Friends and Deal Effectively in the International Marketplace*. New York: Random House, 1985.

"Corporate Culture." *Business Week*, October 27, 1980, pp. 34–38.

Coulson-Thomas, Colin. *Creating the Global Company*. New York: McGraw-Hill, 1992.

Daniels, John L., and Dr. N. Caroline Daniels. *Global Vision: Building New Models of the Corporation of the Future*. New York: McGraw-Hill, 1993.

Davidow, William H., and Michael S. Malone. *The Virtual Corporation: Structuring and Revitalizing the Corporation for the 21st Century*. New York: Harper Business, 1992.

Davis, Stanley M. *Comparative Management: Organizational and Cultural Perspectives*. Englewood-Cliffs, N.J.: Prentice-Hall, 1971.

———. *Future Perfect*. Reading, Mass.: Addison-Wesley, 1987.

Davis, Stanley M., and Paul Lawrence. *Matrix*. Reading, Mass.: Addison-Wesley, 1977.

De Menthe, Boye. *Korean Etiquette and Ethics in Business*. Lincolnwood, Ill.: NTC Business Books, 1987.

———. *Japanese Etiquette and Ethics in Business*. 5th edition. Lincolnwood, Ill.: NTC Business Books, 1988.

Deal, Terrence E., and Allan A. Kennedy. *Corporate Cultures: The Rites and Rituals of Corporate Life*. Reading, Mass.: Addison-Wesley, 1982.

Derr, C. Brooklyn, and Gary Oddou. "Internationalizing Managers: Speeding Up the Process." *European Management Journal* 11, no. 4, December 1993, pp. 435–41.

Desatnick, Robert L., and Margo L. Bennett. *Human Resource Management in the Multinational Company*. Westmead, England: Gower Press, 1977.

Doz, Yves. *Strategic Management in International Companies*. New York: Pergamon Press, 1986.

Dreifus, Shirley B., ed. *Global Management Desk Reference: 151 Strategies, Ideas and Checklists from the World's Most Successful International Companies*. New York: McGraw-Hill, 1992.

Drucker, Peter F. *Managing in Turbulent Times*. New York: Harper & Row, 1980.

———. *The Changing World of the Executive*. New York: Times Books, 1985.

———. *The New Realities*. New York: Harper & Row, 1989.

———. "The New World According to Peter Drucker." *Business Month*. May 1989, pp. 48–59.

Egan, Gerard. *Change Agent Skills A: Assessing and Designing Excellence*. San Diego: University Associates Press, 1988.

———. *Adding Value: A Systematic Guide to Business-Driven Management and Leadership*. San Francisco: Jossey-Bass, 1993.

Elashmawi, Farid, and Philip R. Harris. *Multicultural Management: New Skills for Global Success*. Houston: Gulf Publishing Co., 1993.

Elliot, Jacques, and Stephen D. Clement. *Executive Leadership: A Practical Guide to Managing Complexity*. Arlington, Va.: Cason Hall & Co., 1994.

Ettorre, Barbara. "A Brave New World: Managing International Careers." *Management Review*, April 1993, pp. 10–15.

Evans, Paul. "Management Development as Glue Technology." *Human Resource Planning* 15, no. 1, pp. 85–106.

Evans, Paul, and Yves Doz. "The Dualistic Organization." In Paul Evans; Yves Doz; and Andre Laurent, eds. *Human Resource Management in International Firms: Change, Globalization, Innovation.* New York: St. Martin's Press, 1990, pp. 201–236.

Evans, Paul; Yves Doz; and Andre Laurent, eds. *Human Resource Management in International Firms: Change, Globalization, Innovation.* New York: St. Martin's Press, 1990.

Farquhar, Alison; Paul Evans; and Kiran Tawadey. "Lessons from Practice in Managing Organizational Change." In Paul Evans; Yves Doz; and Andre Laurent, eds. *Human Resource Management in International Firms: Change, Globalization, Innovation.* New York: St. Martin's Press, 1990.

"The Fast Track Now Leads Overseas: Global Companies Now Want Top Managers Who've Been Around." *U.S. News & World Report,* October 31, 1994, pp. 94–95.

Ferguson, Henry. *Tomorrow's Global Executive.* Homewood, Ill.: Dow Jones-Irwin, 1988.

Fisher, Glen. *Mindsets: The Role of Culture and Perception in International Relations.* Yarmouth, Me.: Intercultural Press, 1988.

Fisher, Roger, and William Ury. *Getting to Yes.* Cambridge: Harvard Negotiation Project, 1985.

Fombrun, Charles; Noel M. Tichy; and Mary Anne Devanna. *Strategic Human Resource Management.* New York: John Wiley & Sons, 1984.

The Forum Corporation. *Leadership: Training Workbook.* Boston: The Forum Corporation, 1990.

Gannon, Martin J., and Associates. *Understanding Other Cultures: Metaphorical Journeys through 17 Countries.* Thousand Oaks, Calif.: Sage Publications, 1993.

Garland, John, and Richard Farmer. *International Dimensions of Business Policy and Strategy.* Boston: Kent Publishing, 1986.

Geneen, Harold. *Management.* New York: Basic Books, 1982.

Ghoshal, Sumantra, and Nitin Nohria. "Horses for Courses: Organizational Forms of Multinational Corporations." *Sloan Management Review,* Winter 1993, pp. 23–35.

Gibney, Frank. *Miracle by Design: The Real Reasons behind Japan's Economic Success.* New York: Times Books, 1982.

Gleick, James. *Chaos: Making a New Science.* New York: Penguin Books, 1989.

Goold, Michael; Andrew Campbell; and Marcus Alexander. *Corporate-Level Strategy: Creating Value in the Multibusiness Company.* New York: John Wiley & Sons, 1994.

Gouillart, Francis J., and James N. Kelly. *Transforming the Organization.* New York: McGraw-Hill, 1995.

Gross, Thomas; Ernie Turner; and Lars Cederholm. "Building Teams for Global Operations." *Management Review,* June 1987, pp. 32–36.

Grove, Andrew S. "A High-Tech CEO Updates His Views on Managing and Careers." *Fortune,* September 18, 1995, pp. 229–30.

Hall, Edward T. *The Silent Language.* New York: Doubleday & Company, 1959.

———. *The Hidden Dimension.* New York: Anchor Press, 1966.

———. *Beyond Culture.* Garden City, N.J.: Anchor/Doubleday, 1976.

Hall, Edward T., and Mildred Reed Hall. *Hidden Differences: Doing Business with the Japanese.* Garden City, N.Y.: Anchor Press/Doubleday, 1987.

Hamel, Gary, and C. K. Prahalad. *Competing for the Future: Breakthrough Strategies for Seizing Control of your Industry and Creating the Markets of Tomorrow.* Boston: Harvard Business School Press, 1994.

Hammerly, Harry. "Matching Global Strategies with National Responses." *Journal of Business Strategy,* March/April 1992, pp. 8–12.

Hampden-Turner, Charles. *Charting the Corporate Mind: Graphic Solutions to Business Conflicts.* New York: The Free Press, 1990.

———. *Corporate Culture: How to Generate Organisational Strength and Lasting Commercial Advantage.* London: Piatkus, 1994.

Hampden-Turner, Charles, and Alfons Trompenaars. *The Seven Cultures of Capitalism: Value Systems for Creating Wealth in the United States, Japan, Germany, France, Britain, Sweden and the Netherlands.* New York: Doubleday, 1993.

Handy, Charles. *The Age of Unreason.* Boston: Harvard Business School Press, 1990.

Harris, Philip, and Robert Moran. *Managing Cultural Differences.* 2d ed. Houston: Gulf Publishing Company, 1987.

Harrison, Phyllis A. *Behaving Brazilian.* Cambridge: Newbury House Publishers, 1983.

Hayes, Michael. "Internationalising the Executive Education Curriculum at General Electric: A Case Study of Trends in the 1980s." *Journal of Management Development,* February 1991, pp. 5–12.

Heenan, David A., and Howard Perlmutter. *Multinational Organization Development.* Reading, Mass.: Addison-Wesley, 1979.

Heifetz, Ronald A. *Leadership Without Easy Answers.* Cambridge: Harvard University Press, 1994.

Hersey, Paul, and Kenneth Blanchard. *The Management of Organizational Behavior.* 3d ed. Englewood Cliffs, N.J.: Prentice-Hall, 1976.

Hershock, Robert J., and David Braun. "Cross-Functional Teams Drive Change." *Executive Excellence,* July 1993, p. 20.

Hewitt Associates. "Case Studies: Whirlpool, Nike, Salomon and PSEG." *Compensation & Benefits Review,* January–February 1995, pp. 71–74.

Hickman, Craig R., and Michael A. Silva. *Creating Excellence: Managing Corporate Culture, Strategy and Change in the New Age.* New York: New American Library, 1985.

Hofstede, Gert. *Culture's Consequences: International Differences in Work-Related Values.* Beverly Hills: Sage Publishing Co., 1980.

———. *Cultures and Organizations: Software of the Mind.* London: McGraw-Hill, 1991.

———. "Motivation, Leadership and Organization: Do American Management Theories Apply Abroad?" *Organizational Dynamics,* Summer 1980, pp. 42–63.

"H-P Gives Spain a Global Unit." *Business Europe,* March 15–21, 1993, pp. 7–8.

Hungenberg, Harold. "How to Ensure That Headquarters Add Value." *Long Range Planning* 26, no. 6 (1993): pp. 62–73.

Ibe, Masanobu, and Noriko Sato. "Educating Japanese Leaders for a Global Age: The Role of the International Education Center." *Journal of Management Development,* February 1991.

Imai, Masaaki. *Kaizen: The Key to Japan's Competitive Success.* New York: Random House, 1986.

Johnson, Barry. *Polarity Management: Identifying and Managing Unsolvable Problems.* Amherst, Ma: HRD Press, 1992.

Johnston, William B. "Global Workforce 2000: The New World Labor Market." *Harvard Business Review,* March–April 1991, pp. 115–27.

Kanter, Rosabeth Moss. *When Giants Learn to Dance.* New York: Simon and Schuster, 1989.

Katzenbach, Jon R., and Douglas K. Smith. *The Wisdom of Teams*. Boston: Harvard Business School Press, 1993.

Keirsey, David, and Marilyn Bates. *Please Understand Me: Character and Temperament Types*. Del Mar, Ca: Prometheus Nemesis Book Company, 1984.

Kennedy, Paul. *Preparing for the 21st Century*. New York: Random House, 1993.

Kiezun, Witold. *Management in Socialist Countries: USSR and Central Europe*. New York: Walter de Gruyter, 1991.

Kilmann, Ralph H. *Managing beyond the Quick Fix: A Completely Integrated Program for Creating and Maintaining Organizational Success*. San Francisco: Jossey-Bass, 1989.

Kim, W. Chan, and Renee A. Mauborgne. "Effectively Conceiving and Executing Multinationals' Worldwide Strategies." *Journal of International Business Studies*, Third Quarter 1993, pp. 419–48.

———. "Making Global Strategies Work." *Sloan Management Review*, Spring 1993, pp. 11–27.

Koestenbaum, Peter. *The Heart of Business: Ethics, Power and Philosophy*. Dallas: Saybrook Publishing, 1987.

———. *Leadership: The Inner Side of Greatness*. San Francisco: Jossey-Bass, 1991.

Korn/Ferry International and Columbia School of Business. *21st Century Report: Reinventing the CEO*. New York: Korn/Ferry International, 1989.

Kupfer, Andrew. "How to Be a Global Manager." *Fortune*, March 14, 1988, pp. 43–48.

Labbs, Jennifer J. "How Gillette Grooms Global Talent." *Personnel Journal*, August 1993, pp. 69–76.

Lane, Henry W., and Joseph J. DiStefano. *International Management Behavior*. Scarborough, Ontario: Nelson Canada, 1988.

Laurent, Andre. "The Cultural Diversity of Western Conceptions of Management." *International Studies of Management and Organization* Vol. XIII, no. 1–2 (Spring, Summer 1983). M.E. Sharpe, Inc., pp. 75–96.

———. "The Cross-Cultural Puzzle of Human Resource Management." *Human Resource Management* 25, no. 1 (Spring 1986): pp. 91–102.

Lawrence, Paul R., and Charalambos A. Vlachoutsicos, eds. *Behind the Factory Walls: Decision Making in Soviet and U.S. Enterprises*. Boston: Harvard Business School Press, 1990.

Levitt, Theodore. "The Globalization of Markets." *Harvard Business Review*, May–June 1983, pp. 92–102.

Little, Reg, and Warren Reed. *The Confucian Renaissance*. Sydney: The Federation Press, 1989.

Lussler, Robert N.; Robert W. Baeder, and Joel Carman. "Measuring Global Practices: Global Strategic Planning through Company Situational Analysis." *Business Horizons*, September–October 1994, pp. 56–63.

Macharzina, K., and W. H. Staehle, eds. *European Approaches to International Management*. Berlin: Walter de Gruyter, 1986.

Macoby, Michael. *The Gamesman: The New Corporate Leaders*. New York: Simon and Schuster, 1976.

"Managing a Three-Country Team Project." *Electronic Business Buyer*, May 1994, pp. 68–69.

Marquardt, Michael, and Angus Reynolds. *The Global Learning Organization: Gaining Competitive Advantage through Continuous Learning*. Burr Ridge, Ill.: Irwin Professional Publishing, 1994.

Marquardt, Michael, and Dean Engel. *Global Human Resource Development*. Englewood Cliffs, N.J.: Prentice-Hall, 1993.

Marsick, Victoria J., and Lars Cederholm. "Developing Leadership in International Managers—An Urgent Challenge!" *The Columbia Journal of World Business* 22, no. 4 (Winter 1988): pp. 3–11.

Maruca, Regina Fazro. "The Right Way to Go Global: An Interview with Whirlpool CEO David Whitwam." *Harvard Business Review,* March–April 1994, pp. 135–45.

McCall, Morgan W., Jr.; Michael Lombardo; and Ann M. Morrison. *The Lessons of Experience: How Successful Executives Develop on the Job*. New York: Lexington Books, 1988.

McCaskey, Michael. *The Executive Challenge: Managing Change and Ambiguity*. New York: Harper Collins, 1986.

Miller, Lawrence. *American Spirit: Visions of a New Corporate Culture*. New York: William Morrow and Company, Inc., 1984.

Mintzberg, Henry. *The Rise and Fall of Strategic Planning*. New York: The Free Press, 1994.

Mitroff, Ian. *Business Not as Usual*. San Francisco: Jossey-Bass, 1987.

Mole, John. *Mind Your Manners: Culture Clash in the Single European Market*. London: The Industrial Society, 1990.

Moran, Robert T., and John R. Riesenberger. *The Global Challenge: Building the New Worldwide Enterprise*. London: McGraw-Hill Book Company, 1994.

Moran, Robert T., and Philip R. Harris. *Managing Cultural Synergy*. Houston: Gulf Publishing, 1982.

Moran, Robert T.; Philip R. Harris; and William G. Stripp. *Developing the Global Organization: Strategies for Human Resource Professionals*. Houston: Gulf Publishing, 1993.

Morgan, Gareth. *Riding the Waves of Change: Developing Managerial Competencies for a Turbulent World*. San Francisco: Jossey-Bass, 1988.

Moulton, Harper. "Executive Development and Education: An Evaluation." *Journal of Management Development* 9, no. 4 (1991): p. 8.

Moynihan, Michael. *Global Manager: Recruiting, Developing and Keep World Class Executives*. London: The Economist Intelligence Unit, 1993.

Muna, Farid A. *The Arab Executive*. London: Macmillan Press, 1980.

Myers, Isabella B. *Gifts Differing*. Palo Alto, Ca: Consulting Psychologists Press, 1980.

Naisbitt, John. *Megatrends: Ten New Directions Transforming Our Lives*. New York: Warner Communications, 1982.

———. *Global Paradox: The Bigger the World Economy, the More Powerful the Smallest Players*. New York: William Morrow & Company, 1994.

Naisbitt, John, and Patricia Aburdene. *Reinventing the Corporation*. New York: Warner Books, 1985.

———. *Megatrends 2000: Ten New Directions for the 1990s*. New York: William Morrow and Company, 1990.

Nakamura, Hajime. *Ways of Thinking of Eastern Peoples*. Honolulu: East-West Center Press, 1964.

Nelson, Carl A. *Managing Globally: A Complete Guide to Competing Worldwide.* Burr Ridge, Ill.: Irwin Professional Publishing, 1994.

Nguyen, Andrea, and Brian H. Kleiner. "Quality Management: How Four European Companies Succeed." *Business Credit,* November/December 1994, pp. 32–34.

Nydell, Margaret K. *Understanding Arabs: A Guide for Westerners.* Yarmouth, Me: Intercultural Press, 1987.

Odenwald, Sylvia. *Global Training: How to Design a Program for the Multinational Corporation.* Burr Ridge: Business One Irwin, 1993.

O'Hara-Devereaux, Mary, and Robert Johansen. *Global Work: Bridging Distance, Culture and Time.* San Francisco, Calif.: Jossey-Bass, 1994.

Ohmae, Kenichi. *The Mind of the Strategist.* New York: Penguin Books, 1983.

———. *The Borderless World.* New York: Harper Business Press, 1990.

Overman, Stephanie. "Shaping the Global Workplace." *Personnel Administrator,* October 1989, pp. 41–44 and 101.

Paradigm 2000 Newsletter 1, no. 1 (April/May 1990).

———. no. 2 (June/July 1990).

Pascale, Richard Tanner. *Managing on the Edge: How the Smartest Companies Use Conflict to Stay Ahead.* New York: Touchstone, 1990.

Peak, Martha H. "Developing an International Management Style." *Management Review,* February 1991, pp. 32–35.

Pedersen, Paul. *A Handbook for Developing Multicultural Awareness.* Alexandria, Va.: American Association for Counseling and Development, 1988.

Peters, Thomas. *Thriving on Chaos: Handbook for a Management Revolution.* New York: Harper & Row, 1988.

———. *Liberation Management: Necessary Disorganization for the Nanosecond Nineties.* New York: Ballantine Books, 1992.

Peters, Thomas, and Robert H. Waterman. *In Search of Excellence: Lessons from America's Best-Run Companies.* New York: Harper & Row, 1982.

Pfeiffer, J. William, ed. *Encyclopedia of Team Development Activities.* San Diego: Pfeiffer & Co., 1991.

Phillips, Nicola. *Managing International Teams.* Burr Ridge, Ill: Richard D. Irwin, 1994.

Porter, Michael, ed. *Competition in Global Business.* Cambridge: Harvard Business School Press, 1986.

Prahalad, C. K., and Yves Doz. *The Multinational Mission: Balancing Local Demands and Global Vision.* New York: Free Press, 1987.

Pucik, Vladimir; Noel M. Tichy; and Carole K. Barnett, eds. *Globalizing Management: Creating and Leading the Competitive Organization.* New York: John Wiley & Sons, 1992.

Quinn, Robert E. *Beyond Rational Management: Mastering the Paradoxes and Competing Demands of High Performance.* San Francisco: Jossey-Bass, 1988.

Reich, Robert B. "Who Is Us?" *Harvard Business Review,* January–February 1990, pp. 53–64.

———. "Who Is Them?" *Harvard Business Review,* March–April 1991, pp. 77–88.

———. *The Work of Nations: Preparing Ourselves for 21st Century Capitalism.* New York: Alfred A. Knopf, 1991.

Rhinesmith, Stephen H. *Cultural-Organizational Analysis: The Interrelationship Between Value Orientations and Managerial Behavior.* Cambridge: McBer and Company, 1971.

————. "Americans in the Global Learning Process." *The Annals of the American Academy of Political and Social Science* 442 (March 1979): pp. 98–108.

————. *Bring Home the World: A Management Guide for Community Leaders of International Exchange Programs.* New York: Walker and Company, 1985.

————. "An Agenda for Globalization." *Training and Development Journal,* February 1991, pp. 22–29.

————. "Going Global from the Inside Out." *Training and Development Journal,* November 1991, pp. 42–47.

————. "Global Mindsets for Global Managers." *Training and Development Journal,* October 1992, pp. 63–68.

————. "Open the Door to a Global Mindset." *Training and Development Journal,* May 1995, pp. 34–43.

Rhinesmith, Stephen H.; John N. Williamson; David M. Ehlen; and Denise S. Maxwell. "Developing Leaders for a Global Enterprise." *Training and Development Journal,* April 1989, pp. 24–34.

Ricks, David A. *Big Business Blunders: Mistakes in Multinational Marketing.* Homewood, Ill.: Dow-Jones-Irwin, 1983.

Ronen, Simcha. *Comparative and Multinational Management.* New York: John Wiley, 1986.

Rossman, Marlene L. *The International Businesswoman: A Guide to Success in the Global Marketplace.* New York: Praeger, 1986.

Roure, Juan; Jose Luis Alvarez; Carlos Garcia-Pont; and Jose Nueno. "Managing Internationally: International Dimensions of the Managerial Task." *European Management Journal* 11, no. 4 (December 1993): pp. 485–92.

Schon, Donald. *The Reflective Practitioner: How Professionals Think in Action.* New York: Basic, 1995.

Senge, Peter. *The Fifth Discipline: The Art and Practice of the Learning Organization.* New York: Doubleday, 1990.

Sherman, Stratford. "Are You as Good as the Best in the World?" *Fortune,* December 13, 1993, pp. 95–96.

Simpson, Daniel. "Planning in a Global Business." *Planning Review,* March/April 1995, pp. 25–27.

Siu, R. G. H. "Management and the Art of Chinese Baseball." In Harold J. Leavitt and Louis Pondy, eds. *Readings in Managerial Psychology.* Chicago: University of Chicago Press, 1980.

Smith, David C. "Going Global: Restructuring Aims to Boost Efficiency." *WARD'S Auto World,* December 1994, pp. 39–45.

Solomon, Charlene Marmer. "Transplanting Corporate Cultures Globally." *Personnel Journal,* October 1993, pp. 78–88.

————. "How Does Your Global Talent Measure Up?" *Personnel Journal,* October 1994, pp. 96–108.

————. "Repatriation: Up, Down or Out?" *Personnel Journal,* January 1995, pp. 28–37.

Soros, George. *Underwriting Democracy.* New York: The Free Press, 1991.

Stacey, Ralph. *Managing Chaos: Dynamic Business Strategies in an Unpredictable World.* London: Kogan Page, 1992.

Stata, Ray. "Organizational Learning—The Key to Management Innovation." *Sloan Management Review,* Spring 1989, pp. 64–74.

Steingraber, Fred G. "Managing in the 1990s." *Business Horizons,* January–February 1990, pp. 49–61.

Stewart, Edward C., and Milton J. Bennett. *American Cultural Patterns: A Cross-Cultural Perspective.* rev. ed. Yarmouth, Me.: Intercultural Press, 1991.

Stewart, Thomas A. "How to Manage in the Global Era." *Fortune,* January 15, 1990, pp. 58–72.

Stopford, J. M., and L. T. Wells, Jr. *Managing the Multinational Enterprise.* New York: Basic Books, 1972.

Taylor, Alex III, "Ford's Really Big Leap at the Future: It's Risky, It's Worth It, and It may Not Work." *Fortune,* September 18, 1995, pp. 134–44.

Taylor, William. "The Logic of Global Business: An Interview with ABB's Percy Barnevik." *Harvard Business Review,* March–April 1991, pp. 91–105.

Terpstra, Vern, and Kenneth David. *The Cultural Framework of International Business.* 2d ed. Pelham Manor, N.Y.: South Western Publishing, 1985.

Thurow, Lester. *Head to Head: The Coming Economic Battle among Japan, Europe and America.* New York: William Morrow and Company, 1992.

Tichy, Noel. *Managing Strategic Change: Technical, Political and Cultural Dynamics.* New York: John Wiley & Sons, 1983.

Tichy, Noel, and Mary Anne Devanna. *The Transformational Leader.* New York: John Wiley & Sons, 1986.

Tichy, Noel M., and Stratford Sherman. *Control Your Own Destiny or Someone Else Will: How Jack Welch Is Making General Electric the World's Most Competitive Company.* New York: Doubleday, 1993.

Toffler, Alvin. *Powershift: Knowledge, Wealth and Violence at the Edge of the 21st Century.* New York: Bantam, 1990.

Tourevski, Mark, and Eileen Morgan. *Cutting the Red Tape: How Western Companies Can Profit in the New Russia.* New York: The Free Press, 1993.

Treacy, Michael, and Fred Wiersema. *Discipline of Market Leaders: Choose Your Customers, Narrow Your Focus, Dominate Your Market.* Reading, Mass.: Addison-Wesley, 1995.

Trompenaars, Fons. *Riding the Waves of Culture: Understanding Cultural Diversity in Business.* London: The Economist Books, 1993.

Tuckman, Bruce W., and M. A. C. Jensen. "Stages of Small Group Development Revisited." *Group and Organization Studies* 2, no. 4 (December 1977): pp. 419–27.

Ury, William. *Getting Past No: Negotiating Your Way from Confrontation to Cooperation.* New York: Bantam Books, 1993.

Vaill, Peter B. *Managing as a Performing Art: New Ideas for a World of Chaotic Change.* San Francisco: Jossey-Bass, 1989.

"Wharton Rewrites the Book on B-Schools." *Business Week,* May 13, 1991, p. 43.

Wheatley, Margaret J. *Leadership and the New Science: Learning about Organization from an Orderly Universe.* San Francisco: Berrett-Koehler, 1994.

Winslow, Charles D., and William L. Bramer. *Future Work: Putting Knowledge to Work in the Knowledge Economy.* New York: The Free Press, 1994.

Wolff, John. "The Ancient Art of Globalization: We Truly Will Be a Global Industry only When We Produce Globally." *Vital Speeches of the Day,* 1994, pp. 437–40.

Yip, George S. *Total Global Strategy: Managing for Worldwide Competitive Advantage.* Englewood Cliffs, N.J.: Prentice-Hall, 1992.

INDEX

People
  aligning, 19
  factor in competitiveness, 200–201
  future trends and, 235
  human resource professionals and, 18
  mindsets for managing, 25–29
  open, x
  as resource, 4, 17
Pepsi International, 74, 110
Performance, 123, 216–218
Personal characteristics, 29–33, 35–36, 161–162
Philips
  coordination councils, 121
  global corporate culture, 17, 74, 107, 206
  promotion criteria for managers, 218
  strategy and structure for, 61–62
  weakness in global competition, 125
Planning, global corporate culture and, 116–119
Policies, 81–83, 128, 203, 216
Practices, global, 41
Pragmatism, complexity and, 92–93
Problem solving, systems thinking and, 94–95
Process, principle of trustable, 142
Process mapping, as learning tool, 148
Proctor & Gamble, 61–62, 83, 203
Professional development, multicultural teams
  and, 178–181

Quality, for global competition, 48–50

Reactions, principle of unmanageable, 142
Reentry, 214–215
Reframing, complexity and, 232–233
Regional management, 38
Reich, Robert, 3–4, 19, 64
Reinforcement, change and, 142
Resource allocation, 117–118
Responsibility, 77–79, 100
Retraining, 221
Rewards, globally consistent, 124–125
Rhone-Poulenc, personnel policies, 216
Richards, Sharon, 13
Ringi decision-making process, 95

Samsung, 55, 212
Saw, Gordon, 83
Schavoir, Peter, 82
Schon, Don, 133

Sensitivity, 29, 30, 32, 190–192
Shaping behavior, 183–184
Shell, 74, 107, 131–132, 158
Sheraton, 58–59
Siemens AG, 155–156
Simpson, Dan, 81–82
Siu, Ralph, 133
Socialization, 74
Solomon, Charlene Marmer, 112
Sony, 8, 51
Specialization, functional, 24–25, 198
Stacey, Ralph, 134, 136–137
Staff exchanges, 213–214
Standards, for global competition, 48–54
Stata, Ray, 148
Stereotyping, 175–176
Strategic alignment, personal characteristics
  and, 31
Strategic alliance teams, 158–159
Strategies. See also individual companies listed
  by name
  aligning, 19, 106–107
  chaos as strategy, 132
  global, xi, 10, 15, 59–60, 128
  industry requirements and, 61–62
  international, 55–60
  levers and, 56–58
  mindsets and, 24–25, 198–199
  profitability and, 17
  supported by structure, 60–63
Strategy/structure. See also Strategies
  defined, 15
  global mindsets for, 24–25, 198–199
  international structures, 55–64
  management skills for, 34
  managerial characteristics for, 31
Structure. See Strategy/structure
Success, cross-cultural criteria for, 217
Systems thinking, 66, 94–95

Tasks, global, 41
Teams, project, 159
Technology transfers, 146–147, 158–159, 213
Tesio, Vittorio, 37–38
The Work of Nations, 3–4
Thinking
  outside the box, 54–55
  rethinking boundaries, 218–219
  systems thinking, 66, 94–95
3M, 51, 74, 83, 107, 159

Other books of interest . . .

- *Global Training*
  How to Design a Program for the Multinational Corporation
  Sylvia B. Odenwald
  Co-published with the American Society for Training
  and Development

  Any company searching for ways to research, develop, and implement an
  international training program will find the answers along with how-to tips
  that make the application of the ideas presented as easy as possible.
  1-55623-986-6   240 pages

- *Doing Business Internationally*
  The Guide to Cross-Cultural Success
  Terence Brake, Danielle Medina Walker, and Thomas (Tim) Walker

  Builds a solid foundation for operating in a variety of cultural settings.
  This hard cover training program includes all the information necessary to
  analyze key global trends and their impact on current business practices,
  as well as identify the critical success factors needed to operate across
  borders.
  0-7863-0117-1   225 pages

- *Global Solutions for Teams*
  Moving from Collision to Collaboration
  Sylvia B. Odenwald

  Ground breaking strategies multinational workgroups can use to overcome
  distance and cultural differences in accomplishing common goals. Readers
  will find several examples of how General Electric and other companies
  have turned their international teams into a competitive advantage.
  0-7863-0476-6   200 pages

www.ingramcontent.com/pod-product-compliance
Lightning Source LLC
Chambersburg PA
CBHW011301210326
41599CB00035B/7085